EAT 'EM UP, COUGARS

HOUSTON FOOTBALL

EAT 'EM UP, COUGARS

COUGARS

HOUSTON FOOTBALL

by
Jerry Wizig

THE STRODE PUBLISHERS, INC.
HUNTSVILLE, ALABAMA 35802

To all those Cougars who did so much for so long with so little; and to Maralyn, my great fan. Special thanks are due Ted Nance, the *Houston Chronicle*, and all the Cougars, past and present, who helped.

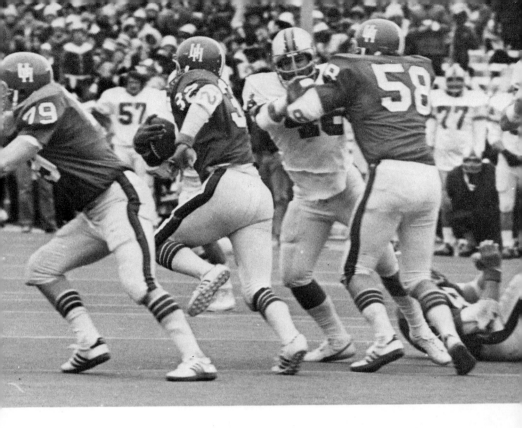

Contents

Foreword

Most universities have been playing football for many years more than the University of Houston Cougars. However, few have had a more meteoric rise to national prominence than the Cougars.

The Southwest Conference co-champions of 1976 came just 31 years after the very first UH team took the field in 1946. Winning the Cotton Bowl game on January 1, 1977, was certainly the culmination of Houston's three-decade trip to the top. However, there were other bowl games and great moments along the way. And, tough times, too.

At times the 31 years have seemed like 300 years. Jerry Wizig's research and description of Houston's battle from post-war infancy to the Cotton Bowl championship is an intriguing tale.

While the history makes interesting reading, Houston's greatest days are, perhaps, in the future. We are looking forward to more bowl games and more Southwest Conference titles.

Nevertheless, there is only one first time for everything. It has been our good fortune to have been a part of a lifetime of "firsts" at the University.

I think you will enjoy reading about them.

Harry Fouke
Athletic Director
University of Houston

In The Beginning

Even level-headed, hard-working Jewell Wallace must have felt a twinge of concern as he faced the first meeting of the first University of Houston football team that steamy September day in 1946.

Of 130 players—young and old, firm and flabby—who greeted Wallace in the school gym, only 10 had ever played college football before. A mere dozen had gone through and survived spring practice.

Their practice field was mowed out of vacant lots where the twin Moody Towers residential dorms stand today. A Quonset-type building with a tin roof and a pot-bellied stove inside served as the dressing room, and the players padded about 25 yards down a walkway to the PE department showers across the street.

Wallace, UH's first head coach, built a notable reputation in Texas high school circles. His only assistants were Alden Pasche, the line coach and also head basketball coach, and Jack Patterson, the B team and track coach. Ned Thompson, the athletic business manager, and Harry Fouke, the athletic director, also lent a hand.

Since there were no student dorms, most of the married players lived in trailers in "Veteransville." Some lived at home, a few bunked on cots upstairs in the Recreation Building, which in World War II had housed cadets in a naval pre-flight training program.

The school began in 1927 as a junior college. A PE teacher named John R. Bender tutored a volunteer football squad and named them the Cougars, after his alma mater, Washington State. The nickname stuck.

About 1,000 students enrolled when UH began operating as a university in 1934, administered by the Houston public school system. Classes were held at night at San Jacinto High School, near downtown Houston.

Three years later, a 112-acre campus was acquired, 95 acres donated by the J. J. Settegast estate and 35 acres by the late Ben Taub. A public campaign for building funds raised $660,000 in 1938, and the Roy G. Cullen Building, the first UH building, was erected from a donation by Mr. and Mrs. H. R. Cullen.

The new campus was occupied in 1939, the Science Building was completed, the Graduate School opened, and enrollment reached about 2,800. The campus grew in size when the Anderson Foundation purchased 90 acres, and Mr. and Mrs. Cullen added 50 more acres. On April 1 the board of regents hired Dr. E. E. Oberholtzer as the school's first full-time president. He had been superintendent of Houston schools and president of the junior college since 1927.

By 1946, with ex-servicemen flocking in under the GI Bill, the school suddenly was struggling to accommodate nearly 11,000 students.

Just a year before, recalls Dr. Franklin Stovall, who was to serve about 20 years as chairman of the faculty athletic council, "there were about 4,000 students, and the whole faculty could almost be seated in one class room."

Johnny Goyen, now a Houston city councilman, was 1941 sports editor of *The Cougar*, the student newspaper, "at a school that had no sports program," he points out. "We had intramurals and got up a six-man team we called the 'Greasy Geese.' We'd sneak into Jeppesen Stadium (then called Public School Stadium) or play on a field on campus."

Goyen then was working part-time and going to UH at night, as many students there still do. "I'd be in line, an 18-year-old freshman, signing up for classes, and there would be people in their forties and fifties next to me. This was their opportunity to better themselves."

Aided by his good buddy, Jack Valenti, Goyen began collecting names on a student petition calling for an intercollegiate football program. In 1942 Goyen, then president of the sopho-more class, and Valenti (later a presidential aide to Lyndon Johnson) were still thinking big. They called a student body meeting. Their purpose—a petition challenging old, established Rice Institute to a football game.

A reporter from the *Houston Chronicle* dutifully asked Goyen how he would finance a football team. Using the logic employed by decades of college students since then, Goyen replied, "That's a problem for the administration."

There were plenty of problems to go around.

"The guys were all fat and out of shape," relates Bobby Brown, the first equipment manager and trainer, then a 17-year-old freshman out of Lamar High. "The practice field was filled with rocks and glass. The players policed the area some times before practice and picked up the junk."

Pasche tells us, "The field was covered with black gumbo, and it got hard like cement. That summer Pat (Patterson) and I were assigned to try to get some grass to grow. We spent all day spreading seed on it and turned the water on. Later we went by to check on it, and you couldn't see the field for all the birds on the ground feeding on the seeds."

With the first spring practice approaching, the school had no equipment. Brown recalls, "One day Fouke came in and said, 'I made a great deal today. I bought all the equipment from Ellington Field (a nearby air base).'

"They'd dumped it in a storage room, and the maintenance man and I went and picked it up."

The order of the day was "improvise." Brown relates, "One day Frank Brady came up to the equipment window for a pair of shoes. I gave him a size 12 and a 10. He looked at me like I was crazy, but I told him, 'That's all I got.' He cut out the sides of the 10 and played in them."

Brown decided the Cougars would look better taking the field in red helmets, "The ones we bought were all painted white. I took them on a bike with a friend, Tom White, over to his house. We went up in his attic and spray-painted them red, with a white stripe across the top. We had red paint on us from our head to our feet when we got through."

There were other perils, too. "It was so hot in that locker room," says Brown, "that I taped while wearing just a pair of shorts. One day Stuart Gordon, one of the ex-servicemen, pulled down my shorts and threw me outside buck-naked with students walking by to class."

Athletic business manager Ned Thompson recalls, "That first spring, there'd be so many mosquitoes in there, they'd be thick as smoke."

Jack Gwin, on the first team, relates an incident in the spring of 1946 that galled Cougar followers for years afterward: "Jewell came out to practice one day that spring and told us, 'We'll just line up and run a few plays against Rice over at their field.' We just wore our old practice uniforms and pooled cars to get over there. We get out there, and they have officials and the field lined off, and the stands are damn near full. They beat us about 77-6." Wallace was as surprised as was his own team.

Pasche says, "That catalogued us and gave us an image that took years to live down. They had guys like Weldon Humble and Huey Keeney, and it was duck soup all around."

The "practice" received detailed coverage in the newspapers and did not do much for the attempted sale of Cougar season tickets.

Wallace notes, "We hadn't been together but a couple of weeks, and some of our players were high school kids who had come over to visit on the weekend and wound up playing. Some people think it was a set-up deal, but I don't think Jess Neely (Rice head coach) would have done that. He was too much of a gentleman."

Meanwhile, Thompson faced other problems in the business end. The coach of the state champion basketball team at Pasadena High School, he reported to work at UH the day after returning from the high school coaching convention at Corpus Christi.

"We had one phone line, no typewriter, no money, no paper—and I even had to bring my own pencil," he recalls. He had to submit the budget "detailed down to the last shoe-string," print tickets (if any were sold), print a program, and arrange for officials and out-of-town transportation. "I'd beat the concrete for awhile selling ads and call on people I didn't even know," he says.

Besides a September 21 opener with Southwestern Louisiana Institute (SLI) the 1946 schedule included West Texas

Members of 1946 Cougars gather for 30-year reunion. Left to right are Bill Cook, co-captain; Alden Pasche, assistant coach; Jewell Wallace, head coach; Tony Ditta, co-captain; and Prentice Jackson, center.

State, Camp Hood (a service team), Texas A&I, East Texas State, Texas School of Mines, Stephen F. Austin, North Texas State, Southwest Texas State and Sam Houston State as the Cougars began the first of their three seasons in the Lone Star Conference.

Thompson arranged for a Pullman car to be hooked onto a freight train for the trip to El Paso, Texas, to play the School of Mines. He found a suitably-priced adding machine at an army-navy store, "mooched a typewriter and got a glass top for the desk at Ellington."

Conditions were such that Thompson was encouraged to spend a minimum of time in the office. He explains, "We just had one desk, and Fouke and Wallace would be sitting at it whenever I came in."

First Kickoff

As Jewell Wallace drilled the Cougars intensively for South-western Louisiana Institute in the Cougars' first collegiate kick-off, their numbers dwindled and injuries mounted in the lengthy scrimmage sessions.

One casualty was Kenneth Hawkins, former all-city guard at Stephen F. Austin High, who suffered a recurrence of an armed services head injury. Luckily for the Cougars, he returned after a few days. So did assistant coach Jack Patterson, who caught poison ivy on the practice field.

The only players with any collegiate experience were 25-year-old quarterback Charlie Manichia, a former Texas A&M freshman who had played for the Cherry Point Marines; Tony Ditta, a former All-Lone Star Conference tackle at Sam Houston State; Pruitt Browning, Texas Tech; ends Stuart Gordon and Evan Weaver, Baylor; halfback Jack Gwin, Texas; back Ralph Porter, TCU; end Warren Settegast, Texas A&M; back Harry Riley, Texas Tech; and guard Roy Fisher, Sam Houston State.

Manichia, however, was in Cleveland, pitching for his Houston Slush Pump Repair Company softball team in a na-tional tournament.

By the final week of practice the 38 remaining players in-cluded "27 grid-rusty war veterans, a squad with an average age of 22, and an average absence from football of nearly three years," wrote George Wright in the *Houston Press*. Former Ala-bama All-American John (Hurry) Cain, the SLI coach, was

16

working with his entire starting line of 1941.

UH's squad ranged from 17-year-old Billy Myers to service vets like Manichia and Ditta, 26 (four years in the army); Hawkins, 24 (three years in the air corps); Bill Hollis, 22 (four years in the navy); Elliott Loy, 24 (a former plebe at West Point); George Nohavitza, 24 (navy); Bill Cook, 20, and Valton Green, 21 (veterans of navy duty in the South Pacific); Buck Foss, 26 (four years in the air corps); Evan Weaver, 23 (overseas with the marines and married, with two daughters); Henry Gomez, 24 (a deep-sea diver in the Seabees); Bill Tingle, 22 (another ex-sailor); and Roy Wallace, 24, Jewell's brother (an army veteran).

Other ex-GIs included Ralph Porter, Manor Smith, Jerry Kelley, John Fenderbosch, Don Domingue, Jimmy Miller, Ken Cockerell, Billy Butler, Alfred Murray, Hans Neumann, Prentice Jackson, Don Purcell, Tom White, Frank Brady, and Roy Fisher.

Ironically, Fouke missed the Cougars' historic first touchdown, Manichia's 32-yard bootleg in the first quarter. "I was

Charlie Manichia (left) scores the first touchdown in Cougar history on a 32-yard run against Southwestern Louisiana in 1946.

down under the stands, checking on things," he says wryly. "I heard the commotion and thought, 'My gosh, have they scored on us already?' I went up and looked at the scoreboard, and WE had scored first." Goyen, too, missed the occasion, for an entirely different reason, "We got there late because my wife, Jody, was fixing her hair."

Gwin remembers, "I looked up from the ground and said, 'He's gonna go.'"

Alas, SLI scored twice in the final 11 minutes to deal UH a 13-7 loss before a crowd of 11,000. The game winner came on a 57-yard pass play with 17 seconds to play, breaking a 7-7 tie.

"Houston has nothing to be ashamed of about its newest collegiate football team as the Cougars played their hearts out...," reported Jerry Ribnick in the *Houston Chronicle*. Johnny Lyons of the *Houston Post* called it "one of the hardest and most interesting opening night college tussles ever staged here."

Charlie Manichia, quarterback of the 1946 Cougars, receives ankle treatment from trainer Buck Hennes.

Crouched on the sideline, Jewell Wallace and assistant Jack Patterson (right, second photograph) sweat out the first Cougar football game with Southwestern Louisiana in 1946.

The program sold that first night had the following message:

It is the policy of the University of Houston to sponsor good sports and recreation of sufficient educational value. Football is one of our greatest American games of sport. It has substantial educational value. We want the support of all friends of the university, and we are all for the team.

Even though the boys had not previously played football together as a team, we believe that they have the right spirit. They will demonstrate their ability, and the high record of the University will be preserved to its educational achievement. So, Hurrah! for the Team. One for all and all for one.

Come join us and be with us at each and every game. All for the University of Houston.

The Bill Hollises also had another reason to remember that day, for their daughter, Patricia, was born a few hours before the kickoff.

The First Triumphs

The Cougars required just one more week for their very first victory, an improbable 14-12 squeaker over the Buffaloes of West Texas Teachers at Canyon. Ken Hawkins kicked both points after touchdown, as UH blocked one conversion by the Buffs and rushed the other into a miss.

UH trailed, 14-2, in first downs and by an amazing 382 yards to a meagre 63 in total offense.

A fumble recovery by Hans Neumann at the Buff seven yard line set up Gene Krus's three-yard touchdown plunge. Another fumble recovery, by Odell Wallace, led to Jackie Gwin's 19-yard sprint and Charlie Manichia's 3-yard scoring run.

The 5-foot-9 Gwin also intercepted two passes and punted 65 yards from near the UH goal to boost the Cougars out of one trouble spot. He preserved the triumph on the game's final play, leaping high in the end zone to knock down a pass aimed for 6-foot-4 Metz LaFollette.

"We rushed back from Canyon to Amarillo to catch the train home," Gwin relates. "They fed us a roast beef dinner at the hotel before we went to the train station. Zarko Franks of the *Chronicle* barely made it in time. I was never so sore in my life, but that first win was as big a thrill as anything."

Brown recalls, "I had to ride home on the train in an upper berth with Bill Hollis."

Again badly outweighed, as they had been in the first two games, the Cougars scalded Camp Hood, 32-7, at Temple, their second win in three starts. As Morris Frank described it in the

Ken Hawkins (left) shows Coach Jewell Wallace the foot that kicked the deciding extra points in Cougars' first football victory, 14-12, over West Texas State in 1946.

Houston Post, "The Cougars took the wheels off Camp Hood's Second Armored 'Hell on Wheels' Division."

Gwin dashed 59 yards for one score and set up another with a 38-yard run. Krus, Ralph Porter, and Manichia scored once each, and Porter passed 32 yards to Floyd Hand for the final touchdown.

"They had a big spread for us afterward," recalls Pasche, "and Frank Brady said, 'Damn, I never saw anything like that until they tried to talk us into re-enlisting.'"

UH's third straight win, its first at home, was a 34-0 runaway over Texas Arts and Industries (A&I) in Public School Stadium. Jewell Wallace's T-formation sprang loose a series of long plays, as Manichia weaved 39 yards, Leon Wallace 30, Gwin 26, and Bill Tingle caught a 45-yard pass from Manichia to set up another.

A 50-member band and about 200 fans boarded a special train, the school's first such outpouring for a football game, for the Lone Star Conference opener at East Texas State. But Cougar mistakes contributed to their 20-14 defeat, despite a signal performance from an injured Manichia.

Playing with his legs taped to the knees because of a broken blood vessel, Manichia went in and out of the game. His 31-yard scamper in the fourth period to end an 84-yard drive hauled UH within striking distance of the Lions of East Texas State.

UH took a 7-0 lead on Roy Wallace's 40-yard pass to Stuart Gordon and Wallace's four-yard TD plunge, but two Cougar fumbles cost them 13 points. Tony Ditta blocked a punt, suffering a broken nose in the process, and Manichia, after a brilliant fake handoff, dashed 17 yards to score, but a holding penalty wiped out the TD.

"Personally, there is not a doubt in my mind," said Coach Wallace, "that we would have won had Charlie been in shape to play more."

Just a 30-man squad made the train trip to El Paso where the Cougars bowed to Jack Curtice's Texas School of Mines team, 21-7. UH drove 80 yards in the fourth quarter, Valton Green scoring from the eight, to avoid a shutout. The El Paso Miners passed for their three touchdowns in the first half.

"Their backs were no better than ours," Coach Wallace

Prentice Jackson (left) and Bill Cook at a 1946 Cougar practice.

said later. "Their front line ruined us."

Manichia, a veteran of three years marine corps service in the Pacific, kept his conference scoring lead, contributing a TD, his seventh of the year, to the Cougars' 16-7 win over Stephen F. Austin, the school's first conference victory.

Gwin and Roy Wallace averaged 41 yards on nine punts, including a 78-yarder by Gwin. Ditta and Buck Foss featured the defense which held the visitors to 47 yards rushing.

Valton Green's 27-yard scoring run and Gwin's interception setting up Manichia's touchdown sent Houston's Coogs ahead, 14-0; then Bill Hollis blocked a punt out of the end zone for a fourth quarter safety. This was to be UH's final victory of the year, however.

The 1946 Houston team is shown after its first collegiate season. Top row (left to right): Gene Krus; Bill Cook; Curly Breeland; Jack Hoeffler; Frank Brady; Elliott Loy; Buck Foss; Charlie Potts; Bill Hollis; Pruitt Browning; Floyd Hand; Bill Tingle; Manor Smith; Billy Barfield; and Willie Davis, manager. Middle row (left to right): Bobby Brown, manager; Roland Kudla; Stuart Gordon; Warren Settegast; Cecil Towns; Dan

Ken Hawkins' 29-yard field goal in the first quarter was the Cougars' only scoring in a muddy 7-3 homecoming loss, to the Eagles of North Texas State, which dropped them out of title contention.

The Eagles' Joe Gieb traveled 32 yards in the third quarter, and they turned back a UH threat at their 30 in the final minutes.

Following a 21-7 loss at Southwest Texas State, UH dedicated its Thanksgiving Night season finale with Sam Houston

Purcell; Henry Gomez; Valton Green; Aubra Dean; Evan Weaver; Ralph Porter; Tony Ditta; Ken Hawkins; Charlie Manichia; Prentice Jackson; Roy Wallace; and Sam Allesandra, manager. Bottom row (left to right): Harold Dixson; Boyd Tingle; Jack Gwin; Jerry Kelly; Don Domingue; Dick Donley; Billy Myers; Harold Maddox; George Nohavitza; Hans Neumann; Odell Wallace; Leon Wallace; and Roy Fisher.

State to its trainer, Buck Hennes, who had reputedly begun the system of athletic training under Knute Rockne at Notre Dame in the 1920s. Ill at home for the past two games, Hennes had attended to such fabled Notre Damers as George Gipp, Frank Thomas, and Harry Stuhldreher.

A budding rivalry had developed with the Bearkats of Sam Houston after the Bearkats scored a pair of one-point decisions over the champion Coogs in the previous LSC (Lone Star Conference) basketball race. As Johnny Lyons wrote in the

Tony Ditta (left) and Bill Cook receive co-captain awards from Coach Jewell Wallace at Houston's first football banquet after the 1946 season. Seated are (left to right) regents Col. W. B. Bates and James Rockwell with Eddie Dyer, former manager of the St. Louis baseball Cardinals.

Houston Post, "For the past four days and nights, each institution has found paint marks and colors of the rival school on its buildings."

Trainer Hennes was badly needed, for several starters, including Gwin, Foss, Hand, Neumann, and Brady were injured.

Again playing in the mud, the Cougars scored first. Manichia's 23-yard pass to Green led to the first quarter score, but they lost, 28-6, to end their first season with a 4-6 record. Manichia, the LSC's leading scorer, was selected as the all-conference quarterback. Ditta and Bill Cook were voted the 1946 co-captains by the team. An estimated 30,000 had attended the five home games.

In the *Houston Press* George Wright wrote, "The University of Houston Cougars, who weren't supposed to win a game in their first season of intercollegiate football, today had ended their initial schedule with four victories against six losses, and were looking for still tougher opposition for next season."

Those were strong words for a team which had placed fifth in a six-team conference.

Jewell Wallace:
"A Prince Of A Guy"

Just 37 when he began "the toughest job in America" as UH's first football coach, Jewell Wallace would have been excused if he felt like 100 two seasons later.

After accepting the job for $4,500 a year, Wallace recalls that his contract was a handshake from Dr. E. E. Oberholtzer, the school's president, and the understanding he could stay as long as he wanted.

"There wasn't much there," says Wallace, "but somebody had to start it."

Wallace had built a unique record in Texas high school coaching, winning state championships in basketball (at El Paso in 1941) and in football (at San Angelo in 1943). A friend, then minister of a Houston church, "camped on Harry Fouke's doorstep" in his behalf, Wallace explains.

In describing his approach to football Wallace says, "It was a game for the boys. They all needed to be treated alike. I let them know what I expected of them.

"Winning isn't everything, but wanting to is.

"If you're going into coaching, go into it with the idea you're going to make citizens out of them. I didn't believe in a lot of rules. I let the kids set up the rules. You can't browbeat these kids; they're too intelligent. They know more about the coach than he knows about himself."

His message to the 1946 Cougars was, "I didn't say you couldn't drink or smoke, because I'd have to be a policeman. But if I do see it, you're going to have to take the consequences."

Wallace adds, "It was just a game then. Now it's big business; there's too much pressure, and the coaches brought it all on themselves." Still nearly as slim and erect as he was then, Wallace notes that his early instructions were, "'Get out and sell them on the school,' but then we had to put them up on the balcony over the gym. You couldn't do much recruiting. For what we had, we did real well."

Jackie Gwin remembers, "Jewell could have told us younger guys to jump off the Cullen Building, and we would have done it. If he had started with a four-year program, he could have done a lot more."

Tony Ditta adds, "His practices were always well-organized. No telling what he could have done with seven assistants like today's staffs."

Dr. Franklin Stovall, former faculty athletic chairman, notes, "Jewell lived in the same neighborhood, and we sometimes drove to school together. He was a prince of a guy."

So, calm and efficient, Wallace set about the difficult task. "I wouldn't want to do it over again, not at my age now," Wallace informed the *Houston Post* 's John Hollis 20 years later. "But I wouldn't give anything for the experience. I learned a lot at the university. You always learn more when you're losing than when you're winning. It's a wonder we won at all."

Charlie Manichia, the Cougars' first quarterback, was well suited to the T-formation offense Wallace installed. "The only teams then using it were Stanford and the Chicago Bears, to my knowledge," says Wallace, who had been one of the first Texas high school coaches to employ the T.

Wallace can still detail UH's first touchdown, Manichia's 32-yard scamper against Southwestern Louisiana Institute in the 1946 opener: "He was a marvelous faker and a good runner. He faked the belly play and circled left end and fooled everybody."

Manichia's fakery was so artistic that it cost the Cougars later. "Against East Texas he ran the same play around right end for a touchdown," Wallace explains. "The official was so sure he'd left the ball with the fullback that he whistled the play dead."

Just one example of Wallace's problems:

"I remember walking into that old tin shack one day and

finding our student trainer passing out cigarettes. I asked him what in the world did he think he was doing. He told me, 'Coach, you've got to remember these guys have been in the service.'

"I told him never mind, they were football players now, and they were going to follow the rules." Wallace agrees he might have been better off running a tighter ship, "but they had had all the orders they wanted. The majority worked hard."

A native of Missouri, Wallace learned football under the masters. He played for three years at Texarkana Junior College for Warren Woodson, then for three years at TCU (Texas Christian University) for Francis Schmidt. "I think he knew more football than anyone I ever knew," Wallace says of Schmidt. "He was a genius."

Wallace was a 178-pound wingback and defensive back on the 1932 Southwest Conference champ captained by John Vaught. Schmidt's TCU teams scored 34 shutouts in five years, never allowing more than 49 points in one season.

After that first season, when the Cougars won four and lost six, Wallace was reading a newspaper account of a coach with the same record at another school being hung in effigy by students. "My son Bill saw the story and started crying," Wallace relates. "He said, 'Daddy, they're not going to hang you, too, are they?'"

Wallace retains warm memories of that first victory, 14-12 over West Texas State, on two extra points kicked by Ken Hawkins, the 24-year-old air corps veteran. "When I found out Ken had a plate in his head from the war, I wouldn't let him do anything but kick."

He described his decision to resign after the 1947 team lost its final eight games, "It was going to take longer than I wanted to fool with it. I never got ulcers, because I never let it bother me that much."

Clark Nealon, then sports editor of the *Houston Press*, wrote, "To us, Jewell Wallace's decision to give up coaching was based on a choice. He could either have gone all out in proselyting, got himself an angel, let down the bars and got the football talent, or he could step down and keep his self-respect. He stepped down, and, we believe, the sport suffers."

Says Wallace, "I never regretted going to UH or leaving. I made a lot of friends, and that's worth more than anything else.

30

That was good experience, and I got my master's degree while I was there. It was the toughest job in America."

Wallace returned to high school coaching several months later and won the state football championship again in 1949 at San Antonio Jefferson. One of his players, S. M. Meeks, was a UH scatback later, and Billy Quinn and Pat Tolar were notable performers for the Texas Longhorns.

After his coaching days, Wallace returned to TCU, where he retired in 1974 as assistant dean of men. He figured up his coaching records as 138-38-8 in football and 238-39 in basketball, "and that's not bad for an old country boy."

Amos Alonzo Stagg (left) is greeted by Jewell Wallace upon arrival for his Houston speaking engagement.

The Second Time Around

For their second collegiate season, the Cougars dressed out in brand-new, peppermint-striped, red and white jerseys. Nineteen of last year's players returned, and a couple of new opponents, like Centenary and Hardin-Simmons, were on Houston's 11-game schedule.

Jewell Wallace faced the problem of replacing quarterback Charlie Manichia, the 1946 starter, during fall practices. Manichia, troubled by old injuries, was advised to give up football.

Sophomore Boyd Tingle, a 1946 squadman, and freshman Aubrey Baker were the major prospects to step in for Manichia. A heavier, more experienced team seemed to be grounds for optimism.

Centenary, trying to rebuild to the success it had known under Homer Norton and Bo McMillen, brought in four teams, two of them schooled in the T-formation and two in the single wing.

"I'm certainly glad to hear we're not supposed to win this game," said Wallace when advised the Centenary Gents felt sure of themselves.

Elliot Loy's recovery of a fumbled punt led to a first quarter touchdown, and a more effective line paved the way for a 19-7 Cougar victory. Jack Gwin's 39-yard punt return preceded Jack Hurst's 16-yard scoring run in the second quarter, but Centenary's Jim Francis returned a punt 85 yards, cutting the halftime margin to 13-7.

Freshman Bill Morrow accounted for the final TD on a

44-yard end-around maneuver.

End Evan Weaver, writing in the *Daily Cougar*, the student paper, said, "Most people agree that the Cougar victory over the boastful Centenary team was a surprise, but the Gents were the most surprised of the two football clubs—proving that the Cougars are ready to battle the cream of the crop and come out on top."

Against McMurry College the next Saturday, Boyd Tingle etched a line in the Cougar record book which was to stand for more than two decades. He swept out from under center, turned wide around right end, sliced past a linebacker and halfback, and tightroped down the sideline for an 81-yard scoring sprint. The run stood as UH's longest from scrimmage until Reggie Cherry covered 84 yards against San Diego State in 1973.

Ken Hawkins' pair of extra points stood up as the difference in UH's 14-13 victory against McMurry College. Tingle also set up the first score with a 23-yard peg to Loy before his 6-yard TD keeper.

Despite the absence of three injured starters, Bill Cook, Loy, and Bill Moeller, the Coogs extended their winning streak to three in a row by defeating Daniel Baker, 35-12. Once again, Boyd Tingle was a standout. As Zarko Franks described him in *The Chronicle*, "The sweet-running Pasadena boy with oiled ball-

Boyd Tingle, 1947 co-captain.

Evan Weaver, 1947 co-captain.

bearings in his hips topped the touchdown parade."

Tingle, listed at 5-foot-9 and 175 (his brother Bill, a half-back, was 6 feet and 175 pounds) scored on runs of 54 and 3 yards. Valton Green, Baker, and Charlie Brightwell scored once each.

Alan Neveux (left) practices handoffs with Jack Gwin in the 1948 season.

Then, a series of injuries, including Boyd Tingle's hurt shoulder, cut into the Cougars' effectiveness. They scored only four touchdowns while losing their last eight games, including shutouts by North Texas, 33-0; Southwest Texas, 2-0; and Sam Houston State, 23-0, in their last three starts.

Alden Pasche recalls the Hardin-Simmons game at Corpus Christi, "They had a police escort for us from downtown to the stadium, and Jewell's son, Bill, said, 'Daddy, wouldn't it be terrible if we lost after all this?' But we did." The score was 33-7 to the team coached by Warren Woodson, Wallace's coach in junior college.

Several days later Wallace, whose only contract was a handshake, turned in his resignation. His two-year record (7-14) is no accurate measure of his contribution.

As Tom Davison noted in the *Houston Post*, "Primary athletic drawback at UH, the second largest college in Texas, is the lack of a dormitory and training table for its athletes."

Line coach Joe Davis of Rice, Bob Berry of East Texas State, and former Rice aide Buster Brannon were among those rumored under consideration. But by the time of the Ex-Students Association football banquet in February, there was still no replacement to greet Notre Dame's Frank Leahy, the featured speaker, and St. Louis Cardinal manager Eddie Dyer, the master of ceremonies.

The new man, Clyde V. Lee, an assistant at Tulsa University, was hired shortly afterwards. *The Chronicle*, in a story from Tulsa, noted, "...players on two Tulsa elevens have nick-named him Simon Legree Lee...."

Tony Ditta And Bill Cook: Among The First

Like most of their teammates on that first UH football squad, Tony Ditta, a stocky tackle, and Bill Cook, their reed-thin center, were World War II service veterans.

Both had played high school ball in Houston, Ditta at San Jacinto, where he was an all-city and all-state selection, and Cook at Stephen F. Austin.

Ditta, 24 years old when he reported to Coach Jewell Wallace, had spent four years in the army after playing two years at Sam Houston State Teachers. Cook, 21, was a three-year navy veteran of the South Pacific.

UH football got off to a pungent start, says Ditta. The Port City Stockyards were nearby, and close to them was a dog food factory. "They kept you hungry and smelly at the same time," Ditta jokes.

Ditta and Cook were elected co-captains of that first team, an honor both still relish. "Jewell told us, 'There will be more said about this first team than any other unless it wins the national championship,'" Ditta recalls. Wallace's prophecy was to hold true for 30 years, until the 1976 Cougars won the Cotton Bowl.

"We had the attitude of, 'Let's go out and give it fits,'" Ditta says. "We were poor GI kids, and we were out there because we wanted to be out there. We were poor, but we had a certain amount of pride. We had respect for Coach Wallace, and he for us. He was a fair man, he told us what he wanted. I thought the school was destined for greatness from the day it

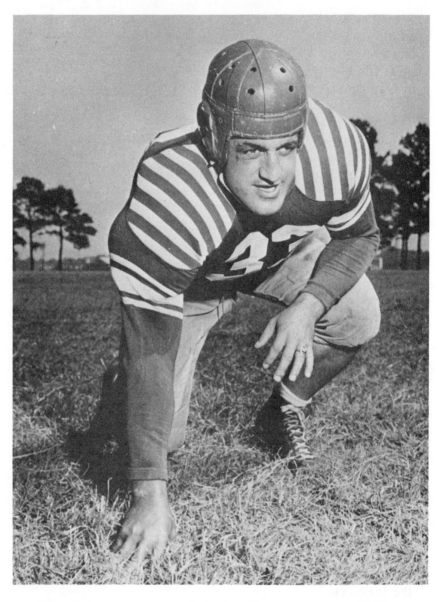

Tony Ditta, co-captain of the first Houston team, in 1946.

opened and it hasn't reached its peak yet."

Jack Gwin, a halfback on that first team, says, "Cook didn't weigh over 165 and hit like he was 250. We called him 'Vitamins' because he was so skinny."

They also vividly recall the team's mode of transportation, an old school bus which they rode to nearby games. "It broke down one night and we had to stay overnight in a hotel," Ditta says. The bus trip back from Camp Hood that first season sticks in Gwin's memory: "Bill Cook and Stuart Gordon both got so sick of riding on it, they got off and hitchhiked back."

Alden Pasche, one of Wallace's assistants, tells this story about Ditta on a trip to East Texas State: "We stopped at a cafe to eat, and there was a slot machine there. Tony kept putting in quarters and putting in quarters. Then Warren Settegast, who was from the River Oaks section, put in one quarter and hit the jackpot. That Tony was so mad, he just kept repeating, 'Damn rich just keep getting richer.'"

Bobby Brown, the school's first trainer, used to ride in the aisle of the bus, seated on a folding chair. "If Bill Cook had weighed 50 more pounds, he would have been the greatest center in pro football," says Brown. "One game at Huntsville against Sam Houston State, Cook got his eye laid open, and we stretched him out on the bench and just sewed it up right there on the sideline."

Ditta, a 220-pounder, "short and squatty" (his description) explains, "All we had was a pair of shoes and a halfway decent hat. We didn't know any better; we thought we were lucky as hell. The school was a lifesaver, where a fellow could go to school and work at the same time. It was a school for the poor man. Half of those players wanted to go into coaching, and we knew it was the only opportunity we'd have."

Ditta, and many of his teammates, took advantage of the chance. He coached for 20 years at Hamilton Junior High, where his teams compiled a 120-32-8 record.

Now an assistant principal, Ditta once told the *Houston Chronicle*'s Bill McMurray, "Junior high coaching, the way I look at it, is where you need more and better coaches. These are the little fellows that you start from scratch and teach everything. You spend more time with most of these boys than their own dads do." Cook, like Ditta, also enjoyed a successful coaching career.

Sitting on the Cougar-red sofa in their home with his wife, Vivian, Ditta describes the singular pleasure of seeing their son, Frank, co-captain the 1971 Cougars. "We kind of expected it because he was captain in junior high and high school." An all-state linebacker, Frank was a three-year starter for the Cougars, returning two interceptions for touchdowns and a blocked punt for another score. His 100-yard interception return against San Jose State in 1971 equalled the NCAA record.

"We ate a lot of steaks because the schools came around to recruit him," says Tony. "Frank did talk about Texas and its traditions," Mrs. Ditta relates. "I asked him how those traditions came about, that it was by sons of the fathers going to the schools their fathers attended. I reminded him it wasn't his traditions at Texas, and UH was a young school."

When Tony Ditta was coaching, he took his sons, Frank and Willie, along on the school bus. Later, Tony says, "I'd be coming home from my game and go out the front door with a sandwich in one hand and a coat in the other to get out and watch them play."

After Tony's senior high school season, he won a *Houston Press* contest as the most valuable player in his district. The prize was a trip to New Orleans and the 1939 Sugar Bowl. His account for the *Press* said, "The TCU-Carnegie Tech football game was the greatest show I've ever seen in my life. And it was a great football game."

A world war and 38 years later, Ditta and Cook reveled in their beloved Cougars' greatest day—in the Cotton Bowl against Maryland.

Jack Gwin,
A Little Scooter

A few weeks after Jack Gwin transferred to UH from the University of Texas, the fuzzy-cheeked little sophomore had heard so many tales of World War II, he felt like a GI.

"We heard a lot of war stories from those guys," Gwin refers to the large group of service veterans on that first Cougar team. "They were a salty bunch of old guys, tough as a boot. Evan Weaver had been in the marines, and he'd tell us, 'You young guys don't let all this influence you.' He wouldn't let me get in the dice games they had before practice."

As a freshman on the Texas varsity in 1945 Gwin had roomed with another smallish player named Emory Bellard, now the head coach at Texas A&M. Bellard helped develop the wishbone offense as a Texas assistant to Darrell Royal, and the Longhorns used it for the first time against the Cougars in their 1968 game.

An all-city back at Lamar High School, Gwin heard from his former coach, Alden Pasche, that UH was going to field its first team. Pasche had joined Jewell Wallace's football staff.

Listed on the school's 1948 roster as only 5-feet-9 and 159 pounds, Gwin co-captained the 1948 team with tackle Cecil Towns. "Jewell always put things on an individual basis, " Gwin recalls, "that it was up to us to get ourselves ready. He rarely raised his voice. One of the few times I remember, he got mad one day at Towns. He kept him after practice and made him run, and he had to be carried to the dressing room. But he made all-conference that year."

Jack Gwin, 1948 co-captain, is aided by manager-trainer Bobby Brown before a Cougar football practice.

Since the school awarded no scholarships until 1948, the players were assigned part-time jobs on campus. "Billy Myers and I went over to Veteransville and mopped and cleaned up the laundry rooms," Gwin says. "The others worked in the cafeteria and painted and cleaned up the gym."

Gwin's wife, the former Dolores Becker, was the school's 1948 homecoming queen.

Bobby Brown, who had attended Lamar High with Gwin and come to UH as the first athletic manager, issued the equipment. "Bobby gave me a pair of lowcut shoes that went from me through my two sons," says Gwin. "During the 1947 season we got new plastic helmets. We thought we were really 'up town.' We wore them for the first time at Stephen F. Austin, but we didn't know how to adjust them, and they kept slipping. Bill Cook got his nose cut, and Towns threw his halfway across the field and told Bobby to go dig his old one out of the sack.

"At Southwest Texas that first year I hurt my ankle, and Jewell picked me up and carried me off the field like a baby," Gwin recalls.

Wallace had to make some allowances for the older players. "Before practice," Gwin relates, "a bunch would sit under the trees and smoke a cigarette. Jewell was against smoking, but I don't think he ever kicked anybody off the team because of it. It was something he had to put up with."

Gwin rates his biggest thrills, "Seeing that first UH touchdown in our first game, that first win over West Texas State, and marching on the field that first time in the school colors. We had a lot of pride. At our 30-year reunion last year, 42 of us showed up out of the 50-odd who are still around."

Charlie Manichia, the Cougars' first quarterback, "would have been as good as anybody who came down the pike," Gwin believes. "He was like Paul Christman and Charlie Trippi, he had the same elusiveness." Christman and Trippi were with the Chicago Cardinals when Gwin went to camp, the first UH athlete sought by the pros.

Some of those first football trips provided indelible memories. Gwin relates, "When we went to El Paso in 1946 to play Texas Mines, a bunch of us went across the (Texas-Mexico) border and put deposits down on cowboy boots. They took our addresses and told us they'd mail them to us. We're still waiting on those boots.

"At Commerce after we'd played East Texas, we had our postgame meal back at the hotel. Later, one of the guys crawled out the window of our room and came back smiling just before it was time to meet down in the lobby. Jewell said, 'Men, I had the best night's sleep I've ever had.' That guy said, 'Me, too, coach.'

"We flew to El Paso in 1948 in a plane converted from a World War II airborne transport. Still had bucket seats in it. It was bumpy, and Buck Miller got so sick he couldn't play. We came back by train."

Gwin recalls going to the airport to meet the first Shasta, UH's Cougar mascot.

Shasta III, Cougar mascot, watches proceedings on gridiron.

In 1948, when Clyde Lee set up the first athletic dorm, Gwin would have nocturnal visits from his more adventuresome teammates: "The fire escape was on my side of the building, and when bed check was over, here they'd come, crawling past my bed to the window. Mrs. Booker, our den mother, was a kindly soul to put up with us."

Gwin played only sporadically at the start of the 1948 season, and gathering his courage, he went to see Lee. "I asked him why I wasn't playing," Gwin says, "and he said, 'Young man, sit down in that chair.' Then he told me in no uncertain terms that I'd start playing when I got the right attitude. He started me in the third game, and I never came out for a down after that."

Hugh Roy Cullen,
"The Father Of UH"

No better title could be bestowed upon Hugh Roy Cullen than "The Father of UH," as he was known at the time of his death, July 4, 1957. Few personal fortunes in the history of U.S. education have been used as generously as Cullen's, and without his personal interest and financial backing the school— and its athletic programs—scarcely could have survived the early years.

Cullen's son-in-law, Corbin Robertson, Sr., a former member of the board of regents and chairman of the athletic committee, became interested in the Cougars through Cullen. Robertson, a familiar figure on the UH practice field for nearly 20 years, believes Cullen's interest in the school stemmed from his friendship with Col. W. B. Bates, another early benefactor and former regent. "Once Mr. Cullen became interested, you got his full shot," Robertson said.

"Mr. Cullen always had the philosophy that if young people had good health and a good education, they could make a way for themselves," said Athletic Director Harry Fouke. "He contributed his resources toward those ends. He and Mrs. Cullen were regulars at all the home games; they'd sweat the losses and wins like everybody else."

Fouke illustrates their interest in the Cougars, "One night at Jeppesen Stadium it was pouring down rain, and they were bundled up on the last row, next to the press box. I invited them upstairs out of the rain, but they said, 'No, thank you, we like to be out here with the rest of the supporters.'"

Johnny Goyen remembers, "Every time they attended a

H. R. Cullen, "Father of UH," with Gen. A. D. Bruce (left), former UH chancellor, and Coach Clyde Lee (right) at Cougar homecoming festivities in 1954.

school function, the students would rise as one. No one told them to do it, they did it out of their love for them. The chemistry between them was the greatest I've ever seen."

Goyen remembers, "Someone had taken Mr. Cullen by the night school at San Jacinto High School in the 30s. He'd seen the college students sitting at those small desks, and the cramped conditions. He said, 'We've got to do something for them.'"

Cullen made his first large gift, $78,000, in 1938. Two months later he announced he and Mrs. Cullen would contribute $260,000 for a liberal arts and cultural center, opened in 1945 and named the Roy G. Cullen Building, for their only son, killed in an oil field explosion in 1936.

On March 28, 1947, Cullen announced the establishment of the Cullen Foundation "for the purpose of aiding educational, medical and charitable institutions" and set aside oil properties on 7,743 acres containing 30-40 million barrels of oil worth $89 million at then existing oil prices. He said he and his wife, Lillie, "are both so selfish that we wish to see our money spent during our lifetime, so that we may derive great pleasure from it."

Just three days after that, in his typical, offhand manner, Cullen told the Houston Chamber of Commerce board of directors that he and Mrs. Cullen "have been thinking this thing over, and we've changed our minds a little bit.

"We've decided to double that figure."

Cullen then disclosed they were adding more than 10,000 acres to the foundation. Its estimated value of $160 million made it the largest charitable foundation in the South and the second largest in the nation. Said Cullen, "It is our hope that the trustees will use both the principal and the income to make Texas Medical Center and the University of Houston centers of world distinction."

One of the world's great philanthropists, Cullen at the time of his death had given away an estimated 90 per cent of his personal fortune, much of it to Houston hospitals and also to Baylor University, besides UH. Yet his first gift—a $5 check to the Salvation Army—bounced because of insufficient funds.

Cullen was to say of that incident, "It's easier for me to give a million dollars now than it was to give $5 to the Salvation Army 30 years ago."

His gifts to the University of Houston alone totalled $50 to $60 million, estimates the UH Office of Development.

Bobby Brown, the school's first athletic trainer, relates one of the many stories (this one possibly apocryphal) of Cullen's generosity:

"At the 1948 football banquet, Mr. Cullen rose to say a few words. He said, 'I really appreciate your inviting Mrs. Lillie and me. I'd like to say that I'm giving $1 million—' About that time Mrs. Cullen began tugging at his coat. He leaned over and they spoke for a moment, then he said, 'I beg your pardon, Mrs. Cullen pointed out that I made a slight mistake—I meant to say I am giving $10 million.'"

Robertson, unaware of that incident, says, "Mr. Cullen didn't get his decimal points mixed like that. But anything he

Corbin Robertson, Sr., former regent, has been instrumental in the rise of the Cougar athletic program.

said, you could put it down in your mind."

Robertson does recall the campus pep rally after the 37-7 victory over Baylor in 1953. Cullen brought world-wide attention to the school by telling the crowd he was donating $2½ million "for their great football victory."

Says Robertson, "He always had a sense of the dramatic. He had already planned to make the gift, and he and his attorneys had gone over it and over it."

Despite that, the flood of world headlines spawned numerous tales, and later Cullen confided to his son-in-law, "I don't know when I'll ever learn to stop throwing in those ad-libs."

Dr. Franklin Stovall, ex-chairman of the faculty athletic committee, remembers that even though the Cougars were financially strapped, "We immediately won the reputation of being a very wealthy athletic department. Harry Fouke and I took a lot of kidding about our sudden wealth at NCAA meetings and such."

An erroneous story of that time, published in a Swiss magazine, reported that Cullen gave $5 million to UH but that a Houston newspaper in a typographical error reported the gift as

$15 million. "After that," the magazine said, "Cullen called the owner of the paper, Jesse Jones, and told him, 'O.K. Jesse, I'll give the $15 million since you've said so, but don't let it happen again.'"

Goyen describes another incident: "We wanted to honor Mr. and Mrs. Cullen at our first homecoming game, and Roger Jeffrey and I went to tell Mr. Cullen of our plan. He asked us, 'How many people will there be?' We told him, 'Three or four thousand.' He told us, 'That's fine; we can handle that.'

"Roger and I thought it was kind of an odd reaction, but we didn't say anything. Then his secretary called and asked, 'What kind of food do you want for the party at Mr. Cullen's home?'"

"I said, 'Oh, no, it's not at his home. We're honoring them at the football game.' But he was perfectly willing to have several thousand people come to his home."

Goyen remembers the Cullens inviting everyone who had worked on the "Cullen Day" festivities at the UH-Baylor game in 1951 to a party that night at River Oaks Country Club: "They stood in the door and shook hands with every person who came."

Brown, who decided to leave as UH athletic trainer for a pro football job in 1948, says, "Mr. Cullen called me to his office and told me my scholarship would always be there. I'd been one of the first four or five to get an athletic scholarship, and I came back in 1951 and got my degree."

Baylor also honored the Cullens at "Cullen Day" ceremonies when the Baylor-UH game was held in Waco. At one of them, says Goyen, Cullen thanked Baylor's officials, then continued, "'I've got to be honest, I want my University of Houston Cougars to win this game.' He had to tell the truth about his feelings."

Cullen's grandfather, Ezekiel W. Cullen, was a Texas pioneer and a member of the House of Representatives of the Republic of Texas. His Cullen Act, proposed to the Republic's Third Congress on January 4, 1839, was to be the keynote for the land-grant plan for free Texas schools. H. R. Cullen, born on his father's farm in Denton County in 1881, grew up in San Antonio, where he left school at the age of 12 to go to work at $3 a week in a candy store.

Young Cullen worked at various jobs until he was 17, when a San Antonio cotton broker gave him a job. A year later, he had learned enough about the cotton business and gained enough confidence to gain a job as a representative for a Houston cotton factor and soon had his own business in Houston.

After going into the oil business and bringing in his first well, Cullen described his early years, "It was a hard life. I've gone a week at a time without sleep and sometimes I was so tired, I couldn't pull off my own boots. However, I can truthfully say I was never discouraged. I taught myself to be optimistic."

His biography, *Hugh Roy Cullen*, tells, "On a visit to Houston Billy Graham asked Cullen why he, who had given millions to Methodist, Episcopal, Baptist, Catholic, and nonsectarian hospitals, had not become a member of any church. Cullen took the evangelist out on the lawn in front of his home and pointed to the sky.

"'See that star up there? It's probably a million light years away. And over there is another star—maybe a million light years away from the first one. My church is up there somewhere, and I haven't been able to locate the exact place where it is.'"

H. R. Cullen (left) and future U. S. President Dwight Eisenhower attend a 1950 Cougar homecoming pep rally. Note the football ribbons on their coat lapels.

The day after his death, classes were suspended and flags flown at half-mast at UH. Dr. Clanton Williams, then the school's president, said of Cullen, "Love of and service to his fellows characterized his life. He was devoted to his family, to his friends and to the youth of this area. He served them as few men are privileged to serve." Dr. Hyman Schachtel of Congregation Beth Israel added, "Mr. Cullen was a man who made philanthropy a religion." Fouke describes the contribution of the Cullens to the Cougars, "They never asked for anything but always gave a great deal."

The first Cougar involvement of Cullen's son-in-law Robertson also was philanthropically oriented. Robertson recalls: "In 1947 I was at a social function of some kind for athletics. Jess Neely (of Rice) and Harry Fouke were there. I was standing in a group of people and commented that I was interested in helping some way. Harry heard me; he was out there in those shacks at the time, and I have accused him since of cutting me out of the herd like a cowboy.

"Harry took me to lunch at the old cafeteria, then to the old gym which was dilapidated, then the locker room, which was nothing. I told him, 'If you're not the No. 1 candidate for help, I don't know who is.'

"My interest then was as a football fan in helping them get going. Once you get interested in one part, you get interested in the others. An excellent athletic program goes hand in hand with academic excellence. I visited more and more with Mr. Cullen, who was then chairman of the board of regents."

A graduate of Northwestern University, where he was an all-conference end, Robertson had flown on B-17s based in Europe during World War II. His crew members got in the habit of rubbing his "lucky" gold ring, and they did not lose a man. Later, *Life Magazine* heard of the story and prepared a picture layout. But it was discovered their bombardier had been interned in a neutral country and was then flying again in the same area, contrary to the Geneva Convention, and the story was scrapped.

"Before Christmas in 1956, Mr. and Mrs. Cullen came over to see the grandchildren," Robertson says. "He and I went up to have a drink before dinner.

"Mr. Cullen said to me, 'Promise me that if anything happens to me, you'll stay on the board of regents until the school is financially stable and its graduate school is approved.' It was the first time I'd ever heard him talk like that, like something might happen to him. We were talking about things years in the future, that he with his foresight was concerned with.

"Less than two months later, he suffered a massive stroke and never recovered from it. When I later resigned from the board, I had all the confidence in the world that under the leadership of Dr. Philip Hoffman (current UH president) the school would fulfill its promise.

"Mr. Cullen had his dream for UH," Robertson says, "and the living proof is out there."

Harry Fouke, The Architect

If Harry Fouke, as young and energetic as he was, had known the enormity of the job he undertook in 1945, he could have been excused for saying, "Thanks, but no thanks."

There were then exactly four buildings on the UH campus, and virtually no facilities or equipment for Fouke's so-called athletic department. He truly was starting from scratch.

"There were no playing fields," Fouke relates more than 30 years later, "and the land was covered with sunflowers. I came here to start from scratch and build a PE program for the students." When the Cougars were invited in the autumn of 1945 to join the Lone Star Conference, which was resuming competition after World War II, the school did not have a single athletic uniform.

Then in his early 30s, Fouke was athletic director of the Houston public school system, a position he had held in San Antonio for three years. As a halfback at Rice Institute, Fouke had helped the Owls win their first Southwest Conference football title in 1934. That team had defeated Purdue on the same afternoon that Texas had beaten Notre Dame to bring the SWC national prestige for the first time.

When Dr. E. E. Oberholtzer, UH's first president, and the board of regents approved Fouke's recommendation to join the Lone Star, the Cougars began by competing in basketball. They started a rich tradition which continues to this day.

Guy Lewis, UH's present basketball coach, was the star of that first team, coached by Alden Pasche. Like most of those early Cougars, Lewis had played elsewhere (at Rice) before the

54

war and had recently been discharged from the air corps. Bill Swanson, Willie Wells, Louis Brown, Charles Carpenter, and Dick Pratt were among others on the team.

UH's first athletic budget amounted to $6.27, and Fouke admits, "We had more nerve than sense." A basketball scrimmage with Ellington Air Force Base, a future benefactor, was the school's first paid athletic event.

Chairs were placed on the gym floor and the teams played crosscourt, Fouke recalls. "There were no leather basketballs to be had because of the war, and we swapped Ellington for a good one with one that was peeling. Their man said, 'You people are really bad off.' We couldn't get regular uniforms, just some old gray sweatsuits."

Fouke recalls that tickets sold for 25 cents (students) and 50 cents (non-students). Dr. Sue Garrison, the women's PE director, manned the ticket booth, "then she'd step outside and tear the tickets as they came in the door," Fouke says.

Under Pasche, those Cougars won the conference basketball crown and competed in their first national competition, the NAIB tournament in Kansas City. Before that, they exchanged their battered old basketballs for a bag of new ones with their friends at Ellington.

"People said I was crazy to come out here," Fouke says, "but I felt this could become a major university with a major athletic program, and I liked the idea of building something from scratch." A UH engineering professor named Dave Williams, who later pioneered the rise of college golf, describes his first impression of Fouke, "That's a mighty young man for a job like this."

Fouke explains, "From the day we started, Dr. Oberholtzer felt this university would develop into a great institution serving this part of the country. I felt the athletic program should be of the same calibre as the total university."

Tony Ditta, a co-captain of the school's first football team, describes one of Fouke's talents, "He can communicate with the Queen of Sheba or the 'roaches' of the Third Ward."

Even then, Fouke pursued his vision of achieving higher and higher goals: "At our first Lone Star Conference meeting we told them that as fast as we could get bigger and better, we'd be moving out." Darrell Tully, then an assistant at East Texas

Harry Fouke, Houston's first athletic director.

State, later a highly successful high school coach and athletic director, joshed Fouke later, "There you didn't even have a football, and you were already talking about getting into a bigger conference."

After three years in the Lone Star, Fouke felt the time had come to move along. "We went into the Gulf Coast Conference because the Lone Star was getting too big," he explains. "It had added Trinity and Midwestern, and we felt it necessary to leave to have the flexibility to schedule larger, better-known schools."

So UH teamed with North Texas, Trinity and Midwestern (the latter two also withdrawing from the LSC) in the Gulf Coast through the 1949-50 seasons. In 1951 the Missouri Valley Conference was the Cougars' lair when UH joined Oklahoma

A&M, Tulsa, Wichita, Bradley, Drake, St. Louis, and Detroit. "We only had to play four conference games," Fouke explains, "and at that time the Valley was probably the best basketball conference in the nation. That was where we learned a lot about basketball."

Then, in 1960 the school decided on another step, one which was to lead through many trials but eventually to Fouke's cherished, never-to-be-forgotten goal of Southwest Conference membership.

"We needed to have dates for nationally recognized schools which would have been conflicting with Valley games," Fouke explains. "We had games with Alabama, Ole Miss, and Mississippi State coming up, and we could see that down the line we were ready to be first class. We've had change, but stability with it, too. The development of our program has received good leadership at every sport level."

But life as an independent quickly proved to be no bed of roses.

The problem really became noticeable after one of UH's most prestigious victories, the 33-19 conquest of Tennessee in the 1953 season finale. "All of a sudden people who never recognized us knew who we were," Fouke says. "That win also hurt. A lot of the teams that had been talking about playing us then decided they wanted no part of us. Scheduling became a constant battle."

Fouke recalls seeing Maryland Coach Jim Tatum shortly afterward, and Tatum deflected the idea of a future game, "I know about that job you did on Tennessee."

Another obstacle was UH's image in its own backyard, where it often played second fiddle to the ivy-covered walls of Rice and its SWC membership. The schools now have a cordial relationship, but even Fouke's diplomacy and tact were tested often in earlier years.

Rice Stadium was UH's home field from 1950 until moving into the Astrodome in 1965, but the Cougars received no parking or concessions revenue and had to take the second choice of dates at Rice.

Fouke made repeated inquiries about SWC membership starting in the late 1940s, supported by Baylor, but when Texas Tech was admitted in 1956, the conference decided members would be admitted by invitation only. Another UH application at the 1956 SWC meeting in Fayetteville, Arkansas, was not acted upon.

Financing of the athletic program became a never-ending battle, but the Cougars kept their heads above the red ink, thanks to the never-ending support of Hugh Roy Cullen and Corby Robertson, his son-in-law.

"Without Corby's assistance," says Fouke, "I doubt we would have been much more than a second class program. He helped get the city behind us." Adds Dr. Franklin Stovall, former chairman of the faculty athletic committee, "We never would have made it without Mr. Cullen and Corby."

Williams recounts one critical juncture, "In the spring of 1952 they were talking about cutting back from 50 or 55 football scholarships to 33 like the NAIA schools. We were almost down for the count, and the 1952 season pulled us through."

Another breaking point was close in 1959. "We were ready to cut out all spring sports," Williams says. "We'd won three national championships in golf, and I told them I could raise enough money myself for our golf program. We sold $9,000 worth of sponsorships for our All-American Intercollegiate Invitational tournament."

Stovall relates a sequence of events when Gen. A. D. Bruce was UH chancellor: "He was ready to recommend to the board of regents that we discontinue all spring sports and keep only football and basketball. I never fought and argued so much in all my life, pointing out that a move like that would mean the end of our entire athletic program. They wanted to save money, but the total budget for spring sports wasn't really that much.

"I remember him telling me that he thought I was a little prejudiced, but he withdrew his recommendation. But it had been on the brink of tottering. That would have been the death knell for us. To my mind, that was the most crucial period, but every year was a battle.

"Corby always picked up the tab to make up the deficit."

Admission to the Texas state system of higher education in 1963 helped relieve part of the financial burden, since UH then became eligible for state tax money for physical education facilities.

Fouke and Stovall always made annual trips to all the SWC

As he arrives to begin his new job as Houston football coach, Bill Yeoman is greeted by Athletic Director Harry Fouke (left) and Sports Information Director Ted Nance at the Houston airport in December, 1961.

schools. "There were few hazards like driving through the hills of Arkansas at night with Harry at the wheel," Stovall says. For years, however, those jaunts appeared to be exercises in futility, even though Fouke never lost sight of the goal.

Then a slow series of events seemed to conspire on the Cougars' side. One was the 37-7 thrashing of Michigan State in 1967 and the resultant increase in pressure upon the University of Texas from UH adherents in the state legislature for the Longhorns to play the Cougars.

The first meeting of the state's two largest universities since 1953 drew a sellout crowd of more than 65,000 at Memorial Stadium in Austin and produced a memorable 20-20 tie.

With the NCAA approval of an 11-game schedule, Fouke quickly asked Darrell Royal of Texas for more dates.

"I'll never forget Darrell's answer," Fouke told Bob Galt of the *Dallas Times Herald.* "He said, 'We don't want to play you again until Houston is just as important to us as Texas is to Houston. Right now there are five or six more games on our schedule more important than Houston, but right now Texas would be the most important game to you.' That made sense to me."

There the situation stood, until Fouke was at the breakfast table with his wife, Virginia, one Saturday in the autumn of 1970. The phone rang, and Mrs. Fouke informed her husband that it was Royal calling.

"Harry, are you still interested in joining the Southwest Conference?" were the words Fouke heard. Controlling his shaking coffee cup Fouke answered, "Well, Darrell, what do you mean?" Royal replied, "If you are, we are thinking about sponsoring you."

After that, Rice joined Texas as a co-sponsor, and UH's membership was all but assured. The Cougars were admitted at the SWC spring meeting in 1971 at College Station, where a five-year waiting period for UH football competition was agreed on.

Another condition of SWC membership was a two-year option period when visiting SWC schools could elect to play either in the Astrodome or Rice Stadium. That option is due to expire after the 1977 season.

Fouke still sympathizes with the plight of Jewell Wallace, the school's first football coach. "I'm not sure Knute Rockne could have handled that group," Fouke recalls the collection of military veterans. "They had had enough discipline in the service.

"Clyde Lee moved us from one stage to a different stage. All of a sudden, we were playing major calibre teams, and our schedules got tougher all the time."

With the move to the Astrodome, "We had an identity of our own," Fouke says. "Every time we reach one plateau there has been some development which has given us new impetus. I'm not sure it could have been done anywhere except in Houston. Being flexible to meet change, that's the secret."

Lovette Hill, who joined Lee's football staff, served under

60

Large, enthusiastic crowds like this attend University of Houston games in the Astrodome.

three head coaches, and coached UH baseball for two decades, recalls, "I just believed what Fouke and Clyde Lee said, and they said, 'We will.'"

Fouke had started his college career at Rice under extreme adversity during the Depression. He had banked his hard-earned savings, matched by his father. "I had just gone downtown and bought some clothes and gave a $50 check, " Fouke recounts, "and before that check could even clear, the bank in San Antonio where I had deposited my money went broke."

His football scholarship enabled Fouke to attend college, and he won Rice's Bob Quin Award, its highest athletic honor.

An eager golfer, tennis and handball player, Fouke and his good friend, Dr. James Whitehurst, usually occupy adjoining seats at the rear of UH charters. They form a smooth bridge or gin rummy duo as they "pick their pigeons."

That is a form of competition, and competition is the core of Fouke's philosophy for the Cougars: "I've always felt the success of intercollegiate athletic program is based on competition between natural rivals. College athletics is part of the culture of this nation. You look at the big games when the whole town closed down to go to the ballgame. It's always been between natural rivals. In college athletics it's Texas-A&M, Army-Navy, USC-UCLA, Georgia-Georgia Tech, Ole Miss-Mississippi State. What we could contribute was where we could compete against our natural rivals."

Aiming For The Majors

In those early years recruiting fans was almost as hard as recruiting Cougar football players.

"It was damn near impossible," recalls Johnny Goyen, the Houston city councilman and former UH alumni director. "We got up a season ticket drive, and one day Mr. Cullen called and said, 'How are you doing?' Then he told us to go see the members of the board of regents.

"A friend, Jack Wilson, and I went to one board member, and he started lecturing us, 'The trouble with your team is, you're playing teams too much better than you are. You need to play teams more on your level, like Lamar High School.'

"I didn't report that to Mr. Cullen, because I didn't want to see a member of the board of regents strangled. We felt frustrated. I'll bet there weren't more than 100 season tickets sold outside of what Corby Robertson bought."

Ned Thompson, the school's athletic business manager for more than two decades, remembers submitting a budget that had to be detailed "down to the last shoestring" and estimates the entire athletic program was financed with about $90,000 annually in the first years.

Clyde Lee, the new coach, needed help fast, and he got valuable aid from the junior college ranks. He recruited quarterback Alan Neveux and speedy Max Clark, 5-foot-9 and 155 pounds, from Kilgore College, his old school.

The returnees from former Coach Jewell Wallace included

Jackie Gwin, Boyd and Bill Tingle, Bill Cook, Cecil Towns, Bill Bidwill, Bernard Purdum, L.Z. Bryan, and Bill Hollis.

Clark quickly paid dividends, returning a punt 70 yards and sprinting 23 yards for the second score in a 14-0 triumph over Texas A&I, Lee's UH debut.

Texas Mines (35-7) and Southwestern Louisiana (21-7) dealt out defeats before the Cougars won a 40-33 scoring duel with Louisiana Tech. Neveux rushed for 103 yards, passed to Gwin for one touchdown and ran for two, and kicked four conversions against Tech. Maurice Elliott's 42-yard interception return was the deciding touchdown. Perhaps coincidentally, the Ex-Students Association announced the next week it was buying two station wagons for the athletic department.

Houston downed East Texas State, 18-7, for its third season victory. Runs of 67 yards by Bo Campbell and 35 by Neveux decided the East Texas game, but three straight losses followed, to Trinity, West Texas State, and Stephen F. Austin.

The Cougars won a mud battle with North Texas, 8-6, halting the Eagles inside the one late in the game. Neveux's punt out on the eight was followed by Buck Miller's safety, the winning margin. Don Willhelm's recovery of a fumbled punt at the three had set up Clark's 5-yard scoring run.

UH offset a 3-0 loss to Southwest Texas with a closing 22-13 decision over Sam Houston State, bunching its scoring total in the second period. Neveux passed 19 yards to Ed Staggs for the first score; then Frank Roddy blocked a punt which Hollis recovered in the end zone. After the Bearkats scored, Clark returned the kickoff 40 yards and later scored from the three. Johnny O'Hara's interception led to Neveux's 37-yard field goal before the half.

Towns was all-Lone Star Conference tackle as the Cougars finished 5-6 for the year and fourth in the seven-team conference at 3-3.

The Cougars then made the first of many applications for Southwest Conference membership. Dr. E. E. Oberholtzer, UH president; Dr. Frank Stovall of the athletic council; Fouke; and Lee appeared at the 1948 SWC winter meeting in Dallas.

As expected, the application was rejected, along with those from Texas Tech and Hardin-Simmons, with a moratorium placed on expansion for at least three years.

Cecil Towns, 1949 co-captain.

H. R. Cullen, chairman of the board of regents, said, "The University of Houston's application for admission to the Southwest Conference should further evidence the determination to provide students and alumni and the people of Houston with a well balanced athletic program on a par with any college in the nation.

"We are attempting to build one of the great universities of the world, and our athletic program is included in these ambitions."

UH, Trinity, and North Texas then withdrew from the Lone Star to form a new conference later named the Gulf Coast Conference.

Prominent among new names on the schedule was William & Mary, a nationally recognized power with preseason All-Americans Jack Cloud and Lou Creekmur. The Indians had tied Sugar Bowl champion North Carolina and defeated Arkansas and Oklahoma A&M in two straight bowl games. St. Bonaventure, Wichita, and St. Louis also were new opponents.

Lee initiated the first athletic dorm on campus, a renovated ROTC barracks building, and a training table. "I remember going down to the furniture store with Clyde to pick out the new beds," Thompson said. "We were so proud, we thought we were moving into the Shamrock."

"Creekmur was one of the most tremendous tackles I ever saw in my life," Lovette Hill recalls 1949 opening night.

"That crowd was vibrant," Thompson still recalls it vividly. "People were talking about it for weeks afterward."

The renowned Cloud scored on two short plunges in the first half and W&M held off the surging Cougars, 14-13. Aubrey Baker and Jack Golden scored TDs, but Neveux's second extra point kick was blocked.

A junior college transfer named Gene Shannon scored twice as the Cougars shook off 11 fumbles to defeat Wichita, 26-6, and they beat Southwestern Louisiana and West Texas for a 3-1 start. UH's ground game and Cowboy John Ford's passes finished in a 27-27 tie with Hardin-Simmons. Losses to Midwestern, St. Bonaventure, and North Texas followed.

The trip to Olean, New York, to play St. Bonaventure was an adventure that required two days through snowstorms in a pair of DC-3s. Lee held a workout alongside the runway near a deserted air force barracks outside Louisville during a fuel stop. Another drill was staged on the dirt floor of a horse show arena in Bradford, Pennsylvania.

Shannon's three touchdowns in the second half helped wipe out an early 21-0 deficit and aided a 28-21 win over Trinity, and the Cougars were within reach of the first winning season in their four-year football history. They blazed to a 35-0 Thanksgiving Day triumph at St. Louis and a 5-4-1 record.

Once again preseason developments made for a lively summer. UH joined the Missouri Valley Conference, signed with Baylor for the first game in the Bears' new stadium, and arranged to play home games with William & Mary and Tulsa in the new Houston Stadium adjacent to Rice Institute. For the first time, their schedule qualified the Cougars as a "major" college in football, and there were new air-conditioned dorms on campus.

But Ted Marchibroda and St. Bonaventure punctured the balloon as the Easterners victimized UH's pass defense. The Cougars jumped ahead, 14-0, before Marchibroda threw scoring passes of 68 and 30 yards and sneaked for another TD.

The Cougars were no match for Baylor the next week in their first game with a Southwest Conference foe, bowing 34-7. Shannon's running was one of the few bright spots for Houston.

A 20-16 loss to Trinity made for a 0-3 start before Bobby Rogers, a new quarterback, got the offense rolling in a 27-7 victory over Louisville. The Cougars had their good days, notably wins over Wichita, 46-6, and a 36-18 trouncing of William & Mary, but their bad days gave them a 4-6 record.

Shannon scored twice against Wichita; Clark ran 45 yards for another; and end Phil Koonce scored on a 26-yard interception return and a blocked punt. Their one-game school scoring record made for pleasant movie viewing of the game films Lee had started the year before.

Ned Thompson recalls that on the first such occasion, the cameraman forgot to remove the lens cover, "and I think that disturbed Clyde more than anything I can remember."

Shannon and Clark staged a cameraman's delight in the 36-18 victory over William & Mary. Clark, calling offensive signals from his halfback post, amassed 198 yards on 18 carries, and Shannon added 157 on 22 carries.

Gene Shannon (24) steps through fallen defenders.

Aubrey Baker's 67-yard dash and Clark's two touchdowns pulled a near upset of one of Tulsa's greatest teams, but the Cougars bowed, 28-21, in the season windup.

With Gov. Allan Shivers among a crowd of dignitaries to honor Mr. and Mrs. H. R. Cullen at halftime, the Cougars hosted Baylor, their first SWC home opponent, to launch the 1951 season. But the Wednesday before the game starting quarterback Rogers twisted a knee, and junior college transfer Bobby Clatterbuck had to step in for the school's "biggest" game.

Quarterbacked by Houstonian Larry Isbell, the Bears

Quarterback Bobby Clatterbuck discusses strategy with Clyde Lee in a 1950 game at Rice Stadium.

wrung out a 19-0 victory before an estimated 60,000. The Cougars reached the 2 and 16 without scoring on the team that was to play in the Sugar Bowl on New Year's Day.

Clatterbuck gained his bearings against Detroit and started a 33-7 rout with an 84-yard pass play to end Vic Hampel. Shannon sprinted 33 and 30 and Bill Bidwell raced 21 as the Cougars piled up a record 608 yards total offense.

Shannon rushed for 126 yards on 15 carries and scored the game's only touchdown on a 33-yard, fourth quarter dash to beat Texas Tech, 6-0.

Shannon caught two touchdown passes and made a 23-yard scoring run in a 46-27 loss to Tulsa.

After winning a scoring duel with Hardin-Simmons and losing one to Villanova in which Shannon had three TDs and 158 yards rushing, UH lost to Wichita and Louisville. Then its defense began making big plays.

Jim Van Haverbeke and Marvin Lackey turned interceptions into touchdowns, and Randy Owens kicked a 34-yard field goal in the first three minutes of a 31-7 humbling of Oklahoma A&M.

Linebacker Paul Carr's 44-yard interception return was the winning margin in a closing 20-14 triumph at North Texas State. Van Haverbeke's interception on the final play of the game negated a successful onside kick by the Eagles.

Discovered in a scrimmage against Ellington Field, where he was a control tower operator, Carr staged a defensive spectacular. He kicked off three times and made all three tackles downfield, and press box observers estimated he must have been in on 75 to 80 percent of the tackles. "In Houston's brief six-year collegiate football history, there have been mighty men up front," wrote the *Houston Chronicle*'s Zarko Franks, "...but it will be conceded that no one player ever dominated the defensive scene like Paul Carr did this bleak afternoon."

The win earned the school's first bowl game, against Dayton University in the Salad Bowl January 1 at Phoenix, Arizona. It may not have been the Cotton Bowl, but it still warmed the hearts of UH followers.

Shannon, who finished the season as the nation's No. 4 rusher, displayed his usual silky running style in the bowl game, outrushing the opposing team's offense for the sixth time that

70

year and scoring all four touchdowns.

With Shannon gaining 175 yards on 28 carries, aided by Warren Ramsey and Owens, the Cougars triumphed, 26-21. Shannon, naturally, was voted the game's most valuable player. The school's first 1,000-yard rusher, he totaled 1,211 yards, a school record that stood until Paul Gipson broke it in 1968.

Ramsey gained 83 yards in 13 tries, and Owens 75 on 9. Buck Miller, Shannon's trusty pulling guard, Howard Clapp, and Lloyd Holloway were among the blocking notables.

Ken Pridgeon, a reserve quarterback and the team's punter, recalls that Lee managed to show a sense of humor under tense circumstances: "Dayton had a good punt returner, and Coach Lee told me to kick out of bounds. They had a good rush on, and I shanked the kick about two yards. When I came back, he said, 'Ken, for gosh sakes, quit following my orders so closely.'"

Clatterbuck's 48-yard pass to Hampel set up the third score, and Jim Van Haverbeke's fumble recovery led to the decisive fourth touchdown.

Lee said later, "Gene's sixth sense on the field made him always seem to do the right thing at the right time. A genius at using his blockers, he was most effective behind Buck Miller. Whenever he won an honor, he claimed it for 'Buck Miller and me.'"

Gene Shannon,
The Gliding Irishman

Before Gene Shannon, the sprouting UH had several good runners, backs like Charlie Manichia, Valton Green, Jack Gwin, Alan Neveux, Aubrey Baker, and Max Clark, Shannon's teammate.

But the calm Irishman from the little Gulf Coast town of Freeport was the first to gain national attention. To this day, he and his faithful blocker, guard Quay "Buck" Miller, own unique distinctions in UH football history.

Shannon and Miller are the only Cougars to own all-conference awards from two leagues, making the 1950 All-Gulf Coast Conference and the 1951 All-Missouri Valley.

"I never weighed over about 180," says Shannon. "I didn't ever realize at the time being a little scared didn't hurt any. Harlan Baldridge played behind me, and he had as much to do with what success I had as anybody. He was my biggest booster, and I knew if I slipped just a little, he'd take my place."

His three-year 1949-51 career rushing figure of 2,507 yards stood as the school record until 1968, when Paul Gipson revised it. Thus far, it has been surpassed by only Gipson and Robert Newhouse.

Shannon's one-year record of 1,211 yards in 1951 was not bettered until Gipson exceeded it in 1968.

His gliding running style and remarkable gift of changing direction are what friend and foe alike remember. "As great as any I've seen," recalls Paul Carr, who played on the San Fran-

Guard Buck Miller lends Gene Shannon a helping hand with his jersey.

cisco 49ers with Hugh McElhenny and Joe Perry. "Speed, moves, toughness—he had everything, and along with it all, he was a great person. I saw him do things that Warren McVea did later. He'd be going full speed, plant his foot and be six feet to one side before you knew it."

"A very fluid runner, not a jitterbug like McVea," says Ken Pridgeon. "He had a slide step where he'd glide right up on

Aided by guard Buck Miller (60), Gene Shannon (24) darts for open ground.

you." Recalls Johnny Goyen, "Gene ran like he was on velvet, and he used the officials to screen people off. He had great peripheral vision."

Buddy Gillioz, one of the school's great defensive tackles, relates, "I can never remember a solid tackle on him the two years I played with him. He'd be a great back today. He'd be running full speed right at you and come to a screeching halt, and slide over. He never got emotional; he was always cool and collected."

After Shannon ran for 148 yards and scored three times against Villanova in 1951, Wildcat Coach Art Raimo noted, "He made me think of Charlie Justice more than once. That boy was dangerous every time he got his hands on the ball." Raimo had played on the same service team with Justice in World War II.

Shannon personally outrushed Detroit, Villanova, Wichita, and Louisville his senior year, and his 68-yarder was the Cougars' only touchdown against Baylor the year before, when he also had 158 yards against William & Mary.

But his greatest day was in the Cougars' first postseason game, the 1952 Salad Bowl at Phoenix. Shannon that day scored four touchdowns and ran for 152 yards on 27 carries in the Cougars' 26-21 victory.

"I got some publicity for it, but I didn't have that good a game," is Shannon's typically modest recollection. "The blocking was great that day."

Shannon ran for 14 touchdowns and caught passes for three more in 1951, when he ranked No. 4 nationally in NCAA statistics. He averaged 7.35 yards per carry that year, a figure bettered among the NCAA top ten by only Oklahoma's Buck McPhail and Tennessee's Hank Lauricella.

"Shannon worked beautifully with Buck Miller," recalls Jack Scott, former UH sports publicist, "He knew every move Buck was going to make, and Gene's first step was from here to that wall."

Drafted by the 49ers, Shannon entered the military service instead. He began his coaching career at New London, where he became head coach, then athletic director, principal and is now superintendent of schools.

Shannon played two years at Tyler Junior College, "the

76

only offer I'd had then," before coming to UH. He still recalls the 1949 William & Mary game his sophomore year, the school's first against a nationally known opponent, "Boyd Tingle started, then he got hurt the next week, and I moved up. Boyd always encouraged me and helped me any way he could. I played some at the end against William & Mary; they were a national power then, and it gave us some confidence, being able to stay with them like we did."

Shannon also tells a story of his passing "prowess": "We had a running halfback pass where I threw to (end) Vic Hampel. In the 1951 Baylor game, we were close to scoring on the last play of the half, and we called that play.

"Vic was wide open and I threw that ball right through the goal posts instead. Coach Lee told Bobby Clatterbuck in the dressing room, 'If you ever call that play again, you'll never play quarterback for me again.'

"That was the last pass I ever threw. I threw five of them at UH, three were intercepted and two incomplete."

Lovette Hill, an assistant coach under Clyde Lee, Bill Meek, and Harold Lahar, describes one of Shannon's unique running talents, "He could put his feet right on the spot he wanted. That sounds simple, but it's not. And he had that split vision, one of the few I've seen who could cut back against the flow. He could pick that thing and break it in places where there didn't look like there was an opening."

1952, The Best Year Yet

Athletic Director Harry Fouke sounded the keynote for the season a few days before the 1952 kickoff with Texas A&M. Said Fouke, "Ever since we first began fielding a football team in earnest, we have been looking forward to 1952. We feel sure that this year we've really got a first rate schedule which will give fans their money's worth."

He must have been believed, for more than 10,000 season tickets were sold (compared to 1,500 the previous year).

UH's first meetings ever with the Aggies, Arkansas, and Ole Miss no doubt whetted appetites following the Cougars' previous game, the Salad Bowl triumph over Dayton.

H. R. Cullen, recovering from serious surgery, noted, "I'm supposed to retire each night at seven o'clock, but the boys can be assured that I'll be there in spirit, listening every minute to the radio report." Since Ezekiel Cullen, his grandfather, wrote the land-grant school legislation that founded A&M, Cullen said, "My ambition for Houston University, aside from it's being a great school, always has been for the Cougars to play Rice. To see them take the field against the Aggies is a milestone next to that ambition."

The largest crowd ever to watch the Cougars, 55,023, paraded into Rice Stadium, but Ray Graves, passing with notable accuracy, directed the Aggies to a 21-13 victory.

Graves completed 10 of 15 passes for 129 yards and one touchdown, and ran for 76 yards and another score as the Cougars rallied too late. UH fumbled at the A&M 32 and 13 in the first quarter and was held on downs at the Aggie 4 as the first half ended.

Operating from a spread formation, Bobby Clatterbuck guided the comeback. S. M. Meeks made a falling catch of a Clatterbuck pass for the final touchdown in the fourth quarter.

Then Coach Clyde Lee made the fateful personnel changes that were to be the making of the unit known at season's end as the "Kimmel Corps." Paul Carr and Jack Chambers were installed at linebackers; Jim McConaughey at defensive end; Buddy Gillioz at defensive tackle; and Marvin Durrenberger at defensive halfback, paving the way to the school's most historic win to date.

End Vic Hampel's clutch receptions, Meeks' squirming, runs, and the ironhanded defense carried the red-letter day for the Cougars' win over Arkansas at Fayetteville, their first victory over a Southwest Conference school.

Vic Hampel, 1952 All-Missouri Valley Conference offensive end.

Harv Boughton wrote in the *Houston Post*, "The most important victory of this or any other year came to the University of Houston Cougars this Saturday afternoon when they fought down the Arkansas Razorbacks for a thorough 17-7 triumph before a crowd of 12,000 who had come to believe their Hogs were at their toughest in their home stadium."

The *Houston Chronicle*'s Bob Wood typed, "Every man in the Cougar defensive wall was magnificent. J. D. Kimmel spent most of the game playing in the Porker backfield...Equally as great in the revamped Cougar forward wall were Buddy Gillioz, Sanford Carr, Paul Carr, Wayne Shoemaker, and Jim McConaughey."

After Arkansas' first loss at home since 1960, Lee said, "It is the sweetest win any team of mine ever won."

Chambers recovered a fumble at the Arkansas 24 on the first play from scrimmage, and sophomore Verle Cray was summoned by Lee to attempt his first field goal ever from the 14 yard line. "My legs were shaking so, I could hardly stand," he admitted afterwards. Refusing to watch the ball after he kicked it, Cray stared instead at the official. When the kick was signaled good, Cray screamed, "Look, look, I did it, I did it! I can't believe it!"

Replacing Arkansas' starting quarterback Lamar McHan, injured in the first quarter, Bob St. Pierre connected with fullback Lew Carpenter on a 62-yard scoring pass in the second period, and Carl Mazza kicked the extra point. Arkansas led at the half, 7-3, but Lee and the Cougars were chortling in glee as they went to the locker room.

"That was the closest we'd ever been to a SWC team at the half," Lee explained later. "I felt we were in pretty good shape." UH's defense held the Hogs to three first downs and 12 yards rushing in the second half and permitted only 70 yards aground for the day.

Hampel's spectacular 30-yard catch from Clatterbuck on fourth down set up Meeks' four-yard scoring dive which sent UH ahead for good, 10-7, in the third quarter. Hampel leaped between two defenders, reached down to snatch the ball away from one of them, and landed on the four yard line. Jackie Howton kicked the first two of his extra points.

After Hampel dropped a Clatterbuck pass in the end zone

the Cougars drove 60 yards on their next series. Again Hampel made a key play, a 23-yard catch at the eight, and Tommy Bailes ran the final four yards with only 4:45 to play. End Joe Tusa, a former seminary student, led the team in prayer at game's end.

Meeks, who rushed for 92 yards on 13 carries, praised "that great blocking, especially by John Carroll." Arkansas Coach Otis Douglas called Carr "all football player, and a great one."

After dining on T-bone steaks at the Mountain Inn, the Cougars boarded their bus to Muskogee, Oklahoma, and the overnight train ride home. Their arrival at Union Station was greeted ecstatically by several hundred fans; Dr. W. W. Kemmerer, UH president; and Corbin Robertson, chairman of the athletic committee. Players and coaches signed the game ball and presented it to Cullen, who chuckled, "I want to put it where I can see it often."

Said Lee, "If we'd beaten the Aggies, we wouldn't have beaten Arkansas. The boys were really keyed up after losing that opener."

Defense was the key to UH's 10-7 struggle past Oklahoma A&M the next week at Stillwater in their Missouri Valley Conference opener.

Held to one first down in the first half, the Cowpokes still led, 7-3. The Cougars lost six fumbles, four of them inside their 35, but the overworked defensive unit allowed just seven first downs, 35 yards rushing, and 27 yards passing.

An Aggie mistake led to Sammy McWhirter's 10-yard scoring scamper with 3:32 to play, the game's only touchdown. A&M's punter was forced to juggle a low snap from center, and he was swarmed under on the 24.

Now it was time for Tulsa and revenge.

Lee showed his squad the movie of the 46-27 drubbing at Tulsa a year ago. "I don't have to say anything to you about Tulsa," he told the players. "Most of you played against them last year. You know what this one means." With Meeks and McWhirter badly bruised, UH was not in good condition for the nation's leader in total offense.

Primed and ready psychologically, the Cougars deflated the Hurricane, 33-7, before a homecoming crowd of 31,000.

Tulsa was held to 200 yards total offense, the lowest since 1949 for the team which set a NCAA record in 1951. UH's defense set up three scores, and Clatterbuck directed long marches of 88 and 72 yards.

Ken Pridgeon's first quarter punt was fumbled. Marvin Lackey recovered on the Tulsa six, and Carr, on offense for the moment, plunged over. After Tulsa tied, 7-7, Frank James blocked a Hurricane punt, and Clatterbuck tossed 48 yards to Hampel, who was racing down the sideline, for a 14-7 halftime lead.

Early in the third quarter, Pridgeon punted out of bounds on the one-foot line, and Gillioz blocked Tulsa's ensuing punt from its end zone and recovered for the third touchdown. Then Cray's field goal try fell short in the end zone, bounced out to the one and was whistled dead. UH got the ball back on the Tulsa 35 after a punt, and Meeks plunged over.

Clatterbuck's 31-yard pass to Hampel, who wrestled the ball away from a defender on the goal line, ended UH's scoring. Hampel caught five passes for 120 yards.

"Carr was magnificent," wrote *The Chronicle*'s Wood. "With what seemed an uncanny sixth sense, Carr was always in the right place at the right time. As a pass seemed headed true to the mark, Carr would suddenly burst from nowhere and bash it down. When a runner shook past the line of scrimmage, Carr seemed to be poised and waiting to hold the gain to a minimum."

Students took an unofficial holiday the next Monday, waving signs proclaiming, "Victory Holiday" and "Go Home, UH Holiday Declared." Lee later praised Kimmel, "J. D. is one of the most interested students of football I have ever had the pleasure to coach. He talks to me about defense every day.... During a game J. D. is standing right behind me every time I look around, drinking in everything that goes on, listening."

After a Saturday off, the Cougars returned to Phoenix, locale of their New Year's Day Salad Bowl triumph which began the year. Arizona State, their foe this time, was formidable, with a high-powered offense which featured a transfer named John Henry Johnson.

Carr's fumble recovery at the Sun Devil seven yard line led to Meeks' touchdown, the only one in a game of missed opportunities by both teams. The UH defense fell on an Arizona State fumble at the Cougars' 31 in the fourth quarter and permitted just 62 yards rushing.

Then, in a 20-7 triumph over Texas Tech at Lubbock, Jackie Howton, brother of Rice All-American end Bill Howton, set a school record by picking off four interceptions. The defense snared six Raider passes, bent for just seven first downs, and gave up 65 yards rushing and 90 passing.

It was a game which was to provide a rich lore of future legends:

Marvin Durrenberger intercepted a Tech pass and inadvertently led to the Raiders' only touchdown. He lateraled the interception at the UH 15 into the hands of Tech's Dean Smith,

Marvin Durrenberger, a standout on the 1952 "Kimmel Corps" defensive unit.

who had an open route to the goal. "Nowadays," says Buddy Gillioz, "whenever we meet Marvin, we walk up behind him and yell, 'Lateral! Lateral!'"

The night before the game, McWhirter and Bailes were in a taxi, headed to a meeting with Bailes' relatives, who had driven in for the game from Littlefield. Their taxi was hit by a car, and McWhirter was thrown out the door. Both were taken to a hospital, then released.

Bailes (13 for 78) ran well the next day, and McWhirter sprinted to haul in a 35-yard scoring pass from Clatterbuck, while gaining 94 yards in 12 carries. So, with five straight wins under their belts, the Cougars awaited their first meeting with Ole Miss.

Like most of UH's future games with the Rebels, this first one was an experience in frustration. Ole Miss's only lengthy offensive push, a 60-yard, second-quarter surge following a UH fumble, ended with fullback Harold Lofton's nine yard slash, the only scoring play in a galling 6-0 defeat. E. J. Oosterhoude, a Gator Bowl representative, called it, "One of the hardest fought games I have seen in a long time. The loss by Houston certainly does not detract from the possibility of their getting a bid from the Gator Bowl."

Each team was forced to punt 10 times, and UH could get no closer than the Rebs' 40 yard line. The Cougar offense totaled 170 yards; Ole Miss gained 279, more than 100 under its average.

At the end Jim McConaughey and Marvin Lackey each had lost 13 pounds in the heat of Rice Stadium; Roland Johnson lost 12; Bob Chuoke had a broken nose; Kimmel suffered a badly bruised hip; and Hampel needed 12 stitches to close a head wound.

The stage was set for Baylor's visit the next Saturday. On the same day as the UH defeat by Ole Miss, the Bears, too, had suffered bitter disappointment, a last-minute 35-33 loss to Texas.

Jack Chambers was a ferocious linebacker for the Cougars, playing against his former Waco High School teammates Bob Knowles, Bill Athey, and Richard Parma. Once again, Gillioz recovered a blocked punt (this one by Wayne Shoemaker) for a touchdown, and the defense also intercepted five passes. The score: UH 28, Baylor 6. Said Athletic Director Fouke, "I can't think of a victory that has meant so much to us. Now, the people of Houston will know we're top calibre."

Like UH, the Bears had injury problems, too, with L. G. Dupre, Allan Jones, and Mickey Sullivan sidelined, but the Cougar defense was unyielding. Baylor showed a minus 3 yards rushing in the second half and 66 for the game. Ken Pridgeon (17-for-68 and two scores) and Jack Patterson (8-for-48, one TD) led UH's best offensive show of the year. Besides his great punting against the wind and his running, Pridgeon also threw a 37-yard pass to Meeks to set up another score.

"That Houston defense lived up to its billing," complimented Baylor Coach George Sauer.

For the first time in the school's seven seasons, UH surfaced in the national rankings the next week, voted No. 19 by both Associated Press and United Press. But the Cougars faced a week's layoff before their next game, and the bowl committees were itchy. Turning down a bid from the Sun Bowl, the Cougars were stunned when the Gator Bowl selected Tulsa, an earlier 33-7 victim. The athletic committee then decided against the Sun and Salad Bowls.

Said Fouke, "I'm both disappointed and confused at Tulsa's selection to the Gator. I'm disappointed in view of the fact they selected a team which we so convincingly had beaten. I'm confused as to how they arrived at their selection."

Thus the Cougars, 6-2 at the time, were left with an empty feeling as they prepared for their final two games, Detroit and Wyoming.

A crowd of 7,200 in Rice Stadium braved the heavy rain and 40-degree cold as the Cougars overcame Detroit, 33-19, and nailed down the Missouri Valley title, their first football championship.

Ted Marchibroda, the nation's No. 2 passer, lofted 33 aerials, completing 10 for 159 yards for Detroit, and UH overcame Ray Zambiasi's 115-yard rushing performance.

They did it partially by blocking their sixth and seventh punts of the season—by Bobby Dorsey and Frank James—while Wendell Collier, making his first start, gained 82 yards on 15 tries, and Bailes 71 on 8 carries. Pridgeon's 26-yard halfback pass to Collier set up quarterback Newton Shows' scoring sneak.

Frank James, kick-blocking specialist for the 1952 Cougars.

Collier's 24-yard dash led to Pridgeon's 2-yard plunge and a 14-7 halftime lead.

Zambiasi's 59-yard sprint on the third play of the second half brought the Titans within reach of a tie, but they missed the point-after. Dorsey's punt blocked at the six led to Collier's 1-yard plunge, and then Meeks darted 40 yards through the mud for a 26-13 lead. Marchibroda's 44-yard toss to Ed Beirne closed the gap to 26-19, but Bailes cut off tackle from the 23, broke three tackles, and stumbled the final few yards with a defender hanging around his waist.

Lee told them, "Congratulations on your victory and congratulations on your championship. You owe it to yourselves because you are the men who did it."

Three days later, eight of the Cougars were selected to the AP All-Missouri Valley team—Hampel (end), Chuoke (guard), and Meeks (back) on offense; Kimmel and Gillioz (tackles), Carr (linebacker), and Howton and Sam Hopson (halfbacks) on defense. UH students received a holiday from class because of the MVC title, but Lee had other plans for his team. One game remained to be played.

Bowden Wyatt's single-wing offense had taken Wyoming to a distinguished record, which included just three defeats on the road since 1948. The Cowboys drove 72 yards to the UH one before being halted late in the scoreless first half.

Don Folks recovered a Wyoming fumble at the nine, and Pridgeon, whose second half punts kept the Cowboys backed up, scored the first touchdown. Then the agile James pulled off his specialty—blocking his fifth punt of the season—when Chuck Spaulding attempted a quick kick. James, who also batted down four extra point kicks during the year, picked up the blocked punt on the bounce in the end zone for the game's final touchdown. James' nine blocked kicks in one season stands as a remarkable statistic.

Kimmel, picked by the AP earlier as the school's first All-American, helped the defense shut off Wyoming with 59 yards rushing in the second half.

A few weeks later, the football rules committee completely changed the collegiate game, reverting to a virtual one-platoon format, with players permitted to return only in the final four minutes of the second and fourth quarters. The

Cougars finished 19th in the final UP poll, their first national top 20 ranking, and 19th in total defense, but the change in substitution rules was to prove a big handicap.

Reflecting now on 1952, Carr says "The school hadn't had a real good season before. We knew it was the toughest schedule we'd had. We talked about starting some tradition, and you don't start tradition until you have a winning season."

J. D. Kimmel, Quiet Leader

Quiet and unassuming J. D. Kimmel earned a unique place
in UH football annals despite playing only one season on the
Cougar varsity. He was the school's first All-American selection,
chosen on the Associated Press 1952 first team.

A 6-foot-4, 235-pounder, Kimmel played tackle on Clyde
Lee's defensive unit which was known as the "Kimmel Corps,"
and it set school records which still stand. In 10 games (8 of
them victories) Kimmel's troopers permitted just 12 touchdowns and 80 points.

In two seasons at West Point, Kimmel already had gained
some national recognition for Col. Earl Blaik's "Black Knights."
An engineering student, he also ranked in the top 30 of his class
academically.

But Kimmel was among about 90 cadets expelled from
West Point because of violations of the Academy's strict "honor
code." He said of that event, "Over the years some of the West
Point rules had been bent. At that time they began to investi-
gate. It just happened. I have no hard feelings. It just
happened."

Decades later, Kimmel was asked to suggest changes in the
"code" after a similar occurrence. He informed former astro-
naut Frank Borman he thought the strict rules should remain as
they are.

Kimmel, born in Omaha, Texas, had played his high school
football at Texarkana under Watty Myers. He won the Point's
heavyweight wrestling championship and helped the Cadets end

Defensive tackle J. D. Kimmel, Houston's first All-American.

Michigan's 25-game winning streak in 1950. Two of his high school teammates, Jerry Norton and Billy Burkhalter, became Southwest Conference notables at SMU and Rice, respectively.

When Kimmel transferred to UH in 1951, he scrimmaged against the varsity and assisted with the freshmen before becoming eligible for the 1952 season. He immediately made an impression.

"He didn't come in like he was the big stud," says Paul Carr. "He fit right in and demonstrated his ability on the field."

Johnny Goyen, who has watched the Cougars from their infancy, recalls, "When I first met Kimmel, I had great respect for him. You could tell he was different. It was obvious he was a quiet leader. When he spoke, you listened."

Ken Pridgeon remembers, "Before long, in the scrimmages, we'd tell Bobby Clatterbuck (their quarterback), 'Let's don't run plays to that (Kimmel's) side.' J. D. impressed me real quick. He was just a big, old mild-mannered boy. He didn't say much, but he was always straight with you. He'd be tough as all get-out on the field, then after practice he was just like a big teddy bear."

After the 1952 season, Kimmel's teammates elected him captain of the defensive unit. They also suggested his No. 78 be retired. It was not, but it has been issued to notable Cougars like Hogan Wharton and Wilson Whitley (both of them All-Americans also), Dalva Allen, and Charley Moore.

"We had a lot of spirit, and we worked together as a unit," Kimmel says of that 1952 team. "When we won the coin toss, we never took the ball, we always kicked off. That's the kind of confidence we had.

"We played as a unit and felt nobody could beat us and went from there," Kimmel sums up. "I was fortunate. I got here in the right place at the right time."

He played both offense and defense in the 17-7 victory at Arkansas, the school's first win over a Southwest Conference school. "It like to killed me," he remembers.

Kimmel notes that West Point's famed Blaik "was a great organizer, and he delegated a lot of responsibility to his assistants. Sid Gillman was his top assistant then; Murray Warmath was the defensive line coach; and Vince Lombardi was the offensive line coach." An ex-West Point center named Bill

Yeoman was a graduate assistant.

"We always went first class," Kimmel recalls. Blaik did not like to fly, so the Cadets frequently went by train. "The first 22 players had roomettes, not bunks," Kimmel says.

Things were different at UH, though. During his redshirt year at UH, the freshmen he was helping to coach bused to Freeport for a game and dined on hamburgers afterwards.

Kimmel still calls Frank James, the Cougars' middle guard who excelled at blocking kicks, "one of the fastest, quickest guys I ever saw on a football field."

The late Charlie Shira played the tackle opposite Kimmel at Army. They were also roommates. Kimmel says, "He'd made some All-American teams and I'd made some in 1950. I think he'd won the conference shot put at Texas A&M when he was 16. I couldn't have carried Charlie's jock."

Kimmel went into the army after his college career and then played professionally with Washington and Green Bay. He received his master of science degree from Rice and notes, "I went to Rice longer than I went to UH."

Elected to the Cougar athletic hall of honor in 1973, Kimmel is president of Houston-based Thermotics, Inc., a manufacturer and designer of oil field equipment with sales of $12 million in 1975. He told the *Houston Chronicle*, "The big thing in life is to have a goal, to have drive, and to work toward that goal." He is on the advisory committee to the school's dean of engineering.

Changing The Rules

Like most coaches, Clyde Lee found himself in a different boat with the new football rules for 1953 which eliminated platoon football. "It caught us with a lot of boys who couldn't go both ways," he said. "We had all-conference selections from 1952 who played very little the next year."

Lee expected a better offense, with Bobby Clatterbuck, Newton Shows, and Les Burton at quarterback, but Paul Carr's battered knees were problems he had to battle all season. Buddy Gillioz and Bob Chuoke, both All-Valley, led the cast of linemen. Defensive backs Jackie Howton and Sammy Hopson, an all-conference pair, had to make the switch to playing both ways.

Billy Polson, Donn Hargrove, S. M. Meeks, Kenny Stegall, and Jim Baughman were reasons for optimism that the running game would be improved, but the schedule began with Texas A&M and Texas, UH's first meeting with the Longhorns.

During the summer a new 10-year contract was signed to use Rice Stadium (formerly Houston Stadium) through 1965. H. R. Cullen signed the new agreement with George Brown, president of the Rice Board of Governors.

Asked if there was any discussion of a game between the two Houston universities, Brown said, "Not since 1950. We discussed it informally then." Cullen noted, "They seem to think it would create too much rivalry. Our boys out at UH are working boys. They don't have time to fight."

Shows conducted the second unit to both UH touch-

Donn Hargrove set a Cougar record with 199 yards rushing against Detroit in 1953.

downs, scored by Sammy McWhirter, in the third quarter, but the game with A&M ended in a 14-14 tie. Howton's tackle of a pass receiver at the UH seven in the final seconds preserved the deadlock.

Lightning hit the Cougars twice in the same place at Austin. They led Texas at the half, 7-2, although a cloudburst made the ball hard to hold. Then, in a ghastly 11-minute period of the third quarter the Longhorns scored four touchdowns while traveling just 124 yards.

Twice, center snaps over the UH punter's head—by two different centers—led to a Texas touchdown, and a fumble on a kickoff cost another in a 28-7 Longhorn victory.

"In 22 years of coaching I never had a snap over the punter's head," said Lee, "and here we had two by two different boys. I never said a word about it to either of them. They felt worse about it than I did, so why should I? I guess lightning always strikes in the same place."

Hargrove, a 6-foot, 180-pounder from Freeport, Shannon's hometown, and wearing Shannon's No. 24, staged a superb example of running like Shannon in the next game. Hargrove shredded Detroit's No. 1 ranked rushing defense with a UH record 199 yards in just 10 carries. He scored the first TD on an 80-yard bolt and set up another with a 54-yarder. Still, UH needed a timely interception by Hopson to hold off the Titans, 25-19.

Then Oklahoma A&M landed a 100-to-1 shot, a 97-yard run with 2:21 to play, that broke a 7-7 tie and dealt the Cougars a 14-7 heartbreaker. Lee wondered, "How many times will a 97-yard run win a game in the last two minutes? Maybe once in 100 games."

Verle Cray's first-quarter field goal stood up as the margin of victory in a 24-20 decision over Arizona State. Hargrove was again the leading runner.

While busy denying reports that he planned to resign at season's end because of ill health, Lee welcomed the return to health of Carr and Gillioz, who had been slowed by injuries. "Beat Houston" signs were plastered all over downtown Tulsa and even the press box. Tulsa rooters wanted revenge for the 33-7 plastering in 1952 of the Hurricane's Gator Bowl team. Tulsa won, 23-21, after a weird series of UH penalties and mistakes, despite an 18-7 Cougar edge in first downs.

UH was a two-touchdown underdog to No. 9 ranked Baylor, which had lost the week before, 21-20, to Texas. Clatterbuck executed brilliantly, and Stegall and Jack Patterson rushed for 236 yards in a 37-7 rout, the Bears' worst non-conference defeat since 1925.

Stegall (12 for 130 rushing) also returned a punt 31 yards, and Patterson (16 for 106) scored twice. Jinx Tucker, the Bears' faithful recorder, describes the blocking of Gillioz, Chuoke,

Bobby Clatterbuck, left, and Ken Stegall helped devastate nationally-ranked Baylor, 37-7, in 1953.

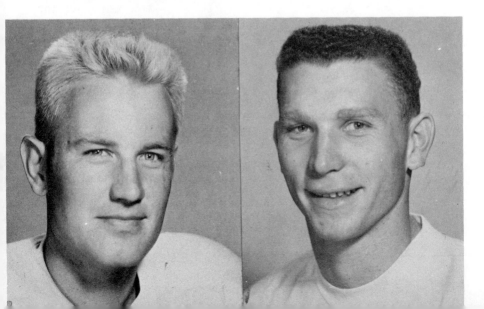

Wayne Shoemaker, Jim Blackstone, and Ed Willhelm, "They picked up Baylor linemen and threw them in the laps of the secondary."

His knee so battered it had to be treated the entire night before, Carr backed the line viciously, with Ben Wilson, Chuoke, and Gillioz helping check Jerry Coody, L. G. Dupre, and the Baylor offense to 91 yards rushing.

Stegall was a 5-foot-9, 165-pounder from Corsicana, only 60 miles from Baylor's doorstep, but the Bears had turned him

The Cougars return from a 37-7 thrashing of nationally-ranked Baylor in 1953.

down because they thought he was too small. "I was hoping I could have a good day against them," Stegall told John Hollis of the *Houston Press.* "And with the blocking we had, it wasn't hard. This was the easiest game we've played. And you know, we weren't particularly fired up, either.

"Going out to the stadium, I looked around at the guys. They were just sitting there quietly, talking. Some of them were yawning. I thought, 'Oh, oh, I got a feeling the boys are going to play a game today.' And they did."

Baylor . . . 7

Chuoke, a fierce blocker and pass rusher, had asked for the game ball weeks before, confident of victory. Center Ken Reese reached down for the ball, watched the final seconds tick off, then walked over to the bench and gave it to Chuoke.

The following Monday, H. R. Cullen made his famous announcement at a campus pep rally of his $2.25 million gift to the university in honor of its great football victory. Cullen had planned the gift for months, arranging it with his attorneys, and a week later donated $1 million to the Baylor School of Medicine. For years, because of the timing and Cullen's exuberance at the time, the public mistakenly associated the grant as a reward for Houston's football prowess.

Texas Tech brought the Cougars down harshly, 41-21,. as Bobby Cavazos gained 121 of the Raiders' 401 yards down the path to the Gator Bowl. Behind 27-7 at halftime, the Cougars closed to 27-21 before Tech, the nation's scoring leader, hung up two quickies in the last four minutes.

Still, the Raiders applauded Carr's performance. "Carr is the greatest linebacker in football," said Tech Coach DeWitt Weaver. Cavazos added, "Carr is the greatest I've ever seen."

Clatterbuck, recovered from the flu, matched his Baylor performance in a significant 33-19 triumph over Tennessee's single wing, a victory that enhanced UH stature in the Southeast.

With the graduation loss of Clatterbuck, Carr, Gillioz, Chuoke, Reese, and Marvin Durrenberger, Lee still was optimistic for 1954. Jimmy Dickey, a great junior college and high school quarterback, would guide an offense fashioned around Stegall, Hargrove, Patterson, Polson, and Tommy Bailes. Ends George Hynes and Wilson, and linemen like Cray, Blackstone, Wayne Geddes, Lavell Isbell, and Shoemaker returned.

Vengeful Baylor retaliated for two straight losses to the Cougars with a 53-13 thrashing in the opener, UH's worst loss in history. Dickey and Baylor's Bobby Jones debuted impressively, but five lost fumbles and the loss of Stegall to a knee injury offset the Cougars' 354 yards gained on offense.

Cray's 11-yard field goal in the fourth quarter and a goal-line stand led to a 10-7 squeaker over the Aggies, with A&M a foot away from the goal at game's end. Dickey passed to Ronnie Emberg for the Cougar TD. Elwood Kettler sneaked for

Exultant Coach Clyde Lee displays the game ball after the Cougar victory over Tennessee in 1953.

the Aggie score, then whipped them to the brink of the goal again. With 10 seconds left after Kettler had been stopped inches short, an Aggie lineman excitedly tossed the ball into the end zone and the final seconds ran out before it could be retrieved for another play.

Aggie Coach Bear Bryant, asked if he considered kicking a field goal for a tie, issued his famous reply, "I'm not interested in ties. I wanted to win. A tie is like kissing your sister."

With 2:23 to play, second unit quarterback Teddy Gray ran 11 yards to end an 88-yard drive and boost the Cougars to a 14-7 win at Oklahoma State. Curley Johnson's running featured the game-turning march.

Dickey's 92-yard kickoff return and 35-yard touchdown

Fullback Jack Patterson (left) and end George Hynes, 1954 co-captains, meet with Clyde Lee.

pass to Don Flynn helped UH to a 28-7 win at Villanova.

The three-game streak was snapped, 9-7, on a bitterly cold day at Wichita. Gray was trapped for a third quarter safety; then Wichita controlled the ball for the last eight minutes after taking over inside its 10. Facing a 25-mile-an-hour wind, Wichita ran 23 straight plays.

Stegall's 13-yard trip and Dickey's 62-yard pass to Baughman in the second half carried the Cougars past Tulsa, 20-7, but Ole Miss shut them down, 26-0.

Eighteen players were stricken by food poisoning the day before the Texas Tech game. Dickey was lame, and the Raiders poured it on, 61-14. Frank Paul, an end, had to do most of the quarterbacking.

Cotton Bowl-bound Arkansas handled the Cougars, 19-0, and a 5-5 record depended on the final game with Detroit.

Just before game time, Blackstone approached one of the few groups of fans in the small crowd, leaned over the railing, and told them, "Boy, are we going to put on a show for you!" They had to wait until the final two minutes, when the teams scored three touchdowns. Dickey weaved 56 yards to score on the season's final play from scrimmage in the 19-7 win.

Two days later Lee resigned. His seven-year record of 37-32-2 does not begin to show the ground the Cougars covered under him.

Clyde Lee,
"Blood And Guts"

His early football days undoubtedly gave rise to Clyde Lee's iron-willed approach. In later years it came to be known as "hard-nosed," and Lee believed in it. So did his players. He saw to that.

Bobby Brown, then the UH trainer, remembers that spring practice of 1948, the Cougars' first under Lee. "It was the toughest I ever saw," says Brown, who later served many years with several pro football clubs. "We scrimmaged every day for two hours, until it was too late to see. A lot of times I just slept in the training room with my clothes on. His favorite exercise was to have the guys roll head over heels for 100 yards."

"One of the toughest coaches you could find," adds Ken Pridgeon. "We'd start and wouldn't stop until we couldn't see the ball; then we'd line up and run wind sprints. When we lost to A&M in the first game of 1952, we felt like we'd run out of gas. The captains went to see him and asked him on a trial basis that if he cut down on practices, we'd give him two hours on the field all-out. He agreed."

Paul Carr, a co-captain in 1953, recalls, "I cussed him out every day, but afterwards I respected him as much as any man I know. I'd have gone to hell and back for him."

During Lee's seven years as head coach (1948-54), the Cougars joined the "major leagues." Their 37-32-2 record in that period does not tell the full story, for the Cougars at times were fighting a tough battle with a short stick.

By Lee's second season, schools like Texas A&I, Louisiana Tech, Trinity, and East Texas State had been replaced by William & Mary, Hardin-Simmons, St. Bonaventure, and St. Louis. By 1951 UH moved into Rice Stadium from Public School Stadium and the Missouri Valley Conference, and a year later the schedule had 10 major college teams, including Baylor, Texas A&M, Ole Miss, Oklahoma A&M, Tulsa, and Arizona State.

"To this day," says Jack Scott, the school's former sports publicist, "people don't have a proper appreciation for what Clyde Lee accomplished."

Scott had an early introduction to the Lee brand of intensity. "In 1949 I was sports editor of *The Cougar*, the student paper," Scott relates, "and I wrote that we'd beat West Texas by four or five touchdowns. Clyde walked in that office and scalded me terribly." The Cougars won, 14-13.

J. D. Kimmel, the school's first All-American, says, "Coach Lee knew football as well as any man I ever saw."

Assistants (left to right) Lovette Hill, Harden Cooper, Elmer Simmons, and Bob Evans flank Clyde Lee.

Lee played for the famed Centenary College teams of 1930-32 coached by Homer Norton, where a teammate was Lovette Hill, later on his UH staff. His first coaching job was at Overton, "the only job I could find open in Texas in those Depression days. They told me they'd give me a job if I'd also play on their semi-pro baseball team."

So, for $90 a month, Lee taught five math classes, a history class, and coached four sports without an assistant. He worked part-time in a cafe for his meals. In three seasons his football teams were 28-3-2.

Moving to Kilgore College, Lee compiled a 61-10-4 record before entering the navy. After military service, he was an assistant to Buddy Brothers for two years at Tulsa.

Lee earlier had been exposed to the enormous potential of UH and the city of Houston: "I'd attended some summer classes when it was a night school at San Jacinto High. I could see it was going to be a great drawing card for the masses of people that would be moving in there. My wife had relatives in Houston, and we would stop off on the way to Port Aransas to go fishing."

Lee conferred with Athletic Director Harry Fouke, Dr. E. E. Oberholtzer, the school president, and H. R. Cullen, then took a look at the facilities. He remembered, "When I walked out there and saw that little tin shack they were using for a dressing room, and the barracks the players lived in, I thought about it a long time before I took the job.

"It was a challenge, a big one. It looked even bigger than that when I went out for the first practice and saw all those fat-tailed ex-GIs."

A big first step was strengthening the schedule with major-calibre teams. "The only way we stood a chance of growing," Lee explains, "was to play good teams.

"We stayed with them all the way," Lee recalls about that first game in the big-time, the 1949 opener with William & Mary, then a national power featuring fullback Jack Cloud and tackle Lou Creekmur, both All-Americans. "They beat us, 14-13; then the next year, we won pretty easily, 36-18. We were always able to get ready for the big teams. It was the little ones that gave us trouble.

"That was a problem for years, but playing in the Southwest Conference will take care of that. They'll be playing against boys and schools they've always heard about."

Lee feels part of the foundation for the great 1952 season was laid the year before, when the Cougars came from behind to defeat North Texas, 20-14, at Denton, and gain an invitation to the Salad Bowl.

"I think they learned about playing under pressure that day," Lee says.

That 1951 season started disastrously. Three days before the Cougars were to play their first game ever in Rice Stadium—against Baylor—starting quarterback Bobby Rogers hurt a knee. "He popped a ligament in a dummy scrimmage," Lee painfully recalls the 19-0 defeat, "but that was a great Baylor team."

The Cougars also lost that year to Louisville in a scoring duel, 35-28, and Lee remembers a freshman quarterback named John Unitas, sometimes throwing from his end zone, who flung four touchdown passes.

The halfback tandem of Max Clark and Gene Shannon was a dandy 1950 duo. "Clark called signals from halfback," says Lee, "and it worked. Max and Gene were so effective, at the end of the year, there was less than 100 yards difference between them in rushing. Clark was faster than Gene. He won two games for us in 1948 with punt returns, but Gene had that deceptive stride. He never seemed to really be going fast."

Lee felt the Cougars were well-armed for two-platoon football by 1952. "We'd had a pretty good year of bringing in boys who could play one way. We thought we had a good nucleus."

After the opening defeat by the Aggies, Lee made some effective position changes, sending Paul Carr and Jack Chambers to inside linebackers; Jack Patterson to fullback from defense; and John Carroll to offensive tackle from defense.

The next week, at Arkansas, occurred that glorious 17-7 victory over their first Southwest Conference foe. Trailing 7-3, Lee led his team off the field at halftime with a smile on his face. "That was the closest we'd ever been to a conference team," he explains the strange behavior. "I told them we were going to beat their tails."

Then, several weeks later, Lee watched UH defeat Baylor, 28-6. "I enjoyed that as much as the Arkansas game," he admits. "John Carroll did an outstanding job of blocking, and

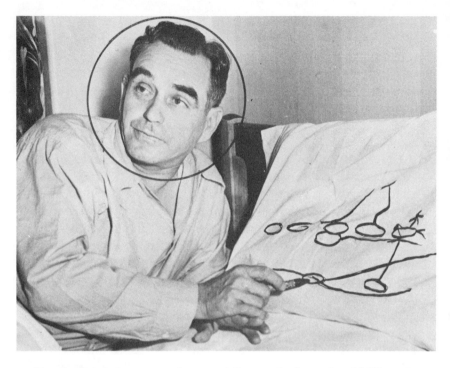

Hospitalized by a respiratory ailment before the 1952 spring practice, Clyde Lee keeps busy.

Ken Pridgeon and Wendy Collier an excellent job of running.

"Then in 1953 Bobby Clatterbuck called an almost perfect game at quarterback. We used audibles on most plays, and he did a beautiful job. We'd lost the week before to Tulsa, 23-21. They'd got ready for one game (Baylor) and forgot the other one."

Several months before the 1953 season, however, fate again seemed to conspire against the Cougars just as they had seemed ready to complete their breakthrough as a major college power.

From two-platoon, unlimited substitution rules, the football coaches association returned to a form of the one-platoon game, with players again required to play both offense and defense.

"We figured we were in great shape," says Lee; "then the rule change threw the hook in us. We had good boys who could play one way that we couldn't utilize sitting on the bench. Then we had to go out and recruit for the all-around boys. I told them, 'In 10 years they'll change back.' They have the best game now they've ever had.

"You have better perfection when you can concentrate on offense or defense. We played with 13 players going both ways when I was at Centenary, and that's drudgery."

The return to the one-platoon format heightened the always critical problem of competing with Southwest Conference schools in recruiting. Two days after the 19-7 victory over Detroit to end the 1954 season, Lee resigned. His contract extended to August 31, 1956, but a settlement was reached.

"I could see we had problems mounting," says Lee. "I wasn't satisfied with the results, and I knew the athletic council wasn't, either.

"I knew six or nine months before that I was going to quit but I didn't tell anybody, not even my wife."

Afterwards, Frank Godsoe, writing in the *Houston Press*, illustrated UH's problem at that stage. He quoted Lee, scanning the 1954 Baylor roster, "I have just counted the names of 29 boys on this year's Baylor varsity whom we knew about, wanted, and made every effort to get at UH." Lee was quoted as saying that, on the other hand, he knew of only two UH players that Baylor wanted badly.

Harv Boughton wrote in the *Houston Post*:

Compared to other, much older schools in the state, Houston's supply of great players has been amazingly small and its supply of really good boys hasn't been consistent or in abundance, yet Clyde Lee had only two losing seasons in seven building years and never failed to win at least four games a year.

. . . but the supply seldom has compared with that of any of the SWC schools, particularly in numbers to befit the sort of schedules the Cougars have been playing, or to satisfy their fans' demands for more victories.

Answering speculation that the school would seek a "big name" coach as Lee's successor, Corbin Robertson, chairman of the athletic committee, said, "I want to make one thing clear; we thought we lost a big name coach."

In Lee's first season, 1948, less than 100 season football tickets were sold. Since 1952, sales had exceeded 10,000.

When he resigned, Lee had decided to coach no more. He has owned an auto agency in Freeport since 1963 and regularly attends UH home games.

"Lee was five coaches in one," Ken Pridgeon praises him. "He always wore the same hat, shoes and coat," recalls Buddy Gillioz. "Corby would always be in the locker room before the game, and Coach Lee would rub Corby's ring for good luck."

Gene Shannon calls Lee "one of the great men I've been associated with. He was a taskmaster. All his workouts were very long and tough. We had no water, even in games. I came to appreciate him more after I left. I thought it was a shame he got out of coaching when he did."

Shannon recalls walking up to a group at the annual Texas high school coaches convention, "They were discussing Coach Lee, and John Vaught said, 'I hated to see him get out because he was five years ahead of his time.'"

"Jayboy," Lee's son, frequently attended practice in those days. He relates, "I was about six or seven years old, and I remember Dad caught two of the guys smoking. He made them run until they dropped, and they had to be carried off on a stretcher."

Jack Scott recalls a scrimmage session, "The temperature was in the nineties and the players were in full gear. When about the sixth player was stretched out on the ground, one of the 'railbirds' came out to help carry him off because the stretcher had not come back yet. This player had a glass eye that had fallen out, and the 'railbird,' said, 'My God, this one is dead.'"

After the banquet following the 1949 season, Cecil Towns, one of the co-captains, rose and announced the squad had decided on an appropriate name for their coach. The name was "Blood and Guts," and no one who played for Lee would argue with the choice.

Paul Carr,
The Cougars' Rock

A transplanted Californian and air force veteran, Paul "Rock" Carr set the standard by which future Cougar linebackers are measured.

"Pound for pound," says teammate Buddy Gillioz, "he was the hardest hitting linebacker I ever played with or against." After UH's momentous 17-7 victory over Arkansas in 1952, Razorback Coach Otis Douglas called him "all football player and a great one."

"We were a close-knit bunch," Carr recalls the 1952 Cougars. "We all got along together; there were no petty jealousies. I respected and admired every one of them. I knew those guys would be there when I needed them."

A 6-foot, 200-pounder, Carr grew up in Azusa, California, and played a season at Citrus Junior College before joining the air force. He was stationed at Ellington Air Base, near Houston, where Coach Clyde Lee heard of him.

Their relationship had its ups and downs. Carr was unanimously elected a co-captain his senior year, 1953, and was selected the team's most valuable player and outstanding back in 1952, when he was also an All-Missouri Valley Conference linebacker.

"One day during two-a-days in 1950, I quit," Carr relates, "but Coach Lee talked me into coming back out. Then later, one morning he'd put us through the mill, and I came back to the room and told my roommate I was leaving.

"I started packing. Then I heard the door shut and looked

Co-captains Buddy Gillioz (left)   and Paul Carr discuss Houston's 1953 prospects with Clyde Lee.

around, and Coach Lee was locking the door. He tried to talk me out of leaving; then when he saw I was serious, he told me, 'Go home and think for awhile, but don't play ball anywhere and lose your eligibility.'

"While I was home, Lee Garl, my best friend, had led California junior colleges in scoring, and he and I went to talk to Red Sanders at UCLA. He came back to UH with me but tore up a knee.

"It was real cold that winter," Carr continues, "and we caught a bus from California as far as Austin. We got off in Albuquerque to look over New Mexico, where we were offered a scholarship, but it was too cold for us. The roads were iced over from Austin to Houston, and we caught a train the rest of the way."

Called "Rock" because of the bone-rattling impact with which he tackled, Carr had the instinct of uncoiling all his strength at the point of contact. One day at practice, a visitor showed up with a machine that measured pounds of pressure at the point of impact. Carr gave a demonstration of his tackling technique which threatened to tear down the contraption.

Following the Cougars' 20-14 victory at North Texas in 1951, Athletic Director Harry Fouke was standing outside the UH locker room when two NT players walked up and asked to see Carr. Fouke recounts, "The boys walked up to Paul, introduced themselves, then told him, 'Carr, we just wanted to meet you off the field and tell you you're the best linebacker any of us ever played against.'"

After the opening 21-13 loss to Texas A&M in 1952, Carr was moved from fullback to linebacker full-time. At season's end he had been named to the remaining nine teams' all-opponent lists.

"We knew we had a tough schedule that year," Carr explains. "We had heard so much stuff about 'Cougar High' and figured we had something to prove. A victory like Arkansas draws a team together. You gain confidence. A lot of times a team plays over its head as a result.

"We felt like we hadn't really lost to Ole Miss (0-6) because the film showed their back's knee hitting the ground before he scored. All the coaches were enthusiastic over the game we'd played. They made us feel 10 feet tall. The positive attitude they took made us feel positive."

In the 33-7 smashing of Tulsa's nationally ranked offensive unit in 1952, Carr figured in on 33 of Tulsa's 38 rushing plays, logging 9 solo tackles and 24 assists.

John Hollis wrote in the *Houston Press*, "Paul's not easily fooled, undoubtedly because he makes a habit of avidly studying each opponent's play over and over, long before game time, asks a thousand questions about the opposition's offense, is never satisfied with his work."

Typical of Carr's personal standard of performance was his reaction after his final collegiate game, UH's 33-19 triumph over Tennessee and its single-wing offense in 1953. Jimmy Wade scored all three touchdowns for the Vols, and Carr, who had played the entire year on injured knees, was disgusted he had not prevented Wade's last scoring run. "My legs wouldn't take me there," he said afterwards.

Carr, drafted by the San Francisco 49ers as a junior, underwent knee surgery after his senior UH season. "He used to keep those cartilages pickled in a jar," recalls a former teammate. "He played on a pair of knees that should have been on exhibit," Corby Robertson describes them.

When two-platoon football was changed to limited substitution in 1953, Carr had to play fullback as well as linebacker. "Tom Wilson never babied anybody, but he knew when you were really hurting," Carr says. "When we went to Baylor in 1953, my knees were so sore, I could barely walk off the plane. We moved a cot for me into Tom's room, and he stayed up all night, putting hot towels on my knees. One week the knees would feel pretty good, the next week not so good."

Carr recalls defensive end Jim McConaughey as "a tough son of a gun, strong and mean. Jackie Howton and Sam Hopson were great little cornerbacks, tough as nails and great tacklers in our 5-4 defense. Jack Chambers (linebacker) was just one steady team man, unselfish as he could be. Buddy Gillioz could have played pro football for anyone. I compare him with Bob Toneff for agility and quickness.

"Bobby Clatterbuck reminded me of Y. A. Tittle. He was meticulous and always tried to analyze everything down to the last detail. Vic Hampel matured late at end; he really came on his senior year. S. M. Meeks was a gutty little devil.

"Hopson and Howton were the team clowns. They'd always kid me about never lifting weights. I came back to the room one day, and there was a set of barbells on the floor. I stooped down to pick them up and one of them snapped a picture of me."

Carr later played three years on the 49ers with Tittle, Toneff, Billy Wilson, Hugh McElhenny, Joe Petty, Bob St. Clair, Matt Hazeltine, and Leo Nomellini. His roommate was Dicky Maegle of Rice. Another teammate was Joe Arenas, now a UH assistant coach.

Even after a near-tragic incident in Houston, Carr continued with the 49ers. Trying to break up a fight at a party he and his wife were attending, Carr was stabbed. The knife nicked his heart.

Johnny Goyen says of Carr, "He would have met a Sherman tank head-on and talked about the consequences later."

Carr was inducted into the Cougar Athletic Hall of Honor in 1977 and is a member of the all-time UH football team picked in 1976 by *Texas Football Magazine.*

Buddy Gillioz, The Agile Giant

As the "other" tackle opposite J. D. Kimmel on UH's 1952 "Kimmel Corps," Maurice "Buddy" Gillioz made a name for himself as one of the school's best defensive linemen.

Gillioz had a modest beginning. His high school at little Santa Fe was so small it fielded only a six-man football team until his junior year. Even then, Gillioz's strength and agility were uncommon, for at 6-foot-2 and 235 pounds he ran on the 440-yard relay and threw the shot and discus.

Jack Scott, the school's former sports information director, recalls, "People from other schools would say, 'Kimmel is a tremendous leader and player, but that agile son of a gun on the other side is the one NOBODY can handle.'"

Adds ex-assistant Lovette Hill, "Gillioz was as good a football player as there's ever been through that school."

Gillioz made the United Press second-team All-American as a junior on the 1952 team which won 8 of 10 games, the school's most successful season up to that time. All-Missouri Valley Conference in 1952-53, Gillioz played in the Chicago All-Star Game and in the Blue-Gray Game, the latter with teammate Bob Chouke.

That Blue-Gray Game gave Gillioz a chance for an interesting observation on his coach, Clyde Lee: "There's no possible way any coach was tougher than Lee. He and Bear Bryant coached the Gray in that game, and playing under both of them, I never saw two coaches more alike."

A co-captain of the 1953 team with linebacker Paul

114

Buddy Gillioz, two-time All-Missouri Valley Conference tackle.

"Rock" Carr, Gillioz and Carr found their responsibilities sometimes put them in a delicate position.

"Every night before a game we all had to be together, that's the way Coach Lee wanted it," Gillioz explains. "We had a choice of going to a movie or to the high school game at Jeppesen. Paul and I went to the dorm to ask the guys which one they preferred. Sixteen of the 22 starters were married, and they said they weren't doing either one.

"I told Paul, 'I'm not going back and telling Coach,' so we both went. He climbed all over us. 'You mean you're the captains and you can't get them to do what you want?' Finally they agreed to go to the game at Jeppesen, but they were damned if they were going to have milk and cookies afterward like we always did.

"Coach Lee said, 'If we lose, I'm going to turn the car lights on and practice until dark next Monday.' We got beat, 23-21, but he didn't do it."

Gillioz does remember that Lee ordered a scrimmage on Friday before the team boarded the bus to Waco for the 1953 Baylor game, where they rapped the nationally ranked Bears, 37-7.

"My high school coach had played for Lee at Kilgore Junior College," Gillioz says, "and he came to our practice one day. Afterwards, he told Lee, 'I didn't know you'd gone soft.' It was so hot the spring of my sophomore year, and he didn't believe in water breaks, that some of the guys were drinking water out of a ditch by the practice field.

"We'd say he invented the white stripe around the ball, he kept us so late at practice. Harden Cooper (the line coach) had played for him at Tulsa, and he claimed, 'You don't know what it is to be worked hard.'"

Gillioz recalls Lee's emotional approach to the game, "My sophomore year when we opened against Baylor, he stood up in the locker room and actually started crying about how much the game meant to him and to the school. The older guys had seen it all before, but he almost had me in tears. He told us to think about it on our own and left the room. One of the older guys stood up and started carrying on like he had, but it wasn't a fake. That was how much it really meant to Coach Lee.

"He could get me fired up because I knew he was sincere.

He could drive you and get everything out of you that you had. I can remember him saying, 'You can get a degree, but it won't mean anything if you don't have a goal in mind.'"

Gillioz continues, "No one was scared of him, because as hard as he worked us, you'd be right back there the next day. I felt I could go and talk to him any time. Nobody was ever scared to walk up the stairs to his office. His wife was the same way. It was like walking up and talking to your mother."

The 1952 defensive unit had a season-long contest for excellence. "I had just learned to use my left arm playing on the 'weak' side when I moved to the other side because Kimmel was going to play there," Gillioz recalls. "Carr said, 'That's okay, we'll take care of our side,' and at the end of the year we hadn't had one touchdown over that side."

UH students in those days had simple accommodations. "My first room was in an old army barracks," Gilloz notes. "Then we moved into an athlete's floor in one of the new dorms. I got married my senior year, and for $30 a month you could rent an apartment that had been converted out of the old barracks. That's where most of the athletes lived.

"There wasn't a whole lot of school spirit when I came," Gillioz says. "I've watched it grow. If you had difficulty you could always go to anybody on the faculty, and they'd sit down and try to help. I never knew a teacher who came out and gave an athlete a grade, but they were always willing to tutor you."

Now an assistant principal in South Houston, Gillioz vividly remembers his final collegiate game, the 33-19 triumph over Tennessee in 1953: "Everything we did was right. Bobby Clatterbuck was a terrific dropback passer, and we stayed on offense the whole day. But I was not as elated over that one as the wins over Arkansas and Baylor in 1952.

"The biggest disappointment was the 1953 Texas game. We fumbled the opening kickoff of the second half and they got the ball about on our 10. The biggest nightmare I ever saw. We put T. Jones, their starting quarterback, on his back; then they put in a little sophomore, Charlie Brewer, and he had a good day."

Gillioz recalls the school's first bowl game, the trip to Phoenix and the Salad Bowl to play Dayton after the 1951 season, "We flew out and stayed at a resort in the desert about

10 days. Being from a small town, the biggest thing I recalled was the big parade they had downtown that week."

The Third Era

The 45-day search for the man to succeed Clyde Lee as head football coach took many twists and turns before Kansas State's Bill Meek was signed to a five-year contract.

Georgia Tech assistant Frank Broyles was an early contender for the job, spending five days in Houston before withdrawing. Gomer Jones, Bud Wilkinson's line coach at Oklahoma; Rusty Russell, former SMU coach; and Mike Brumbelow, Texas Western, also were prominent early candidates.

Ole Miss Coach John Vaught discussed the job with Athletic Director Harry Fouke at the football coaches' convention, set a date for a Houston visit, then took his name out of the hat. Utah's Jack Curtice thought about it for a week, then turned down the job, and Meek was the man.

A single-wing blocking back at Tennessee, Meek had been strongly recommended by his former coach, Gen. Bob Neyland, early in the search when Fouke attended the Southeastern Conference meetings. Corby Robertson, chairman of the athletic committee, disclosed, "We have had Meek under consideration from the very start."

Meek, 33 years old, shaped Kansas State into a conference contender from a perennial cellar-dweller. The school had finished last for 12 straight years in the Big Seven, with one conference victory in 10 years, and 15 wins overall in that time. By Meek's third year the Wildcats were 6-3-1 and second to Oklahoma in the conference, then 7-3 in 1954.

A former army captain and coach of Fort Benning's armed

Bill Meek's 1955-56 teams compiled a 13-6-1 record.

forces champion, Meek put in four years as backfield coach to Jim Tatum at Maryland, where he became grounded in the split-T he used at Kansas State.

Intending to substitute by units, Meek found a fairly good talent pool awaiting him, including quarterbacks Jimmy Dickey and Don Flynn; backs Ken Stegall, Donn Hargrove, Joe Bob Smith, and Curley Johnson; ends Ken Wind, Ronnie Emberg, and Jim Cravens; and linemen Wayne Shoemaker, Lavell Isbell, Wayne Geddes, Dalva Allen, Billy McIlroy, Tom Dimmick, Jim Blackstone, Rod Carpenter, and John Dearen. Among the red-shirts were fullbacks Owen Mulholland and Donnie Caraway.

Jim Blackstone,
1955 co-captain.

Donnie Caraway, all-time
Cougar linebacker.

Physically imposing, with a touch of gray at the temples and a nose broken four times at Tennessee, Meek reminded upon arriving, "You can't win the Derby with a mule." He added, "You have to have talent to build a winning team, and you have to win some games to keep a job."

Meek brought John Cudmore, Jim LaRue, Royal Price, and Clyde Van Sickle with him from Kansas State and hired

Head Coach Bill Meek surrounded by assistants (left to right) Preacher Franklin, Sharkey Price, Jim LaRue, John Cudmore, and Clyde Van Sickle.

Marvin Franklin, from Nebraska State Teachers, to complete his staff. Cudmore was his top aide.

A close follower of UH football recalls Meek's attention to details, "The quarterbacks had to have a brand-new football every day in spring and fall practice. He'd pump them up himself to make sure they had the right pressure. When he left, there must have been 250 footballs in the stock room, all practically new."

Meek's appraisal of his first UH team was, "There are not great players on this squad, but there are some good ones."

One of them who was to make a memorable impression was Caraway, a transfer from Kilgore Junior College. A tough running fullback and good place-kicker, he earned a place among the school's hardest hitting linebackers in history. He wasn't shy about running into people while carrying the football.

One day Homer Norton, coach of Texas A&M's 1939 national champions, was watching the Cougars scrimmage. As Caraway drove through swarms of tacklers, Norton was asked, "See anybody who looks familiar?"

Referring to his former All-American fullback, Norton replied, "Yes, I'd know John Kimbrough anywhere."

Jack Scott calls Caraway, a 220-pounder, "the most destructive player I ever saw play the game. He wore those big lineman's shoulder pads and caved them in."

A perfect example was the 1955 opening game with Montana. Caraway kicked off to start the game, collided with the point man on the receiving team, and sent him off the field on a stretcher. The same player returned for the second half, Caraway again kicked off, hit him again, and the unfortunate one was again carried off on a stretcher. The Cougars cruised to a 54-12 victory to set a school scoring record in their first opening victory since 1948.

Mistakes cost dearly in a 21-3 loss at A&M. An upset Meek said, "The Aggies have a fine ball club, but they're not that much better than we are. You just can't give them the kind of breaks we gave tonight and expect to beat them." Two fumbles and a blocked punt deep in their end crippled the Cougars.

Dickey sneaked the final yard behind Rudy Spitzenberger's block to account for the game's only touchdown in a 7-0 win over Detroit, the Missouri Valley Conference opener. Johnson's 32-yard return of the second half kickoff and his running featured the 46-yard push.

After a three-touchdown first half, the Cougars held off Oklahoma State, 21-13, for their third victory in four starts. "Houston was a magnificent football machine in the first half," reported Dan Shults in the *Houston Chronicle*. Dickey directed an 87-yard drive; Flynn took the second unit 77 yards; and Paul Sweeten's pass interception set up the third TD. Coach of the Cowpokes was Cliff Speegle, the current Southwest Conference commissioner.

A sweet 7-0 win over Texas Tech followed in which the Cougars jammed a 97-yard Tech drive at their one. Dickey, who passed five yards to Stegall for the only touchdown, was knocked cold and missed the entire second half.

The year before, their ranks thinned disastrously by a stomach virus, the Cougars had been trounced, 61-14, at Lubbock.

For the second straight year, two touchdown underdog Wichita upset UH, this time 21-7, scoring once after a fumble and again with an intercepted pitchout. The Cougars also lost Curley Johnson, guard Jim Martin, Donnie Caraway, and Sweeten to injuries.

Tulsa, hit even harder than UH by injuries, used only 20 players in its 17-14 surprise victory. Next the Cougars faced Ole Miss, which would wind up in the Cotton Bowl. UH wanted a good showing in the Deep South, amid rumors of a two-division split in the Southeastern Conference. The League's coaches and athletic directors had been UH guests at a summer deep sea fishing trip to Port Aransas.

UH trailed Ole Miss just 13-11 before the Rebs scored twice in the final six minutes for a 27-11 decision. Eddie Crawford's 57-yard TD run and a Cougar fumble were momentum-switching plays.

The Cougars led, 3-0, on Caraway's field goal, then marched 91 yards to make it 13-11 on Johnson's running and Dickey's 36-yard pass to Ken Wind. Jim Cravens blocked an Ole Miss punt late in the third quarter with UH behind, 7-3, but could not retrieve the ball for a safety before it went out of the end zone. Instead of a 10-3 lead the Cougars still trailed, 7-5.

Stegall, the scatback halfback who had been demoted from the first to the fourth team because of fumbling, found the cure against Villanova. In three runs from scrimmage, he darted 30 and 60 yards for touchdowns while gaining 92 yards in the 26-14 victory.

With Lavell Isbell and Johnson, voted the back of the year, on the All-Missouri Valley Conference team, the Cougars controlled Wyoming's Sun Bowl-bound single wing, 26-14, to complete a 6-4 season.

A week later the Southeastern Conference voted to wait a year before considering UH membership. Ole Miss had sponsored the Cougars' bid.

To launch their second decade—and show their potential as a possible Southeastern or Southwest Conference member—the Cougars staged an intense ticket-selling campaign for 1956.

Besides the important ingredient of more customers, UH added some impressive speed in a backfield quarterbacked by Don Flynn. Sophomores Harold Lewis, a 9.7 high school sprinter, and Don Brown joined the fullback trio of Owen Mulholland, Curley Johnson, and Donnie Caraway. "I've never been associated with a team that has the backfield speed we have here," enthused assistant John Cudmore, "not at Maryland, Kansas State, or anywhere."

Newcomers like center Harold "Burr" Davis, halfbacks Earl Kaiser and Mike Michon, and end Bob "Gunner" Blevins also were on hand. Michon and Blevins were marine corps veterans. Blevins won the Silver Star in Korea for bravery.

UH's largest crowd ever, 56,000, turned out at Rice Stadium, and the Cougars responded with an 18-7 win over Mississippi State. Flynn engineered a 70-yard, second period thrust; then Ken Wind, a superb defensive end this night, shook the ball loose and recovered the fumble. On the next play Flynn connected with Lewis, blazing downfield, for a 44-yard TD pass.

After State's score, Sammy Blount directed a crunching, 66-yard infantry march.

Sixth-ranked Ole Miss, its fans and officials still seething over the recruiting loss of Vicksburg high school star Claude King to UH, scored twice in the first period for a savagely-fought 14-0 decision. Second team quarterback Ray Brown and fullback Paige Cothren, who rushed for 144 yards (to UH's 133) were standouts. When Meek walked across the field to shake hands with Ole Miss's John Vaught, the Rebel coach was absent, evidently still miffed over the King affair.

Meek enlivened the usual hectic week of a Cougar-Aggie game with a charge that A&M spies had watched a secret UH practice. "We are confident the Aggies now have our newly-

Ken Wind is given the 1956 co-captain's award by Coach Bill Meek.

installed defenses," he declared. A&M's Bear Bryant promptly termed the accusation ridiculous. Meek then phoned Bryant, and they agreed to drop the matter.

The teams staged a 14-14 rib-bruiser before 67,001, UH's largest home crowd until their 1976 match with the Aggies. Ranked No. 9 nationally, destined to win the Southwest Conference and finish fifth in the nation, one of A&M's greatest teams was stopped on the one-yard line with 33 seconds to play. Bryant passed up the field goal that would have meant a perfect 10-0 season.

That night remains a yardstick by which Aggie-Cougar games are now compared. On A&M's side were future All-Americans like Jack Pardee, Charley Krueger, John David Crow and Dennis Goehring, and Gene Stallings, who was to coach them to the Cotton Bowl in a different decade.

Sophomore Billy Koons, a third string halfback, was an unlikely Cougar hero. So was defensive end Buddy Boek, who wrapped up Aggie quarterback Roddy Osborne for a six-yard loss on A&M's final play after a 90-yard drive.

Koons had not even suited up for the Ole Miss game at Jackson the week before. He spotted for radio announcers Clive Griffin and Loel Passe. But it was Koons, sent in with the play by Meek, who leaped between two defenders to catch Harold Lewis' 26-yard halfback pass at the five. On the next play Koons swept right end and stiff-armed Pardee to score on his first varsity carry from scrimmage. Flynn's second extra point with 11:03 to play concluded the scoring.

Rudy Spitzenberger recovered an Aggie fumble on the game's first play, and Lewis scored from the eight behind Flynn's block after three and a half minutes of play. Flynn's kick added another point.

Caraway's punt was blocked by Ken Beck, and John Tracey recovered in the end zone for an Aggie touchdown.

The Cougars battered 78 yards with the next kickoff to within inches of the goal. On third down at the three, Caraway and Pardee met in a thunderous collision, and the ball was spotted at the one. "I was head and shoulders over it (the goal)," Caraway said later; "then somebody shoved me to one side." On fourth down Caraway was stopped inches short by Pardee and Jim Langston.

Once again the Cougars threatened, reaching A&M's eight. Flynn was trapped trying to pass, and Caraway's field goal was blocked by Goehring. A&M drove 57 yards to go ahead, 14-7, in the third quarter when Bryant gambled on fourth down at the UH 47. Osborne covered the last 14 yards after a great fake to Pardee.

Mulholland's 58-yard punt was fumbled and recovered by

Crow at A&M's eight, setting the stage for A&M's last drive.

As he had with Koons, Meek sent in the 175-pound Boek from the sideline, figuring the Aggies would run wide. "Man, that was the sweetest tackle I ever made," Boek exclaimed.

Said Bryant, "Houston was a lot more aggressive and meaner. They played contact football. We didn't."

Boek's fumble recovery and an interception by Burr Davis resulted in the touchdowns in a 13-0 shutout at Oklahoma State. The defense again came through, halting the Cowpokes at the three when UH led 7-0. End Bob Borah went to his knees in the end zone to catch Sammy Blount's pass for the second score with 13 seconds left in the half.

Thus, after four games, the Cougars had yielded just 35 points, compared to 42 at the same stage by the great 1952 "Kimmel Corps."

The defense fought off Auburn time after time in a 12-0

Defensive end Buddy Boek, whose key tackle on the goal line preserved a 1956 tie with nationally-ranked Texas A&M.

defeat. The offense gained only eight first downs and 173 yards. Auburn kept the ball for 84 plays to UH's 45.

After scoring just seven touchdowns in the first five games, the UH offense uncovered a spark at Wichita. Lewis ignited it with a 64-yard punt return; then Blount caught the Shockers off guard and sprinted 51 yards on a quarterback sneak. Flynn and Kaiser combined for a 34-yard TD pass, and the Cougars rolled to a 41-12 win.

Ex-players on the 1946 team, the school's first, watched as honored guests while the Cougars throttled Tulsa, 14-0. The victory wrapped up Houston's first Missouri Valley title since 1952.

Once again the defense was superb, doling out just eight first downs and 127 yards. Boek recovered a fumble after Tulsa reached the 9, one of its only two trips over the 50. Flynn took charge of 48- and 81-yard scoring drives, and the offense kept the ball for all but six plays in the third quarter.

The offense continued to improve, pounding out 377 yards in a 26-13 win over tough Villanova. UH trailed at half-time, 7-6, on a pass interception despite giving up only one first down and 35 yards.

Flynn rushed for 110 yards in nine carries, and Kaiser, Gene Ward, Caraway, and Johnson gained steadily. Meek's unit system again wore down the opposition. Offensive linemen like centers Billy McIlroy and Dick McKinney, guards Spitzenberger, Ken Watson, John Peters and Tom Boyd, and tackles Dalva Allen, Buddy Terry, Don Boudreaux, Charlie Brown and Joe Raitano opened the holes.

Caraway's fierce linebacking and bull-like runs were vital to a sweet 20-7 triumph at Texas Tech, where the Cougars, weakened by dysentery, had been routed, 61-14, two years before. Caraway rushed for 77 yards in 16 carries, including a vital fourth down gain on the march to the go-ahead touchdown.

Afterwards, Caraway noted, "It shore was a lot of fun." Did he ever get mad, wondered John Hollis of the *Houston Post.* "I can't say I do. I really don't feel anything. I don't ever get mad at anybody. We're all just out there having a lot of fun."

Another bit of the Caraway legend occurred after another

Houston's 1956 Missouri Valley Conference champions.

DALVA ALLEN

BILLY McILROY

RONNIE EMBERG

VANDERCOOK

KEN WATSON

DON FLYNN

JOE BOB SMITH

SHOP

road game. An out-of-town writer asked Caraway what impressed him about one of the other team's quarterbacks, who had been hurt after a collision with Caraway. He replied, "I sure liked the way he rode that stretcher when they carried him off the field."

Caraway firmly believed that flying was a mode of travel that could be injurious to one's health. Meek used to sit next to him on plane trips to soothe his nerves. "When your number is up," Meek once told Caraway, "you're going to go, regardless of where you are."

Pointing toward the pilot, Caraway responded, "Coach, I'm not worried about my number, I'm worried about his."

With the plane pitching through rough weather on another flight, Caraway unbuckled his seat belt, stormed into the cockpit and tapped the pilot on the shoulder. He growled, "If we go down, and you come to, you better hope I don't."

Caraway, Flynn, Spitzenberger, Wind, and Allen were All-Missouri Valley selections, and Meek was voted the league's coach of the year. Fouke visited Sugar Bowl officials in New Orleans; then several members of the selection committee came to Houston several days before the final game with Detroit. But the Sugar Bowl decided on Tennessee and Baylor.

The Cougars closed with a 39-7 thrashing of Detroit for a 7-2-1 record. Only the 8-2 by the 1952 team surpassed it.

Another bid for SWC membership was turned down in the league's winter meeting in Dallas. Two weeks later Meek was racked between an offer of the head coaching job at SMU or staying at UH.

Significantly, Meek said, "If Houston was in a major conference, they'd have to run me off." Two days before Christmas he announced he was staying, but SMU refused to take no for an answer.

A week later, Meek accepted SMU's "write-your-own-ticket" deal which included a 10-year contract and guaranteed security for Meek and his staff. After two years in which the Cougars had won 13, lost 6 and tied 1, another coaching hunt was on.

The Claude King Caper

One of the most publicized recruits in UH football history, Claude King was the centerpiece of a tug-of-war between Ole Miss and the Cougars that created headlines throughout the South in 1956.

A 16-year-old All-American high school halfback at Vicksburg, Mississippi, where he was also state sprint champion, King was recruited by Cougar Golf Coach Dave Williams, who was aided by the presence at UH of another Vicksburg product, Jim Baughman.

Head Coach Bill Meek's freshmen crop that season probably was the school's most impressive to that point. It included former all-staters and notables like King; Joe Cleveland of Cleburne; Billy Dube of San Antonio; Howard Evans and Ray Ruwaldt of Dallas; Sonny Long of Houston Reagan; Charles McKenzie of Grand Prairie; Joe Glass of Baytown; and Guy Hill of Ferriday, Louisiana.

Williams also had signed up Jim Colvin, a rangy, unknown lineman from Orange, Texas. "They'd lost over 20 games in a row," Williams relates, "and no college recruiters ever came by. When he got here, he said he wanted to have a scrimmage and check out all these all-staters, and boy, he checked them out." Colvin was later to play nearly 10 seasons of pro football with Baltimore, the Dallas Cowboys, and New York Giants.

Coached in high school by Mike Campbell, later Darrell Royal's top aide for years at the University of Texas, King staged a memorable performance when Williams saw him play.

133

"I was looking for big linemen because the good ones are always hard to find," Williams recalls. "Then Claude went about 80 yards on the third play of the game, and I said, 'Oh, Lord.' Then he caught about a 50-yard pass, coming back to take it in the wind. Later he ran through about eight people for a 25-yard touchdown, one of the greatest runs I ever saw.

"He had better balance than Warren McVea. He ran with his whole foot on the ground. He'd run right up in your face and let you snatch at him, then take off."

Hogan Wharton, UH's All-American defensive tackle, recalls, "He'd 'juke' you to death."

Williams describes King's recruiting visit to UH, "I carried his little three- or four-year-old sister all over. She knocked over the phone in (athletic secretary) Margaret Standard's office and raked everything around on the desks, but nobody said a word."

King lived at Baughman's house that summer and had a job at the Quintana Petroleum Corporation air field. "Those Ole Miss coaches got seasick going out to the offshore oil rigs looking for Claude out there," adds Jack Scott, former UH sports publicist.

King takes up the story, "I signed with both schools, then made up my mind to go to Ole Miss. My parents liked Dave Williams, and Jim Baughman came to Vicksburg to visit his parents. I didn't have a summer job from Ole Miss, and when Jim said he and his wife were driving back to Houston one night and offered me a ride, I went with them.

"I was at the athletic dorm one night before practices started. Rich Price and Jack Carter, who had played at Vicksburg and gone to Ole Miss, called and asked, 'Are you homesick yet?' I said, 'Some,' and they said 'Let's go back.'"

King continues, "The UH coaches found out and called mom. I went on to Oxford and told Coach (John) Vaught I was ready to come to Ole Miss. I don't think he knew anything about it. I called mom and she was on the way to Oxford.

"A bunch of us had gone to the movie downtown and were standing around outside. She walked up and grabbed me around the neck and told me to get my little tail in the car. The papers said I'd been 'kidnapped' by Ole Miss, but they weren't taking me against my will."

Williams remembers a 2 a.m. phone call from Meek: "Bill

said the Ole Miss coaches had come over and got Claude out of the dorm and taken him back. I told his mother to go over with her lawyer and see Coach Vaught." Another version is that Mrs. King, accompanied by an attorney, gave Vaught five minutes to produce Claude or she would bring kidnapping charges. It was believed by many that she was advised by the state attorney general, an alumnus of Mississippi State.

King's first freshman game against the Texas A&M frosh was impressive—10 carries and three touchdowns, and King led the UH frosh in almost every category.

Slowed by the injuries which were to hamper him for much of his career, King still averaged 6.9 yards per carry as a sophomore and then led the team in rushing with 438 yards and a 5.8 average as a junior. His 93-yard kickoff return in a 37-26 victory over Miami was then the longest scoring play in school history, but injuries again slowed him in his senior season.

"Coach Harold Lahar knew as much football as any man I've ever known," King says, "and he gave me a bunch of chances. There wasn't that much interest down here in Missouri Valley Conference football, and UH had been known as a secondary school and a bunch of outlaws. That's why you fought so hard when you played Southwest Conference schools.

"The game I'll never forget is Oklahoma State my junior year (1958) at Rice Stadium after we'd won our first three games. They crossed our 50 once, and we were inside their 10 four or five times. Then we lost to Tulsa, 25-20."

Dave Williams describes runners on UH teams of the late 1950s, "When we had Lonnie Holland, Harold Lewis, Don Brown, Pat Studstill, Don Mullins and King, we had one of the greatest collections of backs in the country. Lewis had run a 9.7 at Pampa weighing over 200 pounds, and that was unheard of back then."

Besides King and Lewis, Williams also recruited Mullins and Studstill, both from Shreveport, Louisiana. He recalls, "I took Don downtown to lunch to show him the opportunities in Houston. I had lunch with him several years ago, and he gave me a check for the Cougar Club. He asked me, 'Remember that day you took me downtown to lunch? Well, I own that building now.'"

King, an assistant coach at Ball High School in Galveston,

Claude King, object of a heated Ole Miss-Houston recruiting battle, and Coach Harold Lahar.

says he got his greatest satisfaction "from just seeing the place grow and playing with good football players like Don Caraway and Don Flynn."

Hal Lahar: A New Image

Less than two weeks after Bill Meek had left for SMU, UH had its new man—an Ivy League Okie named Harold W. Lahar.

In five years at Colgate, the East Coast independent in New York State, Lahar earned a reputation as one of the nation's most imaginative offensive-minded coaches. The Raiders had the leading passer in the East, Guy Martin, and had played a memorable 46-55 game with Army as the teams set a collegiate one-game scoring record.

Later, Earl Blaik, the esteemed West Point coach, said of Lahar, "I regard him as one of the really fine football coaches in the country. He worked in a tough job, without a lot of boys, yet he has always been able to give a good account of himself."

UH officials had interviewed, among others, Dan Devine of Arizona State and Jim Owens, Bear Bryant's top aide at Texas A&M, who was then also negotiating for the job he was to take at Washington.

An All Big 7 guard at Oklahoma, where he played on the school's first bowl team, Lahar had coached Colgate to a 24-17-4 record despite difficult circumstances. The school had only 1,700 male students and operated under the Ivy League code of restricted athletic scholarships and no spring practice.

A native of Durant, Oklahoma, Lahar grew up in Oklahoma City. His Sooner teammates included Bill Jennings, hired that winter as Nebraska's new coach; Frank "Pop" Ivy, later a head coach of the Houston Oilers; and Cliff Speegle. Speegle, an assistant for a time at Colgate for Lahar, now is Southwest Conference commissioner. Lahar is the assistant commissioner.

138

Head Coach Harold Lahar (left) with assistants (left to right) Jasper Flanakin, Casto Ramsey, Swede Hill, Red Conkright, Hank Watkins, and Andy Zubel.

Lahar's Colgate teams lost only three games to Ivy League schools in his last three years. His first four products ranked in the nation's top ten defensive units.

Released from his Colgate contract which had three years remaining, Lahar was contacted by both Iowa State and UH at the 1957 NCAA convention in St. Louis. "Both schools wanted me to visit," he recalls. "I went to Houston first; they offered me the job, and I accepted."

Lahar notes, "It was a very difficult situation, stepping in like that. The previous staff had decided it could not recruit the good high school prospects, although there were some good recruits like Claude King, Harold Lewis, and Don Brown.

"We made an effort to recruit players in order to build from underneath. We always had good defenses and good linemen; we worked the smaller schools but could never get the top backs.

"We had tremendous difficulties recruiting against the SWC," Lahar echoes the problem which was to plague the school for years. "We were a kind of safety valve. The only pitch we had in recruiting was the city of Houston. The school was young, it had great colleges like business, architecture, and pharmacy. We really sold the city. In the Missouri Valley (from which UH withdrew in 1959) we had nothing to sell.

"I didn't realize when I took the job the position you were in if you didn't belong to the SWC or any conference," Lahar continues. "The kids then were SWC-oriented, and their coaches were, too. It was a tough, hard sell. We worked hard to find boys in the small schools."

Lahar describes his first priorities, "If it were possible, in the long run you had to build with athletes who were recruited and came as undergraduates. We insisted on academic efforts, compulsory study halls, and class attendance.

"We weren't trying to cut up other schools in our recruiting. I developed a pretty good relationship with Jess Neely at Rice. You could see if the school survived, it was going to be great, and you had to build your own program."

Lahar explains, "The image of the independent in our part of the country was much better. In Texas the Missouri Valley Conference didn't mean a damn thing. We'd be a lot better off to schedule as an independent, and we continued to play the best teams in the Valley.

"In 1960 we knew we had a chance to become a state school. We had developed good relationships with the SWC schools. I felt we had overcome some of the black marks. We had shown, 'This is the kind of house we're trying to run.' We were out of the bottom of the barrel financially. The Astrodome was going to be built, and we were fairly sure that would be our home.

"Three people held it together—Mr. Cullen, Corby Robertson, and Harry Fouke. You can lay it at their doorstep. At the toughest times Corby was the guy who hung in there."

Lahar continues, "I only saw Mr. Cullen three times. Once he told me he'd been very lucky to have made so much money, that if a person had good health and an education, he had a chance to succeed in life. That's why his charities went to things connected to those. He believed in Houston, this was the big thing to him."

Defense became a primary concern during Lahar's UH tenure. "We always gave defense the first choice of personnel up front and linebackers," he says. "The offense got first choice of backs. We felt our best opportunity of winning was with a strong defense. If you have defensive ability, you can take more chances and know that you're going to get the ball back. We always felt our strength should be on defense, and in one platoon football we always picked on the basis of defense. "

But Lahar's teams also showed they could score a lot of points, as in 1958. "We scored 117 points our first three games," Lahar points out, "39-7 over A&M, 34-13 over Cincinnati, and 44-0 over Wichita." At that point the Cougars were the nation's offensive leader. "Then we lost to Oklahoma State, 7-0, and to Tulsa, 25-20. Tulsa had a man hit on the one yard line and roll into the end zone."

The Cougars could not have started the Lahar era more impressively than they did in the 1957 opener against Miami of Florida, ranked No. 1 in some preseason polls.

"Fran Curci was their quarterback," Lahar says, "and we had noticed he was 87 percent left-handed (in play-calling). Charles Caffery, our defensive guard, would crash inside the left guard to destroy their belly play. We were taking a chance, but it worked. They never threatened us. We used a five man line and overshifted the left end to the inside of the offensive end if they were on the right hash mark. We showed everybody how to beat them; they lost seven or eight games that year."

Lahar recalls Kenny Bolin, a 155-pound halfback, as "a fantastic competitor. He was one of the toughest, physically and mentally, you could ever see. He had no physical qualifications at all but a great heart.

141

Ken "The Spear" Bolin, leading rusher for the 1960-61 teams, with Coach Harold Lahar.

"Billy Roland was a great little quarterback. His dad was coach at Alvin. He had marvelous hands and a great sense of timing. He didn't look good, he wasn't fast, but he had a lot of little funny moves.

"Joe Bob Isbell had been a high school fullback at Little Cypress. He had great strength and was a great block protector. He never gave a blocker a solid shot at him. Danny Birdwell was a very intense center and defensive guard with pure, unadulterated strength. Hogan Wharton also had great strength, and he had a little fire in him.

"Demaree Jones (linebacker) was like Bolin; they had a total disregard for their bodies. Bob Borah was a great 185-pound end. Don Brown, Don Mullins, and Pat Studstill were fine runners. Studstill developed into a great kicker in the pros. Swede Hill recruited Bobby Brezina, another fine runner, and through him we got the whole Brezina bunch."

Lahar resigned after the 1961 season opener, a 7-7 tie with A&M. He had signed a three-year contract upon arriving at UH, then another three-year pact after his second season. "We had a meeting in the summer and I asked for a new contract," Lahar says. "They declined. I felt they had overlooked the program, and some of the things we had done. I felt our records were no less commendable than any of the others, in spite of the fact we never won big. We'd had great defensive teams, but we were criticized for not being imaginative offensively, and we'd had some bad crowds."

Still a fine golfer, Lahar was a member of the Oklahoma collegiate team. Corby Robertson recalls an example of Lahar's skill: "We were playing Champions one day with Jackie Burke, who was getting ready to rejoin the pro tour the next week. Hal had outdriven Jackie every hole coming up to No. 6 or No. 7. Hal did it again, and Burke, who'd gotten madder and madder, went down the fairway to his ball. He looked farther down toward Hal's ball, and said, 'Coach, I know what's wrong with your football team—you play too much golf.'"

Lahar's final team ended its 1961 season on a high note. "The last two games I coached were great, great games," Lahar says, referring to the wins over Florida State, 28-8, and Oregon State and future Heisman Trophy winner Terry Baker, 23-12. "They were very emotional, and the kids played closer to their capabilities."

With the Cougars now a full-fledged member of the South-west Conference, Lahar discerns a fundamental change for a typical UH alumnus: "Football is an identification catalyst. I have a different position with my coffee klatsch, friends or lunch crowd. I'm in a different spot when I can say, 'That was a great game we had with Texas Saturday' instead of 'We beat the heck out of Wichita.'"

No Rose Garden

Rare is the new head coach who finds a rose garden awaiting him, but few face the problems Harold Lahar encountered as he took up his task.

Among 15 lettermen were just four full-time returning starters and there were 26 sophomores on a 48-man squad to play seven road games. Their 10 opponents had compiled an overall 65-29-6 record the year before.

Sammy Blount, Don Flynn's understudy, was the only experienced quarterback. Halfback Harold Lewis, fullback Owen Mulholland, guard John Peters, and tackle Charlie Brown represented most of the previous season's game experience.

Halfback Claude King headed the sophomore group, and King's varsity debut was eagerly awaited. "All that buildup makes it kind of tough," he admitted. "It puts more pressure on me, but I'm working twice as hard so I won't let Coach Lahar and the team down."

Brown predicted, "Claudio is going to be every bit as good as they say he is. He left his press clippings back in Mississippi, and he's out there working just as hard—if not harder—than the rest of us."

Unfortunately, no one could have lived up to the feats expected of King.

Miami of Florida, a top 10 outfit the year before when it was 8-1-1 and had the nation's No. 1 defense, arrived for Lahar's first UH game ranked as high as third in preseason polls. The Hurricanes were quarterbacked by 150-pound sophomore

Fran Curci. Junior college transfer Billy Ray Dickey started for UH.

King began his career with two big plays that aided UH's 7-0 triumph. He recovered a fumble at the UH 48, then slithered 21 yards on a double reverse. Lewis bolted through the left side behind blocks by Burr Davis and Mulholland and covered 26 yards to the game's only touchdown.

The Cougars were fired up, none more so than center Joe McDonald. Later the head coach at Houston's St. Thomas High School, he recalls, "Coming down the ramp at Rice Stadium, the excitement was so great my stomach muscles knotted up when I bent over to take pregame calisthenics. I played the entire game without being able to raise up."

McDonald also met an old friend from his Fort Benning days on Miami's team: "He was a linebacker and a salty old dog. After every play I'd pull his shoe off down in the pileup and keep my head down so he wouldn't recognize me. He'd complain to the officials every time. The last time I did it, he got so mad he put a half nelson on me and pulled me down. The officials were coming over to break up a fight when he recognized me."

Lahar was named coach of the week by International News Service and United Press. A flu bug which struck before the Miami game weakened more than half the team as it prepared

Burr Davis, all-time Cougar offensive lineman and 1957-58 All-Missouri Valley Conference.

for Baylor's Sugar Bowl champs. The Bears were in a nasty mood when Villanova coach Frank Reagan called them over-rated after Baylor's 7-0 win.

Quarterbacks Buddy Humphrey and Doyle Traylor passed effectively as the No. 11-ranked Bears beat UH, rated 14th, by 14-6. Lewis' 63-yard kickoff return set up his fourth down three-yard pass to King for UH's only score, one of only five passes the Cougars tried.

At Cincinnati a 35-yard punt return by Lewis left only 25 yards to cover, and King gained the final four in a 7-0 victory. An altercation between Charley Mallia and a Cincinnati player nearly provoked a full-scale fight. During the affray Earl Kaiser chased a photographer off the field.

Third-ranked Texas A&M was primed and ready after the 14-14 tie the previous year. The Aggies exacted revenge, 28-6. McDonald remembers, "John Crow was like King Kong. Every play you'd hit him as hard as you could, and the next play he'd come right back like a freight train. I had cleat marks all over my body afterwards."

King suffered a strained knee ligament, a season-long problem. Then Mulholland, the leading rusher and punter, was ruled ineligible the week of the Missouri Valley opener with Oklahoma State. The Cougars salvaged a 6-6 tie, scoring in the last seconds after Hogan Wharton blocked a punt.

All dressed up in their new red leggings, the Cougars suffered their worst homecoming defeat in history, 48-7, to No. 1-ranked Auburn, which scored 16 points within eight minutes of the first quarter.

Lloyd Nix passed 71 yards to Red Phillips on the Tigers' first play. UH bobbled the kickoff, resulting in a safety. Two plays after the free kick, Auburn's Bryant Harvard went 35 yards to another TD. The lone bright spot for UH was Paul Sweeten's school record 89-yard interception return.

McDonald recalls, "Hal made us take off those red socks after the game and told us, 'These will never see another ball game.' Then he took them out and burned them."

A three-touchdown underdog against Ole Miss, the Cougars gained a 7-7 halftime tie with a 93-yard drive before bowing, 20-7, at Jackson. Back from his knee injury, King scored twice and averaged 12 yards per carry in a 27-12 win over Mississippi

Southern.

Amid blowing sleet and numbing temperatures Brown and Dickey ran well in a 27-6 triumph at Wichita that brought the second straight Valley title. Brown rushed for 117 yards and Dickey, installed at halfback when King reinjured his knee, added 95.

"We were all hiding under our parkas, trying to keep warm," McDonald said. "The sleet was whirling around, and there was Ray Ruwaldt (a defensive back), just standing stock still for about five plays. He never even moved. He was so cold, like he'd been frozen in place."

A satisfying 13-7 win at Tulsa, their first ever in T-Town, closed out a 5-4-1 year for the Cougars. Wharton, voted the league's lineman of the year, Davis, and Lewis were chosen on the All-Missouri Valley team.

At the team's postseason banquet Fouke made an unexpected announcement—the school would pursue Southwest Conference membership exclusively, dropping thoughts of the Southeastern or any "super" conference. Said Fouke, "We feel our right place in athletics is in the place where we exist. We feel the place we belong is in the Southwest Conference. Nothing will be left undone until we accomplish that goal."

As for the relationship with Rice, Fouke said, "There are those who say Rice and UH cannot be members of the same conference, that we would conflict. Such is not true. We respect Rice. It's a fine institution, with a fine athletic program, but I also say there's no reason why two fine schools like Rice and UH can't go forward together in a great city like Houston."

Fouke also contradicted the old argument that UH's admission would eliminate the SWC round robin schedule, "We could replace, and command more interest, than most nonconference teams who are on the schedules of SWC members."

Lahar, perplexed by the new two-point conversion written into the rules, jokingly suggested a press box of experts. "After each touchdown you guys wave a red flag if you want us to kick for one point. If you want us to run for two, wave a green flag," he said. Assistant Lovette Hill added, "I could have spent two solid weeks, 24 hours a day, changing rules, and I never would have thought of that one."

With a stable of fine runners like Brown, King, Lewis,

Dickey, and sophomore Don Mullins, Lahar retooled his split-T to a split wing, with a flanker set wide on almost every play. Don McDonald, sophomore Pat Studstill, and Oklahoma transfer Lonnie Holland were the quarterbacks, fronted by linemen like Wharton, Howard Evans, Jim Colvin, Charlie Brown, Davis, and sophomores Charlie Patterson and Jim Windham.

The offense meshed beautifully in the 1958 opener, a surprisingly one-sided 39-7 smashing of Texas A&M. King dashed 47 yards for one touchdown and set up two more, gaining 90 yards in just seven carries. King and Brown accounted for 160 of UH's 356 yards total offense. The Cougars did not lose a fumble or throw an interception.

UH's "assassins in scarlet" rolled past Cincinnati, 34-13, to take over the national scoring lead. Brown's 35-yard interception return in the fourth period was a key play, while Cougar passers completed 13 of 21. The Cougars also surfaced in the

1958 Houston quarterbacks (left to right) Pat Studstill, Lonnie Holland, and Don McDonald.

top 20 in both national polls.

They enhanced their scoring average with a 44-0 rout of Wichita in which Studstill made several big plays. He returned an interception 76 yards in the third quarter for the game's third touchdown after a sluggish UH start, caught a 38-yard TD pass and punted for a 38.6 average.

Tackle Tom Pierce, playing at the request of his father, who had died the night before, was awarded the game ball after clearing away the final defender on Studstill's runback.

With 117 points scored in the first three games and ranked sixth nationally in total offense and third in rushing defense, the Cougars met Oklahoma State minus McDonald, their top passer, and fullback Jim Kuehne. Then Windham, a starting offensive guard, separated a shoulder and was lost for the year in the Oklahoma State game.

Cliff Speegle, Lahar's former teammate and roommate at Oklahoma and later on his Colgate staff, fashioned the Cowpoke defenses to cut off King's long runs. It was an unusual game.

The Cougars ran off a record 85 plays from scrimmage, penetrated the 30 six times without scoring, held the Cowpokes to 26 yards the second half, and lost 7-0. They had a first down on the two in the fourth quarter, but Holland was stopped inches short on four straight quarterback sneaks. They reached the two again and incurred a delay of game penalty on fourth down.

"If anybody says anything against Lonnie," Wharton rumbled, "there's gonna be a big line waiting to belt him one, and I'm gonna be right up there in front. The linemen called for those quarterback sneaks, and it was our fault, not his, that we didn't score."

The next three weeks were a study in frustration.

Fumbling their way into a 0-13 hole, the Cougars lost to Tulsa, 25-20, their first conference defeat since 1955. They also lost Brown for the rest of the year with a broken elbow.

There followed a 56-7 nightmare at Ole Miss, UH's worst defeat ever, and a 10-6 loss at North Texas State.

"Hal put up tarps around the practice field before the Ole Miss game and changed our entire offense," Joe McDonald recalls. "We used three centers in the middle to create a bal-

150

anced or unbalanced line. My brother, Don, was the quarterback. On the first play I was to pull and trap as the right guard, and everybody on Ole Miss's defense yells, 'Here it is.'

"Hanson Churchwell, their tackle, caught me under the chin with an elbow when I pulled and turned. I cleared the ground and flew back into the quarterback and fullback. When I looked up, the official is telling me, 'Son, it's a penalty to assist the runner.' Both my jaws were knocked out of their sockets, I lost 12 teeth and split both cheekbones, and I'm 'assisting the runner.'"

Jack Scott, the school's former sports publicist, remembers the gloom after the North Texas loss, "One of our radio broadcasters asked Harry Fouke, 'This was to be the great year for UH, where do we go from here?' For the first time in my life, I saw Harry at a loss for words." The radioman was Dan Rather, now with CBS, who assisted with Cougar football broadcasts in those days.

Their fullback corps practically decimated, the Cougars outscored Miami of Florida 37-26. King's school record 93-yard kickoff return deflated the Hurricane after Miami pulled to 29-20. Lahar had to move guard Dewey Wade to backup fullback behind Hilmer Potcinske, who had played just 13 minutes. When Wade hurt a knee in the first half, Joe McDonald moved from center, changing to a backfield number.

Holland's eight for nine passing, Borah's eight catches and Lewis' 64-yard punt return helped a 22-17 closing victory over Texas Tech and a 5-4 season.

Ole Miss and Alabama, the first two games, presented a tough hill to climb at the start of the 1959 season. Lahar stationed Studstill as a flanker, with King expected to be the hub of the running game in his senior year.

Some Mississippians still had not forgiven King. "King, in going to Houston," said the Jackson, Mississippi, *Clarion-Ledger,* "passed up the big league for the bush league."

Bob Khayat's 52-yard interception return led to the Rebs' first score as the Cougars dominated the first half, yet trailed, 7-0. Then Ole Miss charged to a second TD and a field goal on its first two series of the second half to stow away a 16-0 win. King, running just seven times, was held to six yards.

Alabama kicked a third quarter 15-yard field goal that

stood up for a 3-0 victory. The Cougars were penalized out of field goal range at the end of the half when kicker Gerald Ripkowski was sent into the game for the third time that quarter, an illegal substitution. A 13-12 victory over Cincinnati was followed by losses to Texas A&M when King's career ended with a separated shoulder; Oklahoma State, 19-12; and North Texas State, 7-6.

Directing the No. 2 offense, sophomore Don Sessions figured in every point for a 22-13 win at Tulsa, scoring two touchdowns, throwing a 67-yard touchdown pass and a two-point conversion. Sessions also sparked the offense at Wichita, directing a three-touchdown rally in the third period climaxed by Mullins' 32-yard double reverse in a 28-13 win.

But defeats by Texas Tech, 27-0, and Washington State, 32-18, meant a 3-7 season, the worst since the school's second campaign in 1947.

Two months later the Cougars resigned from the Missouri Valley and became an independent, a role they were to play for the next 16 football seasons. The crunch developed when UH signed a contract with Mississippi State and decided to drop Wichita, leaving the Cougars and Wichita short of the four required conference games.

Facing the first season as an independent, Lahar labeled the 1960 Cougars "the best team I've had to start a season with here." He was referring to quarterbacks Sessions and Larry Lindsey; fullback Charlie Rieves; ends Randall Dorsett and Errol Linden; and linemen Joe Bob Isbell, Wiley Feagin, Jim Windham, Jim Norris, and Murdoch Hooper.

Ahead just 7-0 at the half, Ole Miss bombed the Cougars with passes in the second half of a 42-0 rout in the opener. Jake Gibbs threw for three touchdowns, Doug Elmore for two, and Glynn Griffing for one as the Rebs scored six aerial touchdowns.

Lindsey, hit in the throat on the opening play, came back and turned apparent losses into gains in a 14-10 comeback at Mississippi State. Ken Bolin scored both TDs on runs of 56 and 10 yards.

After a 29-20 loss to Oregon State in which they totaled 391 yards, the Cougars blanked the Aggies, 17-0, behind Ses-

1960 tri-captains (top to bottom) Jim Kuehne, Wiley Feagin, and Jim Windham with Gen. A. D. Bruce, former university chancellor.

sions' sharp passing and the running of Bolin and Lindsey. They stopped Oklahoma State at the seven in the last minute of play to preserve a 12-7 decision. Alabama crossed midfield only four times but won anyway, 14-0.

In a 41-16 trouncing of North Texas State Bolin darted 25 and 21 yards to score, and Sessions threw TD passes of 46 yards to Bob Barnett and 38 to Bolin. At Cincinnati, Bolin's 46-yard punt return started a two-touchdown burst in the final six minutes which led to a 14-0 victory. Bolin, the 155-pound "Spear," bolted 19 yards to set up the first score; then Sessions passed 29 yards to Gene Ritch for the second. Bolin's 12-yard reception from Sessions and Eddie Mitchamore's extra point wrung out a 7-6 verdict at Florida State.

But once again, an enemy aerial game, this time by Tulsa's Jerry Keeling, inflicted severe damage, and the Cougars closed out with a 26-16 defeat and a 6-4 record.

Among 26 lettermen for Lahar's fifth UH team were 13 seniors for another no-holds-barred schedule. Reasons for optimism were quarterbacks Sessions and Billy Roland; fullbacks Rieves, Larry Broussard and Bobby Brezina; and halfbacks Bolin, Lindsey, Jerry Kruse, and Bill McMillan. A veteran interior line looked like a strong point, with Danny Birdwell,

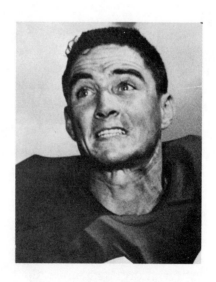

Kenny Bolin, "The Spear."

154

Red Wright, Isbell, Hooper, Ken Chancellor, and Bill Brown prominent.

An opening 7-7 tie with A&M was followed by a 10-7 loss to Mississippi State. The Bulldogs used flat zone passes to pick away at the corners. Boston College was the season's first win, as Bolin intercepted three passes and ran 80 yards from scrimmage. Then the Cougars actually led No. 1-ranked Ole Miss, 7-6, and trailed just 13-7 at the half. The Rebels' Glynn Griffing, Doug Elmore and Perry Lee Dunn triggered a second half avalanche and a 47-7 licking.

Bolin's 80-yard scoring sprint, his second in three weeks, aided a 13-7 win at Cincinnati, but fourth-ranked Alabama handled the Cougars, 17-0.

Four days before the Tulsa game, Lahar suddenly announced his resignation. The previous year's 26-16 upset by Tulsa had cost a 7-3 season, and Lahar had been given a win-or-else ultimatum when he had asked for a new contract. He turned in his resignation letter to Fouke the day after the Mississippi State game. It was to be made public after the season.

The move stunned the city and his squad. Alabama's Bear Bryant said, "He's a sound, fine football coach. I don't think I could take his material and beat ours."

Corby Robertson offered to resign as chairman of the athletic council to clear the way for a new two-year contract, but the offer was not accepted.

Vowing to hand Lahar four straight wins to close the season, the team was keyed too high and had to struggle past Tulsa, 14-2. Oklahoma State beat them, 28-24; then Roland and Sessions passed the Cougars past Florida State, 28-8.

Oregon State, the end of Lahar's five-year era, held the key to a winning season and winning record. The Cougars scored all their points in the last 24 minutes to overcome Terry Baker and the Beavers, 23-12. Roland scored twice, Sessions passed for another TD, and Isbell trapped Baker for a safety. The team gave Lahar an emotional farewell after the victory.

Lahar was gleefully tossed in the shower, and Birdwell told him, "Thanks for an education and the chance to play for you, coach. I've enjoyed every minute of it."

Said Lahar, "I'll always remember this one." The 1961 team bettered the total defense record held by the 8-2 team of

1952, and Sessions broke Bobby Clatterbuck's career pass completion record.

Best of all, the closing victory meant a 5-4-1 season and an overall 24-23-2 record for Lahar. He deserved to go out a winner.

"There's one thing I have always told my football players," said Lahar. "I have always told them when they walk off that field, I only ask one thing of them. I want them to be able to ask themselves, 'Did I give it everything I had?' If they can honestly say yes, then they've succeeded.

"I've put my coaching on the same principle."

Hogan Wharton, Amiable And Tough

Like many of the Cougars of his era, Hogan Wharton began his college football career elsewhere. Like them, he played with distinction at UH and later in the pros.

A transfer from SMU, Wharton was a friendly, 6-foot-2, 240-pounder from Orange, Texas. Twice chosen Missouri Valley Conference lineman of the year (1957-58) and twice All-MVC, Wharton was UH's second All-American, voted on the 1958 football coaches team.

"Burr Davis, Harold Lewis, John Peters and Bob Borah were about the only ones who hadn't transferred from another school," says Wharton. "Lonnie Holland and Don McDonald, our quarterbacks, had gone to Oklahoma and TCU. There wasn't a better halfback in the U.S. than Don Brown in 1958 until he got his elbow broken. He ran with reckless abandon; running into people didn't bother him a bit.

"We won the Valley both my years, but people figured, 'So what?' There wasn't that much talk in those days about the Southwest Conference; we kind of figured eventually we'd get in."

Wharton remembers Auburn's 1957 national champion as "the best I ever played against. They had Red Phillips (end), Jackie Burkett (tackle) and Billy Atkins (fullback)."

As is his nature, Wharton recalls some of the lighter moments: "We had the biggest gang fight on the field you ever saw at Cincinnati in 1957. After the game Earl Kaiser runs off the field with the ball. We're on the bus waiting to leave the

157

stadium, and this guy gets on the bus and wants their ball back. Earl ran him off the bus.

"We were a bunch of rowdies," Wharton says. "Coming back on the plane one night, Hal Lahar tells us, 'Okay, if you want to smoke, light up.' So everybody lights up, and the smoke gets so thick, Hal turns around and says, 'Good grief, if there's any of you who don't want to, you don't have to.'"

Wharton relates, "One day in our meeting Andy Zubel (an assistant) tells us, 'We're going to attack these people methodically.' Then he asks Don Boudreaux, 'Do you know what that means?' Boudreaux tells him, 'Yes, sir, bordering on mediocrity.'"

Wharton recalls another coach telling a team meeting, "Out of this formation, they do two things—run or pass."

Still, Wharton knew just one way to play the game: "I never separated one game from another. You want to win every time out, no matter if it's Valley Normal or Notre Dame. I learned early that Valley Normal might have a tush hog in front of you just like Notre Dame."

By the time Wharton came to UH "our facilities were as good as any school in the SWC," he says. "We had an air-conditioned dorm and the best food and equipment."

Billy Ray Dickey, a back in those days, sticks in Wharton's memory: "Pound for pound he was about the toughest son of a gun you could find at 158. If he'd weighed 200, you'd have needed a license for him."

Wharton also recalls the 1958 game at Ole Miss: "We scored first and it was just 7-14 at the half."

But the Rebels deluged UH in the second half for a 56-7 rout. Jack Scott, then the school's athletic publicist, was driving back to Memphis with John Hollis of the *Houston Post* and Dan Shults of *The Houston Chronicle*. They stopped for gas, and the attendant, taking them for Ole Miss fans, asked, "Been to the game?"

"Yep."

"How was it?"

"Not worth a damn."

"What's the matter, give too many points?"

Scott says, "All year I'd promised Hogan he'd be on the All-American team on Ed Sullivan's TV show. After we lost at

Hogan Wharton, 1958 All-American tackle.

North Texas, I got a wire to collect a plane ticket for Hogan to fly to New York after our game at Miami.

"When I told Hal Lahar, he was so thrilled he was in tears. But he told me Hogan was in the hospital with the flu. Both teams had so many guys hurt the *Miami Herald* was calling the game the Hospital Bowl.

"I told Hogan, 'You play at Miami and I'll have you on Ed Sullivan's show in New York on Sunday.' He played one of the most fantastic games I ever saw. I went to the dressing room and they were cutting Hogan's uniform off, he was so exhausted."

That was the way Wharton played the game, befitting an All-American on a team that won five and lost four.

"We had a lot of pros come off our teams," Wharton points out, "Jim Colvin, Errol Linden, Jim Norris, Charlie Rieves, Wiley Feagan, Joe McDonald, Hal Lewis, Claude King, Burr Davis, Pat Studstill, Don Mullins. We had good players, as good as anybody. We just didn't have enough of them."

Starting An Era

With 15 players departed to the pros, Bill Yeoman would never have admitted it, but it was a tough way for a fellow to start his first head coaching job. Especially with a 155-pound squirt at quarterback and a lack of experience just about everywhere.

Yet, there were the Cougars playing like wild men in Yeoman's first night on the UH sidelines, and Byron Beaver was plucking Baylor passes out of the air like oranges. A hard-nosed sophomore running back named Joe Lopasky hammered out three touchdowns, Beaver collected five interceptions, and the Cougars gave Yeoman a heady 19-0 opening night present.

"The defense was as spirited as has been seen on the Rice lawn in ages," wrote Dick Peebles in the *Houston Chronicle*. "The Cougars went after it from the opening whistle, and their pursuit was so strong that rarely was one white-shirted Bear felled by one red-shirted Cougar. The redshirts usually were in the majority by 3-1."

Roland directed them smartly, and the 10 sophomores among the 28 Cougars who played performed like veterans. Beaver, the part Indian from Lawton, Oklahoma, shared the credit: "You don't intercept passes by yourself. Those linemen have to rush the passer and hold their hands up in his face and make him throw it up in the air."

Demaree Jones, a teammate of Beaver's, later described him, "He was the only guy I ever saw who never broke a sweat on the field and always did things right. He had a natural eye for the ball."

Roland and Gene Ritch combined for the perfect story against Texas A&M. "UH Strikes it Ritch," reported the *Houston Post* after the Cougars' 6-3 triumph.

Facing 80 yards of grass with four minutes to play, Roland flung a long pass for Ritch before Billy was leveled by the Aggie pass rush. A 9.7 sprinter, Ritch caught the pass and ran to A&M's 18 for a 62-yard gain. Lopasky hurtled the final 3 yards with 2:38 to play, and for the second time in their short history the Cougars defeated their second Southwest Conference opponent in one year.

Seventh ranked Ole Miss, as usual, brought the Cougars down to earth, 40-7. Rebel quarterback Glynn Griffing passed for four touchdowns. The game was moved to Jackson from Oxford because of the turmoil on the Ole Miss campus over the James Meredith integration situation.

The brutal schedule continued, sending UH to Alabama to play the No. 1 nationally ranked Tide, led by quarterback Joe Namath. Alabama's Leroy Jordan recovered a fumble in the UH end zone after a high center snap on a fourth down punt. Ritch's 69-yard interception return of a Namath pass had led to Billy McMillan's 30-yard field goal, but the Cougars spent the rest of the day fighting off the Tide.

Beaten, 14-3, UH managed only three first downs and lost 49 yards rushing during the day. Namath completed just 4 of his 10 passes for 56 yards.

"I loved those games against Alabama and Ole Miss," said Jones. "You could walk among a team like Alabama and just feel the confidence and assurance oozing from them. It was the mental thinking of a winner."

Their lack of scoring punch cost the Cougars twice more. A Mississippi State receiver, Odie Burrell, outdistanced limping Beaver for a 24-yard touchdown pass with 1:43 left, and the Bulldogs had a 9-3 victory. Boston College dealt a 14-0 defeat, the fourth straight loss, when UH's offense totalled four first downs and 71 yards.

Starting his first game, Frank Brewer rushed for 122 yards and Bobby Brezina scored the only touchdown of the game in the fourth quarter in a 7-0 decision at Florida State. Suddenly, the offense began producing sparks, and the Cougars edged

Tulsa (35-31) and Louisville (27-25) before an easier time with Cincinnati (42-14).

Clem Beard's 42-yard return of a Tulsa punt blocked by Jones helped decide the outcome. After the game Athletic Director Harry Fouke accepted an invitation to the Tangerine Bowl at Orlando, Florida against Miami, Ohio.

Roland passed for 155 yards and Billy Smith ran for 11 in the 27-25 victory at Louisville.

Beaver intercepted his 10th pass of the season against Cincinnati to end as the national leader despite missing three games. "He would have set a record that would have stood up for 20 years if he hadn't been hurt," Yeoman said.

Yeoman and his assistants found themselves all wet at the Tangerine Bowl, where they were dunked in the showers after the 49-21 spanking of Miami.

Lopasky scored four times, and Roland performed brilliantly in his final game. Bruised up against A&M after his three

Billy Roland, cool operator of the 1962 Cougars.

touchdowns against Baylor, Lopasky equalled the school record Gene Shannon set in the Salad Bowl 11 years earlier. Lopasky weaved 70 yards on a punt return, caught a 13-yard TD pass from Roland, and plunged over from the four and three. Brezina averaged five yards a try and caught a 44-yard touchdown pass from Roland.

Voted the game's most valuable player, Roland completed 11 of 19 for 199 yards and three TDs. Jones recalled, "They had shot off their mouths all week, and once we got them down, we never let up." Jones called Roland "one of the coolest guys I ever saw at quarterback. He'd collect people together. He portrayed the air that he always had things under control. The year before, Danny Birdwell would center the ball back so hard, it'd blister his hands, and that was the only time you'd hear him complain about anything, no matter how hard he got hit. He was always dependable."

Jones remembered Brezina as "another guy you never worried about. He played his heart out all the time. He'd never say die."

After the Cougars scored the most points on Miami in 20 years, Coach John Pont had an appropriate summation, "You just kicked the hell out of us."

Another bone-bruising schedule in 1963 awaited a mere three returning regulars, six seniors, and a squad with an average age of 19.7 years. No need for razor blades to shave. Obviously the Cougars would need the combativeness of their coach (Yeoman had fouled out in 24 of 30 basketball games in 1945 at A&M). Baylor (Bluebonnet), Ole Miss (Sugar), Alabama (Orange), and Mississippi State (Liberty) would all go bowling after the 1963 season.

Lopasky's 82-yard punt return closed a 21-0 gap to the final 21-14 loss to Auburn, and Baylor blanked the Coogs, 27-0. Ole Miss scored twice in the last half after a slim 7-6 halftime lead for a rugged 20-6 decision, and six turnovers cost the Cougars dearly in a 23-13 loss to the Aggies. Mississippi State cashed in a fumbled snap on a fourth down punt to begin a 20-0 triumph, and Alabama made it an 0-6 season for Houston, 21-13. Joe Namath's fourth quarter, 12-yard pass to Ray Ogden brought the decisive score. The 6-foot-4 Ogden leaped to take the ball away from 5-foot-10 Mike Spratt. A sophomore, Spratt

The 1963 all-time Cougar team included linemen (left to right) Vic Hampel, end; Hogan Wharton, tackle; Joe Bob Isbell, guard; Burr Davis, center; Frank James, guard; J. D. Kimmel, tackle; and Bob Borah, end; and backs Don Brown, halfback; Donnie Caraway, fullback; Don Flynn, quarterback; and Gene Shannon, halfback.

caught 41- and 75-yard scoring passes from Jack Skog.

An eight-touchdown barrage, including a UH record 103-yard kickoff return by Ronnie Powledge, blitzed Detroit, 55-18, before adversity struck again at Tulsa. Jerry Rhome passed 42 yards with 70 seconds to play, then winged the winning two-point conversion for a 22-21 Tulsa triumph. Memphis State drubbed the Cougars, 29-6, to complete its 9-0-1 season.

Spratt's two scoring sprints and Skog's passing yardage record featured the 21-7 triumph over Louisville, the end of a 2-8 season. Skog bettered Bobby Clatterbuck's mark with 1,145 yards passing for the year.

Significant news was made off the playing field. Dr. Philip G. Hoffman, UH president, announced that the school would recruit black athletes who measured up academically and athletically. Then the board of regents decided to again seek membership in the Southwest Conference, and also agreed that the

Cougars would play their home football games indoors in the Astrodome, starting in 1965.

The newest bid for SWC membership ended in bitterness. UH officials thought they had assurances from Rice that that school would sponsor the Cougars at the annual spring meeting of the conference.

Days before the meeting convened in Lubbock, Rice's president announced the Owls would not sponsor UH. He suggested that the Cougars instead join other state supported schools (all of which were much smaller) in a new conference.

Four days later, the SWC announced a decision not to expand beyond its eight members.

In midsummer Yeoman won the recruiting battle for Warren McVea, the state's most highly sought high school prospect. After signing UH's first black football player, Yeoman said, "I think the biggest factors were the domed stadium and the fact he didn't want to be far from home."

Three touchdown passes, two by Skog and one by Preasley Cooper, helped an unimpressive 34-7 win over Trinity in the 1964 opener. Jimmy Sidle, Tucker Frederickson and a fierce Auburn defense then manhandled the Cougars, 30-0.

End Horst Paul's five-yard scoring pass from Skog in the first quarter and Jim Dyar's 28-yard field goal in the third period produced a 10-0 victory over Texas A&M at Jeppesen Stadium. Paul, also a standout in the defense that held the Aggies to minus 28 yards rushing the second half, was awarded the game ball. It was to be the Cougars' last win of the year.

Amazingly, a Dyar field goal and Skog's TD pass to Dick Spratt, Mike's brother, sent the Cougars ahead, 9-7, at halftime against Ole Miss. It was the first time in the 12-game series UH had been in that position. But the Rebels regrouped for a 31-9 decision, and the Coogs lost close ones to Tulsa, 31-23, and Mississippi State, 18-13.

UH allowed State its scoring total in unique fashion—three field goals, a safety and a 73-yard kickoff return.

Sophomore Bo Burris directed two scoring drives in the fourth quarter in a 13-13 tie with favored Florida State as Fred Biletnikoff, the Seminoles' gifted receiver, watched with an injured leg.

The physically battered Cougars were no match for Penn State (a 24-7 loss), and the same applied to the windup with

166

Horst Paul (third from right, back row) among honorees at the 1964 National Football Hall of Fame banquet. Paul won a Col. Earl Blaik Fellowship.

Cincinnati. Brig Owens and Al Nelson featured the Bearcats' 20-6 triumph, and the Cougars finished 2-6-1 for the year.

Horst Paul, an academic All-American, was awarded an Earl Blaik fellowship by the National Football Hall of Fame, based on scholarship, athletics, leadership, and campus activities. Sophomore Dick Post rushed for 528 yards, the team high and a school record for a rookie.

Demaree Jones, a 1963 co-captain, recalled an incident when Post was suffering from homesickness, "He came to my room and said he was leaving. I talked to him for two or three hours and talked him out of it. Post was the type you always wanted on your side. He didn't play for the big glory—he'd do it if there was nobody in the stands."

Indoor Football

Dick Post said about the Astrodome, called the "Eighth Wonder of the World" and in 1965 the Cougars' new home football field, "Whenever I walk in that place, I get chills up and down my back."

As the Cougars readied for Tulsa, their opponent in college football's first indoor game, Yeoman was busily answering questions on the possible differences in outdoor and indoor football.

With no weather factors to worry about, what about strategy, coach? "What factor do you have when you have to play with numbed hands and feet?" Yeoman replied. "All it does is detract from the players' capabilities."

Cotton Guerrant, the UH captain, even shipped the last of his pet bears to a zoo to get ready for the unique season. Bo Burris was stepping in at quarterback, Dick Post looked stronger than ever (if that were possible), sprinter Mike Spratt was at split end, and Warren McVea was beginning an expected fabulous career.

In short, the Cougars were young, but they also seemed to possess explosive potential.

Tulsa Coach Glenn Dobbs visited the Domed Stadium the previous winter, when his team was in Houston for the Bluebonnet Bowl. He figured the game a natural opener for the NCAA television schedule and the network agreed, so a nationwide audience would be tuned in.

Like many of the players, McVea was troubled by the

Cotton Guerrant, 1965 captain.

footing on the dirt floor (grass would not grow indoors). But Warren also could not hold the football.

McVea returned the opening kickoff 35 yards, then the outstretched hand of a Tulsa defender who had been blocked to the ground tripped him up. In 11 carries from scrimmage he gained a paltry 21 yards and fumbled three times. A fourth fumble occurred after catching a short pass, and McVea retired to the sideline for the second half. Crouched miserably alone, he watched the 14-0 defeat.

"That field was the worst I've seen, hard as a rock," he said. He had slipped several times with open ground ahead and noted, "My cleats just wouldn't go in."

Howard Twilley, Tulsa's All-American split end, caught 11 passes from Billy Anderson for 111 yards, including a six-yarder in the second quarter for the first touchdown under the Dome. "It's like running over rocks," Twilley agreed with McVea. "Then you come to that soft infield dirt, and it's like trying to walk on water."

A few blades were all that remained of an attempt to grow grass, for not enough sunlight was admitted through the roof. It had been painted in the baseball season to reduce glare. The footing was improved a week later by watering the ground, but UH's offense was still missing in a 36-0 drubbing by Mississippi State.

The Cougars did not score in their $31 million home

(which belongs to Harris County) until the fourth period against Cincinnati, a string of 11 scoreless quarters. McVea's 30-yard reception from Burris preceded Dick Woodall's 16-yard pass to Ken Hebert, who scored behind McVea's downfield block.

Finally, the Cougars were able to see the $2 million scoreboard light up for the first time like a pinball machine.

George Nordgren and McVea added the second and third touchdown in a 21-6 triumph, and the Cougars jubilantly carried Yeoman and his aides off the field.

"It was just a matter of pride," explained linebacker Joe Rafter, "after all the things that were being said during the week about coach Yeoman. We just had to prove to the people that they were wrong, and we had to prove something for ourselves, too."

But failure to pass and catch effectively hamstrung the Cougars again in a 10-7 loss to Texas A&M, their last meeting until UH began Southwest Conference competition more than a decade later.

Tom Beer was wide open in the end zone late in the game, but Burris' pass was yards too short and intercepted. Yeoman disdained a tieing field goal. Instead he called for a fourth down pass from the nine yard line. "You never go for the tie, always for the win," he said afterwards.

The Cougars hit the bottom of the well with their performance at Miami, Florida, a 44-12 embarrassment which included just eight first downs and 10 yards rushing, and three lost fumbles offensively. The most disastrous flub of all occurred when McVea failed to pick up a kickoff in the UH end zone and Miami recovered for a touchdown.

Woodall, starting for Burris at quarterback, threw 30 yards to Hebert for an early 6-3 lead. That was the high point of the night in the Orange Bowl. As the *Miami News* put it, "The most impressive member of the Houston entourage was a 110-pound Cougar named Shasta."

Tennessee officials decided in midweek to go ahead with their UH game at Knoxville after the death of two assistant coaches. Bobby Jones and Bill Majors were killed and assistant Charlie Rash was critically hurt in a car-train accident at a grade crossing.

With Nordgren, Post and linebacker Mike Payte injured,

170

UH prospects seemed dim against the 14th ranked Vols, yet the Cougars played it to the hilt. The first half was scoreless before Tennessee cashed in a piling-on penalty, an interception return for a touchdown, and a fumbled punt for a 17-8 decision. Burris directed a 67-yard drive in the final minutes that provided a glimmer of hope.

The Cougars honed their passing game in a 40-7 runaway past Chattanooga, and Yeoman decided it was time to fully test his new veer offense.

To have a chance against Ole Miss, UH's annual tormentor, Yeoman and his staff knew they would have to pass effectively and protect the corners against Jimmy Heidel's sprint-outs. The Cougars succeeded beyond their dreams.

McVea, maligned almost as much as Yeoman, streaked downfield from his wide receiver spot to haul in 80- and 84-yard touchdown bolts from Burris, and the defense battled fiercely to hold the Rebel offense to 59 yards rushing.

The results: a 17-3 victory that suddenly stilled Yeoman's critics, firmed up his faith in the veer, and proved to the Cougars they could play with anybody.

Old Miss settled for a second quarter field goal when Dick Spratt overhauled Mike Dennis after a 66-yard pass play. Hebert had toed a 29-yarder in the first quarter.

Defenders like Royce Berry, Paul Otis, Ray Dudley, Cotton Guerrant, Rafter, and Payte rose up to stop the Rebs after a fumbled punt deep in UH territory in the third period. Ole Miss missed a short field goal, and three plays later lightning struck.

McVea winged down field, defensive back Billy Clay barely missed Burris' pass, and Warren scurried 80 magnificent yards to the end zone. With Post and Mickey Don Thompson hacking out tough yards aground to keep the defense from ganging up on Burris, the Cougars added the final touch.

The defense forced another missed field goal in the fourth quarter, and Burris and McVea again worked their act, this time for 84 yards. UH had won its first victory over Ole Miss in 13 tries.

McVea's mother was home sick in bed, "but she's feeling better now," McVea grinned. "She was right beside the radio. I'll bet she's smiling like I don't know what."

171

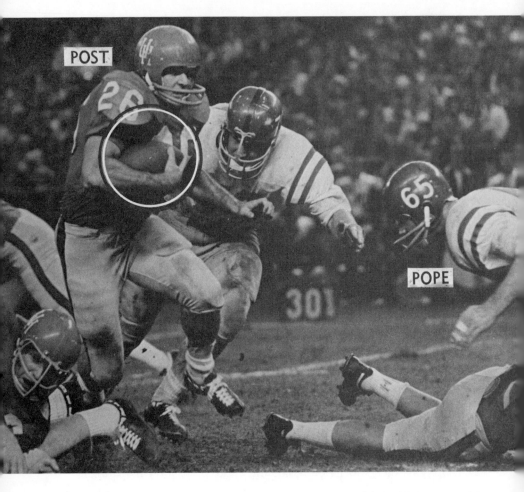

Dick Post (26) stomps out yardage in Houston's 17-3 upset of Ole Miss in 1965, its first victory ever over the Rebels.

Mac added, "I owe everything to Bo tonight."

"You can't overthrow a guy like that," Burris said. "On the first one I was about to get hit and just threw the ball. I didn't see him catch the ball. I was on the ground and didn't know what happened.

"I'd throw the ball and see him catch it. I'd be on the ground and see everybody running down the field. It's a great sight."

Yeoman later put the stunner in its simplest terms: "If

your O can't block their X, then you're in trouble."

Discussing the efforts of a faction that wanted him out of his job, Yeoman said, "When all that talk started, I was the least concerned fellow around...When they nip on my fanny, it's all right. When they chew on Burris, they're chewing on the one chance we have to be a good football team...."

Then he described the Ole Miss game's significance, "Some kids like to be pioneers. We may beat Ole Miss 50 times between now and Lord-knows-when, but this group will always know it was the first one."

Rick Norton, a great passing quarterback, led 10th-ranked Kentucky into the Astrodome, where Cotton, Gator, and Bluebonnet Bowl scouts awaited the Wildcats. Coming from behind five times, the Cougars scored their second eye-popping upset, 38-21. This one showed the Ole Miss victory was no fluke.

Burris threw for four touchdowns, Mickey Don Thompson fought for 17 yards for the first one after Hebert's 61-yard run from punt formation, and the defense intercepted five passes.

Norton passed for 255 yards in the first half, including 75 and 54 yard TDs. With UH ahead, 24-21, in the third quarter, Dick Spratt intercepted a Norton pass in the end zone. His brother Mike caught two touchdowns from Burris, who broke Bobby Clatterbuck's one season record for passing yardage.

"I almost came unglued," was the way Yeoman described Hebert's run from punt formation. What did he say to Hebert? "Good run." And if it had not worked? "Bad run."

With a chance to finish the year with a winning record if they beat Florida State, the Cougars heard talk they would receive a Bluebonnet invitation if they won. But the afternoon of the game, the bowl took Tennessee, and UH tied the Seminoles, 13-13.

Burris summed up the season, "I never dreamed we'd beat Ole Miss and Kentucky. I knew we could but before them, I wasn't so sure."

Clearly, the team that came in from the cold faced the future bright-eyed and bushy-tailed, but a cloud soon formed.

In January, 1966, the NCAA placed the school's football program under a three-year probation, barring it from bowl games and NCAA television. The violations cited free transportation home for athletes and parents, excessive entertainment,

173

and out-of-season spring practice.

The violations occurred from 1962 through 1965. Before the probation ran its course, the Cougars would compile a three-year record of 21-7-2, and Yeoman's veer offense would radically change college football.

The Veer Hits High Gear

Defensive coordinator Bum Phillips sounded the warning for 1966:

"The hardest thing to realize is that we just don't automatically start where we were when we beat Ole Miss and Kentucky. A lot of sweat has to go under the bridge."

When the Cougars sweated indoors in the Astrodome, they would perspire on a new $250,000 green rug. An artificial grass surface called Astroturf had been laid over the rock-hard bottom, replacing the original dirt floor.

Before they worried about which of several styles of soccer-type shoes suited them best indoors, the Cougars had other problems—like trying to win a game on the road, namely their season opener at Florida State.

Not since the Tangerine Bowl triumph over Miami, Ohio, at the end of 1962 had UH won away from home, a string of 12 losses and a tie.

The Seminoles quickly staked out a 7-0 lead on a 92-yard drive in the first quarter. Quarterback Bo Burris got that back on one play, an 80-yard scoring pass to Warren McVea; then Tom Paciorek's interception positioned the Coogs for Burris' 26-yard TD pass to Ken Hebert.

Dick Spratt's 81-yard punt return early in the third quarter sent UH ahead, 21-7, but the Coogs spent the rest of the sultry night with their backs to the wall.

First, they made a goal-line stand at their two yard line. After FSU cut the margin to the final 21-13, a 68-yard TD pass deflected into Ron Sellers' hands was wiped out by a penalty. Then sophomore Johnny Peacock, making his first start, intercepted a pass on the UH three with 31 seconds to play.

Paciorek intercepted three passes; the defense was on the field for 38 of 60 minutes. FSU ran 91 days from scrimmage, most ever by a UH foe, including 28 inside the Cougar 25 yard line.

Six nights later, UH and Washington State played the first football game ever staged on man-made grass. Like the playing field, it was unusual.

The Cougars won, 21-7, after a 99-yard Burris-to-McVea pass play in the third quarter broke a 7-7 tie. The play officially covered 99 yards because it statistically could not be longer. It was the longest pass play in an NCAA game since 1947 and equalled the NCAA record.

Burris said, "I couldn't believe it" when Yeoman sent him on the field with the play following a punt. "Get it to Warren and get them off our backs," Burris repeated Yeoman's instructions.

McVea explained, "I didn't even go into the huddle. I knew what the play was, so I just lined up. I caught the ball out in front of me, and the defensive back swung at it and missed, so he must have been right on me. After that, I didn't see anybody."

Somebody asked, "Who downed the punt?"

A Cougar replied, "You mean who set up Warren's touchdown?"

Burris also passed to Dick Post for 11- and 29-yard touchdowns, the latter on third-and-one. The visitors ran off 84 plays to UH's 51, but Burris completed 11 of 19 for 240 yards. McVea caught 3 for 128 and Post rushed for 100 yards on 21 carries.

Burris, the senior from Lake Jackson, continued his sensational passing through the next game, against Oklahoma State. The Cowpoke secondary concentrated on the speedy McVea, and Burris threw a school record five touchdown passes to other receivers—three to tight end Tom Beer covering 15, 5, and 17 yards; a 5-yarder to Post; and a 48-yarder to Hebert.

After UH's 35-9 victory, Burris had broken Bobby Clatter-

The school's first 1,000-yard rusher in 15 years, Dick Post (26) heads for the end zone in 1966 against Washington State.

buck's school career passing record with 2,204 yards. Hebert caught seven for 140. In their first three games, 10 of the Coogs' 11 touchdowns had been by passing.

Yeoman was calling every play from the sideline, using a signal system. Elwood Kettler, an Oklahoma State assistant coach that night, disclosed a decade later, "We knew every play they called. We had their signals, but every touchdown went to a secondary receiver. We'd broken their system of signals, but it didn't do us a bit of good."

Mississippi State, the next opponent, tried to put a strong rush on Burris, but the Cougar running game came alive while Burris flipped short passes to his backs. The result was a 28-0 victory before 47,870, the Cougars' largest crowd to date in the Astrodome.

Post, George Nordgren, and Paul Gipson scored on touchdown runs, the first of the season by the UH infantry, and Burris threw a 12-yard TD pass to McVea. The former fifth string quarterback accounted for 149 yards total offense, breaking Gene Shannon's career total offense record with 2,649 yards. The defense intercepted 3 passes, running its total to 12 for the year.

However, a hand injury suffered by Beer turned out to be a broken bone, McVea turned an ankle, and Gipson was bruised on the collarbone he had broken his freshman year.

The Cougars headed for Memphis and their meeting with Ole Miss carting a 4-0 record and a No. 11 national ranking in the UPI poll. Yeoman noted a difference in the preparation following UH's 17-3 upset of the Rebels a year ago, "I got quite an inkling that they are viewing us differently than in past years when they wouldn't trade game films with us."

Even before the kickoff, it was a day when everything went wrong for the Cougars against the nation's second best defensive unit. Gipson, the starting fullback, was left home because of his injured shoulder; then the Cougars were informed they would have the bench across from the press box.

Burris threw seven passes into enemy hands, and Ole Miss needed to cover a total of just 76 yards to three touchdowns and a field goal in its 27-6 win. Wearing a foam rubber pad on his broken hand, Beer could not bring in a pass in the end zone from Burris, and McVea dropped another in the end zone.

Yeoman later heard that Ole Miss, like Oklahoma State, also had learned the Cougars' signal code. By watching the Cougar bench across the field from the press box, the Rebs had a clear view. Suspecting as much, Yeoman later in the season began sending in plays from the bench by alternating Bill Cloud and Larry Perez at offensive tackle.

"We knew Ole Miss would come at us," Post said later. "Now we just have to go on from here. I think we're going to win the last five." He was within one point of being correct.

The Cougars rebounded with a 48-9 rout of outclassed Tampa. Hebert staged a school record pass-catching show. He caught four touchdowns from Burris—three of them in the second quarter—and kicked five extra points for a 30-point production.

Burris raised his touchdown pass total to 16 in six games, and the defense intercepted 6 more passes (a total of 19 for the year).

An emotional UH team awaited Tulsa. Besides bearing the stinging reminder of last year's nationally televised 14-0 loss to the Hurricane, the first game in the Astrodome, the Cougars were dedicating the game to offensive tackle Charlie Fowler.

Fowler's father, an ardent UH booster, died during the week, and Charlie missed several days while attending the funeral in Hendersonville, Tennessee. He did not return until the morning of the game.

Aiming their slashing runners straight ahead, the Cougars wrecked Tulsa, 73-14. The carnage included school records of 25 first downs, 586 yards total offense, 433 yards rushing, and the skittering punt returns by Don Bean.

A transfer from Southern Missouri Junior College, Bean returned punts for 66 and 63 yard touchdowns and totalled 199 yards on five runbacks. It was also a night to remember for Warren McVea. *The Chronicle* noted, "McVea, victim of four fumbles last year against Tulsa, came back to haunt the visitors like a stutter-legged ghost."

McVea ran for 158 yards on 12 carries, Post for 124 on 16 tries, and the defensive unit clamped down on the country's No. 1 passing team.

"As I told Coach Yeoman," Tulsa Coach Glen Dobbs related, "I think, tonight, this was the finest football team I've ever seen."

Fowler was presented the game ball. Defensive tackle Jim Dyar told David Fink of the *Houston Post*, "My best friend is Charlie Fowler, and there was no doubt about it, in the back of my mind, and I'm sure in the mind of everyone else who plays for this team, that this game was won for Charlie Fowler. It's not everybody that can come back only three days after losing his father, and play the kind of game that Charlie played tonight. He was an inspiration to all of us."

179

Like Fowler, a 6-foot-2, 295-pound graduate of a Tennessee prep school, Bean was an unusual recruiting "find." A 9.7 sprinter at Beaumont's Hebert High School, he ran on the same relay team with Mel Farr and Jerry LeVias but was only 5-foot-8 and 150 pounds.

After a year at Drake University, he went to junior college, where Bum Phillips heard of him. En route to re-enter Drake, Bean was chased down in the Oklahoma City bus station by a friend, who told him the Cougars wanted him.

Like Ole Miss, Kentucky was aching for a return bout with the Cougars, mindful of the 38-21 affair the previous year. Kentucky scored first and led, 6-3, late in the opening quarter. Then Post's 71-yard sprint was nullified by a clipping penalty before McVea flashed 62 on the next play behind Hebert's down-field block.

All-Americans Warren McVea (left) and Ken Hebert show their running and pass-catching styles.

A touchdown flood then engulfed Kentucky, 56-18, as the Cougars pulled off the unusual feat of scoring twice in the last 15 seconds of the first half for a 36-6 lead.

McVea's third touchdown of the day, an 11-yarder, 15 seconds before intermission, was followed by Jim Pat Berger's recovery of an onside kick at the Kentucky 41. On the last play of the half, Post traveled 40 yards to score on the draw play, a staple of the UH offense.

Thanks to the blocking of Bill Pickens, Barry Sides, Rich Stotter, Cloud, and Perez, the Coogs again broke school records with 29 first downs and 649 yards total offense.

Two days later Yeoman received a new five-year contract.

Then Memphis State put a 14-13 blot on the UH record. The Coogs missed a two-point conversion after scoring their final TD with eight minutes left, and Hebert's 31-yard field goal with 1:14 to go was barely wide. Their final drive covered 67 yards.

The Tigers, learning that afternoon their hometown Liberty Bowl had ignored them, covered 19 yards after a UH fumble before the Cougars drove 82 yards. Memphis State led at the half, 14-7; then Hebert caught his second TD pass of the night from Burris.

Yeoman explained the two-point try, "We were having trouble stopping them, and I don't play to tie. I wanted to get the lead, and then let them play ball control all they wanted."

Post gouged out 152 yards on 26 carries and joined Gene Shannon as the school's only other 2,000-yard career runner.

In their final game, the Cougars pummeled Utah, 34-14, to equal the 8-2 record of the 1952 team as the school's best ever. Hebert caught a 10-yard TD pass from Burris on the last play of the season to wrap up the national scoring title with 113 points.

Post, chosen earlier in the week for the *Houston Chronicle* award as the state's outstanding football player, also staged a memorable finish. He rushed for 172 yards on 28 carries, raising his season total to 1,061 yards, only the second UH runner in history (with Shannon) to crack 1,000 yards. Bean's 60-yard punt return behind Greg Brezina's block started the UH scoring, and Burris' pair of touchdown passes gave him the national lead in that category with 22.

Post finished his career with 2,219 yards rushing after five

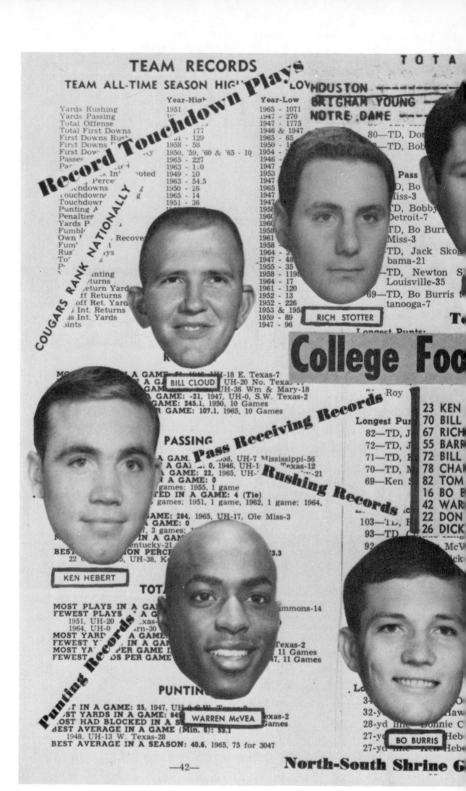

TEAM RECORDS

TEAM ALL-TIME SEASON HIGH'S LOW

TOTA

	Year-High	Year-Low
Yards Rushing	1951	1965 - 1071
Yards Passing		1947 - 270
Total Offense		1947 - 1775
Total First Downs	177	1946 & 1947
First Downs Rush	51 - 129	1965 - 65
First Downs	1958 - 58	1950 - 1
First Dow	1950, '59, '60 & '65 - 10	1954 -
Passes	1965 - 227	1946 -
Pa	1963 - 1;0	1947
In...ted	1949 - 20	1953
Perce	1963 - 54.5	1947
...chdowns	1950 - 26	1965
Touchdowns	1965 - 14	1947
Touchdowr	1951 - 36	1947
Punting A		1958
Penalties		1960
Yards P		1960
Fumbl		1958
Own Recove		1961
Fum...t		1958
Rus ...ys		1964 - 3
To		1947 - 48
P		1955 - 35
...nting		1958 - 1198
...turns		1964 - 17
...eturn Yard		1961 - 120
ff Returns		1952 - 13
off Ret. Yard		1952 - 226
Int. Returns		1953 & 195
ss Int. Yards		1959 - 89
ints		1947 - 96

HOUSTON ----------
BRIGHAM YOUNG ----------
NOTRE DAME ----------

80—TD, Do
—TD, Bob

Pass
D, Bo
iss-3
TD, Bobby
Detroit-7
TD, Bo Burri
Miss-3
TD, Jack Skog
bama-21
—TD, Newton S
Louisville-35
69—TD, Bo Burris
tanooga-7

RICH STOTTER

Longest Punts

COUGARS RANK NATIONALLY

Record Touchdown Plays

Pass Receiving Records

Rushing Records

Punting Records

BILL CLOUD

MOST...LA GAME...1048...UH-18 E. Texas-7
A GA...UH-20 No. Texa
GAM...UH-36 Wm & Mary-18
GAME: -21, 1947, UH-0, S.W. Texas-2
R GAME: 245.1, 1950, 10 Games
R GAME: 107.1, 1965, 10 Games

College Foo

Roy

23	KEN
70	BILL
67	RICH
55	BARR
72	BILL
78	CHA
82	TOM
16	BO B
42	WAR
22	DON
26	DICK

Longest Pun
82—TD, J
72—TD, J
71—TD, B
70—TD, M
69—Ken S
103—TD, H
93—TD G
92

PASSING

A GAM...98, UH-7 Mississippi-56
A GA...0, 1946, UH-1
Texas-12
A GAME: 22, 1965, UH-...21
A GAME: 0
games; 1955, 1 game
...ED IN A GAME: 4 (Tie)
games; 1951, 1 game, 1962, 1 game; 1964,
...AME: 284, 1965, UH-17, Ole Miss-3
A GAME: 0
...3 games; 194
...IN A GAN
BEST...ON PERCE...3.3
22 6...UH-38, K...
Kentucky-21

KEN HEBERT

TOT

MOST PLAYS IN A GA
FEWEST PLAYS A G...mmons-14
1951, UH-20 ...xas
1964, UH-0 ...rn-30
MOST YARD A GAME
FEWEST Y...IN A GAME...Texas-2
MOST YA...ER GAME I...11 Games
FEWEST...DS PER GAME...7, 11 Games

PUNTIN

WARREN McVEA

T IN A GAME: 25, 1947, UH-0 S.W. Texas
ST YARDS IN A GAME: 849 ...exas-2
OST HAD BLOCKED IN A S... ...ames
BEST AVERAGE IN A GAME (Min. 6): 53.1
1948, UH-13 W. Texas-28
BEST AVERAGE IN A SEASON: 40.6, 1965, 75 for 3047

Lo
34
32-y...haw
28-yd line...onnie B
27-yd line...Ken Heb
27-yd line...Ken Hebe

BO BURRIS

—42—

North-South Shrine G

FENSE
AYS YDS PERGAME TD*
78 4372 437.2 44
4006 400.6 36
3915 391.5 44

etroit-19
cinnati-

1965, UH
pel, 1951
, 1965, UH
1963, UH-13,
pel, 1951, U
1965, UH-40, Chat-

se

UNIVERSITY OF HOUSTON · FOUNDED 1934

Attendances Keep Climbing

Scoring Records

RUSHING

ST CARRI ... AME: 28
Gene Shanno. Salad Bowl, UH-26 Da
Gain: 182 Loss. '75 TD: 4
OST CARRIES IN A ... - 171
Gene Shannon, 1951.
Gain: 1250 Loss: 39 N TD: 7
CARRIES IN A CAREE.
Shannon, 1949, 1950, 19
Gain: 2632 Loss: 125 Net: 250
YARDAGE IN A GAME: 199
nn Hargrove, 1953, UH-25 Detroit-
rries: 10 Gain: 199 Loss: 0 TD: 1
YARDAGE IN A SEASON: 1211
ene Shannon, 195
arries: 171 Gain: TD: 7
YARDAGE
nes)
arries: 397 D: 24
T AVERAG ON
imum 60
Ken Bolin
Carries: 7 42 TD: 4
EST AVERA ER
Minimum 180
Gene S es)
Carries 507 TD: 24

BILL PICKENS

CHARLIE FOWLER

's Greatest

.... SE
.... LT
.... LG
.... C -13
.... RG
.... RT
.... TE
.... QB
.... HB
.... FLK 18
.... FB

6

Passing Records

MOST ATTEMPTS I
Bo Burris, 1965, UH ky-21
Comp: 22 Int: 0 Gain: TD: 4
MOST ATTEMPT
Jack Skog, 19
Comp: 100 In
MOST ATTEMPTS IN A CAREER: 310
Don Sessions, 1959, 1960, 1961 (26
Comp: 145 Int: 25 Gain: 1680 TD:
MOST COMPLETED IN A GAME: 22
Bo Burris, 1965, UH-38, Kentucky
Att: 30 Int: 0 Gain: 175 TD: 4
MOST COMPLETED IN A SEASON:
Jack Skog, 1963, 10 Games
'92 Int: 9 Gain: 1145 TD:
TED IN A CAREER:
, 1959, 1960, 1961 (26
At 25 Gain: 1680 TD:
MOST YARD SE IN A GAME: 284
Bo Burris, 1965, UH-17, Ole Miss-3
Att: 19 Comp Int: 0 TD: 2
MOST YARD EASON: 1256
Bo Bur
Att: 1 TD-12
MOST Y R: 2125
Bob 2, 1953 (28 Gam
Att TD: 12
MOST 4
Bo uc
air
MOST N:
A ain: 1256
MOST : 13 (Tie)
Ja Games)
Att 1631
Bo
Att 20 Gain: 1582
BEST CO TAGE ONE GAME: 83.3
Jack S etroit-18
Att: 12 0 Gain: 140 TD: 0
BEST COM ENTAGE ONE SEASON
(Min. 60 Att.)
Lonnie H 9, 10 Games
Att: 76 Comp: 45 Int: 9 Gain: 423
BEST COM ENTAGE I
(Min. 180 A
Billy R 1967
Att: 212 Comp: 114 Int TD: 12

TOM BEER

Hula Bowl Game

Punt Return Records

DICK POST

H-3
-3, No
UH-11, Ole Miss-27
38, K
6, Fla

DON BEAN

(Contin at page)

—39—

183

Royce Berry, Jerry Drones, and Cliff Larson (left to right), members of Houston's all-time defensive unit.

straight 100-yard games. The stumpy 5-foot-9½, 195-pounder, recruited by assistant Melvin Brown from little Pauls Valley, Oklahoma, compiled some notable achievements. A starter from the second game of his sophomore year, Post gained 528 yards in 1964 for a team which won just two games and played four bowl teams. He added 630 as a junior.

Post's backfield and track coach had quarterbacked Brown's first team at Southeastern Oklahoma State. Dick was the first of a long line of 1,000 yard rushers over the next decade.

In one of the finest seasons in NCAA history, the football team ranked No. 19 in the final UPI poll; UH's golf team won the school's 10th NCAA championship in 12 years; the baseball team finished second in the College World Series; UH's basketball team was third in the NCAA tournament; and the Cougar cross-country team placed 10th in the NCAA meet.

Bo Burris, Unlikely Hero

Perhaps no Cougar arrived on campus with less acclaim and departed with more accomplishments than James "Bo" Burris.

The first quarterback in Bill Yeoman's new veer triple option offense, Burris was as unknown as Yeoman's newfangled attack. An all-district defensive back and part-time quarterback at Brazosport High School, Burris had been coached by Harden Cooper, a former assistant on Clyde Lee's UH staff.

Burris was recruited almost as an afterthought when the Cougars took three high school teammates. He was never even asked to the campus for a visit.

"Chuck Fairbanks (a UH assistant) was at our playoff game with Galena Park," Burris recalls, "and he introduced himself, but I never saw the campus except for the times I'd drive my sister there for some classes she was taking.

"I was high jumping at the regional track meet at Jeppesen Stadium (on the UH campus) and qualified for the state meet; then I went to play in a baseball game. When I came back to Jeppesen to watch my friends run that night, Coach Yeoman came up and told me I had a scholarship if I wanted it.

"I had a football-baseball offer from Sam Houston State, and I'd always wanted to prove that I could play. When I came to UH, I was down at the bottom of the list of about seven quarterbacks. I worked my way up to be the starter on the freshmen."

A starting safety his sophomore year, Burris also backed

QUARTERBACK BO BURRIS

NATIONAL LEADER IN TOUCHDOWN PASSES - 22
10TH IN TOTAL OFFENSE - 1846 YARDS
SET ALMOST EVERY UH PASSING AND TOTAL
    OFFENSE RECORD
MEMBER OF SOUTH ALL-STAR TEAM
HONORABLE MENTION ALL-AMERICA

Bo Burris (16) arrived at the University of Houston unnoticed and rewrote almost every school total offense and passing record.

up Jack Skog and Preasley Cooper at quarterback, then drew his first start as quarterback against Mississippi State.

"I couldn't comprehend playing that much before I saw the way it was," he admits. "I was in awe of the other players, and I'm not a go-getter type. The spring after my freshman year, Coach Yeoman started saying nice things about me."

Burris reconstructs his high school career: "I'd been an end

in the ninth grade, and the coach said I ought to play quarterback, but the first couple of days in the spring I jammed my
thumb and quit. In the tenth grade I was the last team quarterback on the sophomores. I'd grown four or five inches that
summer. The JV Coach, L. Z. Bryan (a UH ex), took me on a
couple of trips when I was in the tenth grade, and that
encouraged me. I threw a touchdown pass in one game, and that
made my year. I was going to be the starting safety my junior
year but dislocated my ankle in the last scrimmage and missed
nearly the whole year."

Burris's UH quarterbacking career also had a rocky start.
"In the Tulsa game of 1965 we were running about 25 different
things, just trying to find something that worked. We weren't
together as a team, and I was just out there.

"Miami (a 44-12 drubbing) was the lowest point of my
career. The first series we fumbled two or three times, and
coach put in Dick Woodall at quarterback. Next week, before
the Tennessee game, I'm on the defensive field and backing up
Woody at quarterback."

Then occurred one of the incidents that Burris and his
teammates refer to as a turning point in UH football history.
"At Knoxville the next week to play Tennessee, we were at the
stadium loosening up the day before the game," Burris says.
"We were late getting there because of plane trouble and
couldn't work out. That's when Coach Yeoman told us I'd be
starting at quarterback. I felt he was showing confidence in me.
We got beat (17-8), but we were competitive; then we beat
Chattanooga and scored some points (40-7).

"Coach gave me a second chance, but that's the kind of
guy he is. I think he said to heck with the boo birds. There was
some dissension; some of the players were talking about where
they were going to transfer, and I overheard one of the
offensive linemen one day saying, 'What we need is a new
quarterback.' I'm sure that was the low point of coach's career,
and I could see the opportunity I had was gone. Then the next
week it was turned around. At Tennessee I was on pins and
needles.

"Coach Yeoman took up for you. He was always very easy
on me. He knew how to handle me, and he has a way of han-
dling others. He has a way of getting his message across. I just

wish I'd been a more aggressive person and could have helped
get things together a little faster."

Burris could feel a distinct difference before the 1965 Ole
Miss game: "From the first of the week, I was really into it.
There was some enthusiasm on campus for the first time, and I
felt we'd really play well. Those touchdown passes (84 and 80

*Bo Burris (16) delivers an 84-yard touchdown pass to long-gone
Warren McVea (42) in the 1965 triumph over Ole Miss.*

yards to Warren McVea in UH's 17-3 upset) were fine. But they weren't the game; our defense and running game were.

"Kentucky the next week was probably the best game I ever had. They had a bunch of super players—Rick Norton, Bob Windsor, Larry Seiple, Sam Ball, Rick Kestner. Those were my favorite touchdown passes; they were precision. I remember

throwing one through about four arms. Maybe I was just lucky, but I seemed to zip the ball in there better."

Burris completed 22 out of 30 passes for 175 yards that night including 4 scoring passes, 29 and 10 yards to Mike Spratt, 19 to McVea, and 5 to Ken Hebert.

"Hebert running on fourth down from punt formation won the game for us as much as anything," Burris says of the 38-21 victory. "I was sitting on the bench at the time, and I remember thinking, 'Coach, you didn't really call that play, did you?'"

Burris remembers the next year and the 1966 games at Kentucky and Ole Miss: "Kentucky stopped us on our first series, and when I came off the field, Coach Yeoman had a funny look on his face, like 'What happened?' I told him, 'Don't worry, we're going to score.' They drove it down and scored first before we got rolling. Before the half Post breaks a draw play right after they called back McVea's touchdown.

"I'm half-walking along behind the play, watching Post break tackle after tackle, and he dives over the flag into the end zone, and the clock has run out.

"Nobody wants to call the touchdown, and I'm thinking, 'They better give him that touchdown.' When we go off the field at the half (leading, 36-6) the people are looking at us like we're the Green Bay Packers.

"The year before, when we'd beaten Ole Miss for the first time, the pressure wasn't on us. This time we just basically choked. And we were using signals from the sideline to call plays. On every play they were hitting me and the back before we could function. It seemed like they knew what we were going to do. The thing I remember most, they gave me an interception on the last play of the half when their guy caught the ball three yards out of bounds. I thought later, 'I really only had SIX interceptions, not SEVEN.'"

Burris describes those 1966 seniors as a "weird group. We were kind of a melting pot. Tom Beer (tight end) was a transfer (from Detroit); Rich Stotter (offensive guard) had come without a scholarship; Larry Perez (offensive tackle) was a short, little guy; Barry Sides (center) was about the only highly recruited player; they'd been worried about Post's size."

Burris remembers, "Coach Yeoman told us, 'I can't

promise you a lot of things, but before you leave here, you're going to bring a certain amount of national recognition. You're going to be the start of it.'

"I don't really think of him so much as a coach now. I believe his ultimate goal is not really winning all his games as much as he feels an overall responsibility to the school and his players."

When Burris ended his UH career, he owned almost every school passing and total offense record, was voted the team's most valuable player, and went on to play in the Chicago All-Star Game and the Coaches All-American Game.

A Golden Day
In East Lansing

Warren McVea was finally, firmly stationed at running back, but the Cougars faced some gnawing uncertainties in the summer of 1967.

Bill Yeoman, referring to his shuttling of McVea between wide receiver and halfback, said, "Sometimes it creates interest to keep people wondering—like 'Where is that dumb Yeoman going to play McVea this week?'"

Yeoman, of course, realized the potential inherent in Duffy Daugherty, his former boss, agreeing to play the Cougars at East Lansing. Michigan State was an established, nationally-renowned football power, sharing the nation's No. 1 spot in the polls the year before with Notre Dame after the Irish ran out the clock on their 10-10 tie. Clinton Jones, George Webster, and Bubba Smith were gone, but the Spartans were still No. 3 in the preseason rankings.

Dick Woodall, a fifth-year senior, was stepping into Bo Burris' quarterback role, and Paul Gipson had to come through at fullback, vacated by Dick Post's graduation. Perhaps worst of all, defensive end Royce Berry would miss the season because of knee surgery. Berry was hurt on the final series on the final spring game, a few hours after Yeoman informed him he had been elected team captain.

First, however, there was Florida State in the season's opening game. Greg Brezina's interception and return to the 14 began the year in great shape. McVea swept the final 10 yards two plays later. Woodall sharply executed the option for

192

Dick Woodall, quarterback of the 1967 Cougars who led the nation in total offense and rushing.

7 yards and a 13-0 lead, and McVea went to the locker room with 103 yards on 15 carries. He did not play in the second half.

Early in the third quarter Woodall suffered a bruised hip, and Ken Bailey, a redshirted sophomore, stepped into the crisis. He completed 7 of 13 passes for 107 yards and directed three more scoring drives for a 33-0 lead. Coach Bill Peterson's aerial game produced two fourth period scores for the Seminoles to narrow the final margin.

"I didn't have time to think," Bailey described his rescue operation. He was visiting on the sideline with Burris, his cousin, when Woodall limped off.

"Michigan State Bows, 37-7," exclaimed the multiple column headline September 24, 1967, on the front page of the

Linebacker Greg Brezina (65) helped the Cougars rank No. 10 nationally in defense in 1967.

53 GREG BREZINA

L-AMERICA LINEBACKER GREG BREZINA

y member of the nation's 10th ranked
fense in 1967...one of team leaders
tackles with 139 for the '67 season...
so team co-captain...nominated for
tional lineman of the week after

New York Times sports section. It added, "McVea's Running and Passing by Woodall Down Spartans."

The lead headline on page one of the *Houston Post* read, "Cougars Shell-Shock Michigan State, 37-7." Bordered in red on the front page of the *Houston Chronicle* were the words, "UH Stomps Michigan State." Said *Sports Illustrated* (SI), "The Spartans get stabbed by Mac the Knife."

SI reported, "Led by the 180-pound McVea, it looked as if everyone on Houston's team could run the 100 in 8.6....No one in East Lansing would be surprised if Yeoman's splendid pair of offensive guards, Bill Pickens and Rich Stotter, aren't 9.5 men, too."

Hebert's 44-yard field goal and McVea's 50-yard sweep furnished a 10-7 halftime lead and began the Spartans' worst loss in 21 years. Throwing from deep in UH's end of the field, Woodall connected with Hebert for 77 yards and a 17-7 lead in the third period. Then he found Don Bean streaking down the sideline in the fourth quarter and delivered a 76-yard TD pass. Bailey, subbing for Woodall, threw to Hebert for 32, and sneaked the last two yards for the fourth TD. Mickey Herskowitz of the *Houston Post* called that "the day's biggest surprise. Michigan State didn't know the Cougars could score from that close in." Mike Simpson added the final note with a 41-yard interception return.

A tigerish Gipson sent three Michigan State defenders to the sideline, and McVea gained 155 yards in just 14 carries. "This was kind of a grudge game for me," Warren said. "Tody Smith and the other Texas boys on Michigan State's team kidded me during the summer so much. They acted like it was a big joke, us playing Michigan State."

Assistant Melvin Brown recalled years later, "I got a phone call at 7 a.m. that day from Mac. He never got up that early. He said,'Gabe (Gipson) isn't gonna play.' Billy Willingham and I went over to talk to him and settle him down. Early in the game he takes a pitch from Woody and runs over a guy and goes for about 15. That made him as a football player."

Stotter, a constant escort on McVea's darting runs, recalls, "Being from Cleveland, Ohio, where all they know is Big 10 football, I took a lot of razzing that summer about how the Houston game would be nothing more than a warmup exercise

Rich Stotter, 1967 All-American offensive guard.

for Michigan State. I was the game captain that day, and more than 20 of my relatives and friends had come to the game. Playing before 75,000 hostile fans, and against the previous year's co-national champs, was a bit awesome. As the Big 10 has discovered over the last 10 years, you have to do more than line up big people and run right over them if you're playing another good football team."

Said Yeoman, "We've been trying to tell people as politely as possible for three years now about Warren. The same with Ken Hebert. Kenny led the nation in scoring last year, and that was the best-kept secret of the year. He didn't get any national recognition at all, and not having Warren on the All-American made it ridiculous."

Like McVea, Bean also had personal reasons for wanting to play well. "Shoot, this was for the city of Beaumont championship as far as I was concerned," he referred to four Beaumont high schoolers on the Spartans. "They were recruiting me when I was in high school. Bubba Smith was showing me around. He's 6-foot-9 or so, and you can imagine the picture we made. Then I guess Duffy decided I was too small. I bet he doesn't even remember me."

A cheering, sign-waving crowd of about 7,000 students and fans greeted the Cougars when they returned that night. One placard proclaimed, "Poland in Nine Days!" Mark Godfrey, the *Houston Chronicle* photographer at the scene, could not get off the team bus through the jubilant crowd and was forced to ride back to the campus.

The Coogs were ranked No. 3 by the AP, which picked McVea as back of the week. UPI, which had UH No. 4, voted Yeoman coach of the week.

Houston Chronicle sports editor Dick Peebles predicted correctly. "The Cougars will reap the fruits from this one victory for a long time."

"What made it all so sweet," wrote *Chronicle* columnist Wells Twombly, "was the way in which the school's alumni came out of hiding. On the Monday after Michigan State's bloody carcass was discovered prone on the turf, downtown Houston looked like the British army at Saratoga. Red coats were everywhere. People who used to let the impression get around that they'd really gone to Baylor or Texas A&M or Rice dropped their masks."

Tripped By
The "White Shoes"

Three quick touchdowns in the first quarter against Wake Forest showed the Cougars were not still celebrating their Michigan State spectacular.

UH led, 21-0, before Wake Forest managed a first down. Houston won easily, 50-6, even throwing in a brief shoving match between Warren McVea and Ken Hebert to keep the 41,769 fans interested. Hebert chided McVea for not blocking on a pass play, and one shove led to another before teammates separated them. Playing despite the pulled groin muscle he had suffered in the summer, McVea was replaced before the next snap.

Before that, Hebert's block had helped McVea turn a simple swing pass from Dick Woodall into a 70-yard scoring play. Hebert caught three touchdown passes of 50, 8, and 13 yards, kicked six extra points and ran over a two-pointer after a bad center snap in a 26-point night.

Woodall completed 11 of 17 for 266 yards and four touchdowns, compiling a one-game record 361 yards total offense. The Cougars totalled a team record 695 yards total offense and 32 first downs. The AP rankings listed UH No. 2, its highest before or since, and UPI listed the Coogs third.

Then came the "White Shoes."

North Carolina State's defensive players, wearing shoes painted white, put McVea out of the game in the first quarter. The Wolfpack stunned the Cougars, 16-6, before an Astrodome crowd of 52,483.

UH lost three of their seven fumbles, threw two interceptions, and managed just 222 yards total offense against the Wolfpack, a three-touchdown underdog.

Trailing, 10-6, the Cougars messed up a fourth down pitchout after Jerry Drones recovered a fumbled punt at the Pack's 23. Dennis Byrd, the 256-pound defensive tackle who sent McVea out with a shoulder injury, explained, "We tried to jam up the middle with our line and leave the outside stuff to our linebackers and deep backs."

"Our own mistakes killed us," reasoned Bill Pickens, UH's offensive guard.

With McVea held out to recuperate for the next week's Ole Miss encounter, George Nordgren and Don Bean shared his running back slot at Mississippi State. The Cougars won handily, 43-6. Bean scampered 63 yards with a punt return and ran 9 yards from scrimmage for a second TD. Nordgren's 20-yard bolt capped an 80-yard thrust with the opening kickoff.

Bean returned six punts for 172 yards. A 50-yard return set up a TD and a 76-yarder led to a field goal. The "Mad Dogs," UH's defensive bunch, permitted just one first down and 20 yards total offense in the first half.

Seemingly the epitaph whenever the Cougars played Ole Miss, the game accounts read, "Coogs Trapped by Own Mistakes, 14-13," and "Erring UH Stopped by Rebs."

Ole Miss, 41-3-2 the past 20 years at Oxford, was a five-point underdog to UH, back to No. 9 in the polls. Bean's 74-yard punt return sent the Coogs to a 7-0 lead, but Bruce Newell's 28-yard peg to Mac Haik evened the score. Haik was wide open after safety Gus Hollomon slipped down.

Hollomon, one of UH's finest defensive backs ever, was unlucky again in the third period. He had an interception lined up on the UH two yard line when reserve tight end Hank Shows leaped over him, plucked the ball from his grasp and tumbled into the end zone with a 37-yard touchdown. Jimmy Keyes' pair of extra points proved to be decisive.

Woodall passed 42 yards to Calvin Achey for UH's second score with 13:40 to play, but Hebert missed the extra point. Ken had also missed a 10-yard field goal in the first half, and McVea, en route to an apparent touchdown at midfield, fell down in the open. Nordgren played the entire second half for

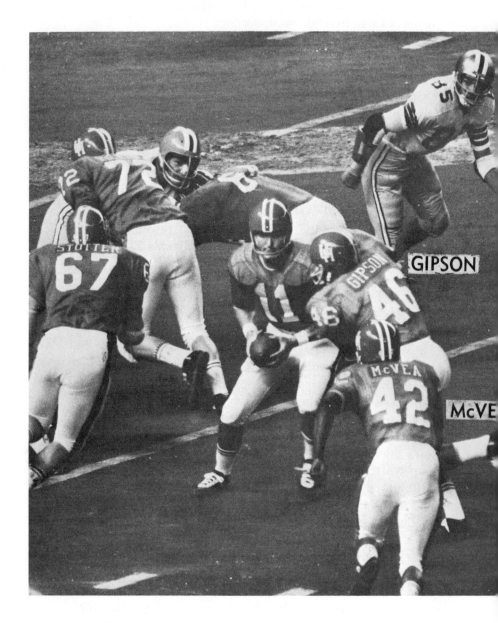

Three Cougar All Americans are shown, as guard Rich Stotter (67) leads a sweep by Warren McVea after a fake to Paul Gipson in the 1967 game with Florida State.

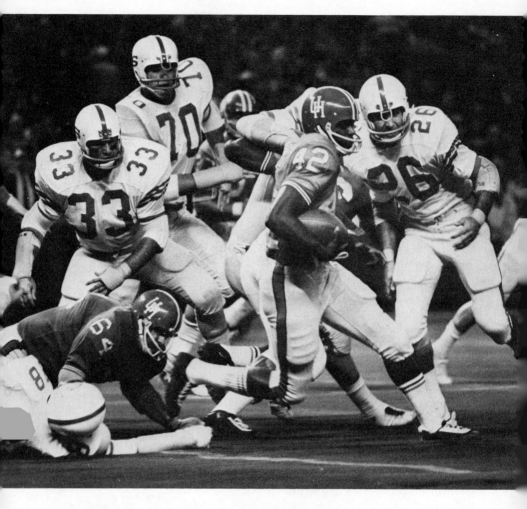

Warren McVea (42) slips through the opposing defense, but the Cougars suffered a 16-6 upset by North Carolina State in 1967.

McVea.

With a standing-room-only crowd assured for the Georgia game, Houston Sports Association publicist Bill Giles noted, "This may be the only event in the history of the Dome when even I can't find a ticket."

McVea, who had played only 33 minutes in the four games since Michigan State, acknowledged, "I didn't know I was that far off, but I was. I hadn't done enough running to work on my moves. I don't think you'll see me fall down anymore."

Oddly, the unranked Coogs were a five-point favorite over No. 5 ranked Georgia. They fell behind, 14-0, then, overcoming a rash of fumbles, edged the Bulldogs, 15-14, before 53,356.

Yeoman later described it as one of the school's most significant triumphs "because it showed them they could come back against a great team."

Fittingly, Gipson scored the winning two-point conversion on a pitchout from Woodall with 4:27 to play. He pounded out a school record 229 yards on 29 carries against the nation's No. 2 defense. UH's "Mad Dogs" also were a stirred-up bunch, permitting two first downs and 48 yards in the second half while the offense overcame five lost fumbles during the night.

Hebert fled down the sideline for a 57-yard Woodall pass for the second touchdown. He had noticed that defensive back Terry Sellers was shaken up tackling Gipson on the previous play. Gipson's 25-yard TD rumble on the first play of the final quarter started the comeback.

Sellers' 71-yard interception return set up Georgia's second score, and Coach Vince Dooley second-guessed himself for not calling timeout for Sellers before Woodall's touchdown pass. "They noticed he was hurt, and they took advantage of it," Dooley said.

The AP selected Gipson its national back of the week, and he was also chosen for UPI's backfield of the week. It had been a long trail for "Gabe."

Orphaned at age two and raised in Conroe, Texas, by his grandmother, Gipson suffered a broken collarbone and missed his entire freshman season. He was practicing without shoulder pads at the time. Then he was dismissed from the squad for a curfew violation during his sophomore season, dropped out of school in the following spring, and worked at a Conroe country club.

To be academically eligible for 1967, Gipson needed to attend both summer school sessions. "I got up at 4:30 a.m. five days a week for the first session," he said. "I'd get out on the highway and thumb a ride to Houston. After class, sometimes I'd get a ride back with someone from school, sometimes not. The second session I shared an apartment with some people from Conroe who worked at NASA." He also was about 30

Paul Gipson scores the winning two-point conversion behind Rich Stotter's block in the 15-14 victory over Georgia in 1967.

pounds lighter, at 193, than he was the previous year.

Gipson and the McVea of the Michigan State game led a 35-18 pummeling of Memphis State. Gipson, shaken up making a tackle on a punt return, scored three times in a 154-yard performance. "All I know is that after I hit that guy, my nerves just sorta tingled all over my body," he said. "We were well into the second quarter when I sort of woke up." McVea gained 109 yards on 16 carries and sat out the final quarter.

In their final home game the Cougars brushed off Idaho, 77-6. Yeoman pulled most of his regulars early in the third quarter and told his quarterback not to pass in the second half. Gipson rolled up 193 yards, McVea streaked 58 yards in his final home game, and Hebert, another senior, caught two touchdown passes.

Thus, it came down to Tulsa, whose players obviously remembered the previous year's numbers—73-14. Announced defensive tackle Joe Blake, "Houston doesn't have a chance against us this year."

Their worst performance of the season cost the Cougars an 8-2 season and their first Top Ten finish. They lost six fumbles, threw two interceptions, and lost, 22-13, to a team which had been beaten, 54-12, the week before.

Tulsa threw only one pass in the first half, and UH managed a 13-3 lead early in the third quarter. But a new quarterback passed the Hurricanes most of the way on a 65-yard drive. An interception led to their go-ahead score, and a fumble applied the clincher.

Stotter, Hebert and McVea were selected on various All-American teams, and the Cougars led the nation in total offense and rushing and were 10th in total defense. With 1,100 yards Gipson was the nation's No. 7 rusher, and Bean was third in punt returns.

Warren McVea,
The Wondrous Runner

Like a thunderbolt, the news out of San Antonio that
sweltering Saturday afternoon in 1964 shocked the state's football circles and surprised the nation.

Warren McVea, the nation's most publicized high school
runner, was coming to the University of Houston. Wondrous
Warren, the speedster of a thousand moves, would become a
Cougar. Bill Yeoman, accompanied by Ted Nance, the school's
sports information director, got Warren's signature on the
dotted line.

It was an event that made headlines across the state of
Texas. For the first time in memory the Cougars had recruited
the No. 1 football player in Texas. It was an omen of things to
come, for that same summer UH also enrolled Ken Hebert, who
was later to lead the country in scoring; linebacker Greg Brezina; defensive back Gus Hollomon; runner George Nordgren;
offensive guard Bill Pickens; and others who were to be the seniors of 1967.

"Mac the Knife" and "The Hummingbird" were just two
of the many nicknames anguished sports writers tried to pin on
McVea as they feverishly described his running style. "His legs
are like computers— they think on their own" was one of the
more analytical descriptions.

After McVea's shining day in the bright sun at Michigan
State in 1967, Dan Jenkins wrote in *Sports Illustrated*, "A run
by Wondrous Warren seems to last six or seven minutes."

Said Duffy Daugherty after the Cougars had slashed his

Warren McVea (42) follows guard Rich Stotter (67) to a long gain against Michigan State in 1967.

Spartans, 37-7, "I found myself admiring McVea as a runner."

Yeoman later was to say, "The only one I've seen that I can compare him with for sheer speed was Glenn Davis, and Davis didn't have Warren's moves. You see one like Warren in a lifetime, and he's mine."

Recruited by nearly every major university in the Midwest and West, McVea was the first black football player recruited by UH, which earlier that summer had signed up basketball players Elvin Hayes and Don Chaney, its first black athletes. Those days were before Southwest Conference schools integrated their athletic programs.

McVea says, "The only schools I ever seriously considered were USC, Kansas, Nebraska, Arizona State, and Oklahoma. Mike Garrett showed me around when I visited USC, but I got homesick there in three days. I thought, 'What would it be like in nine months?'

"The more I visited other schools, the more lonesome I got. I come from a close-knit family—five brothers and three sisters. I enjoy being around home. They weren't scared of losing me out of state. I'd come to Houston and visit and in half a day I was ready to go home. I worked for the Judge (Roy Hofheinz) that summer; I'd visit groups and explain the layout of the Dome. Then, it was nothing but a big hole in the ground. I quit in two weeks because I was homesick."

McVea recalls, "When I visited USC, Charlie Hall (an assistant coach) had a story in the paper that I was the best high school player he had ever seen. Raymond Johnson and his brother Cliff (a major league baseball player) lived around the corner in San Antonio. Raymond was in school at USC then, and they found him. Mike Garrett took me to a Dodgers game, and Willie Brown took me out to a couple of clubs. We saw Wilt and Pete Beathard and Hal Bedsole.

"Then they took me to see John McKay. He was sitting behind his desk smoking a cigar. All he said was, 'I hear you're the best high school player in the country (puff). I've seen you on films, and you're everything they say (puff). We'd very much like to have you here (puff).' He said about 30 words, and that was it. That was all I saw of the head coach. I said, 'Hell, they don't want me.'"

McVea continues, "All the coaches I met were class peo-

208

ple. My mother thought the world of Coach Yeoman and Dan Devine. I never even considered UH at first; I'd never heard of them. But they were so nice. Ted Nance was always willing to help. I never even met the other SIDs where I visited. When Coach (Bob) Devaney (of Nebraska) came to the house, my mother was asleep. He didn't want to wake her, he was so considerate. I really liked him. I was so proud of my mother. I wanted everybody to meet her.

"Johnny Roland and George Seals showed me around Missouri. But the town was so small. Arizona State started writing me when I was a sophomore, when I'd scored something like 22 touchdowns. I'd run 9.9 in the eighth grade."

McVea recalls his visit to Tempe, "Joe Caldwell, Henry Carr, and Ulis Williams showed me around, and they sent me a photo album with their autographed pictures. I cherished that album. The weekend I was in L.A., I went to the Coliseum Relays. Henry Carr told me he was going to win the 220, and after he beat Bob Hayes, he came up in the stands and sat with me.

"Then I got on the plane home, and there were Tom Williams and his Grambling track team. They were the hottest thing going that year. I sat next to Tom. He knew how much I loved track, and he told me, 'We're going to let you lead off our 440 relay next week.' I never heard anything more about it."

During the mid- and late-60s UH was one of the first integrated major college teams to play in Tennessee, Florida, Kentucky, Georgia, and Mississippi.

"I lived in an integrated neighborhood in San Antonio," McVea says. "I had integrated Pony League and never had any trouble. The thought never entered my mind. I got the worst letters from Florida. One of them said they were going to shoot me. When I went to see coach about it, he said, 'Son, if they were going to do it, they would have done it already.'

"At Starkville, Mississippi, my senior year I didn't play, and they were giving me the business from the stands—nothing racial—just the usual. I knew D. D. Lewis (Mississippi State linebacker), and after the game I was on the field talking to him. Jack Littlefield (the UH equipment manager) would always wait for me, and we'd go to the dressing room together. I looked up and all the people in the stands were heading down

209

to the field. I got so scared, I didn't know what was going on.

"They got right up to Jack and me, and we were surrounded. I didn't know what was going on. Then they started asking me for my autograph. I've never been so scared in my life, and those were the nicest people I ever met."

McVea remembers the next week at Oxford, "Coach called me to his room the night before the game, and we talked outside on the balcony at the motel. I was really depressed. I wanted to quit. I was so fed up, because my teammates had started to doubt me. Working out that summer, one day Otis Taylor and Charlie Frazier and everybody from the pros were there.

"Otis caught a pass and lateraled to me, and I took off. I felt something pop. Three nights before the Florida State game,

Faking a tackler off his feet, Warren McVea turns the corner against Florida State in 1965.

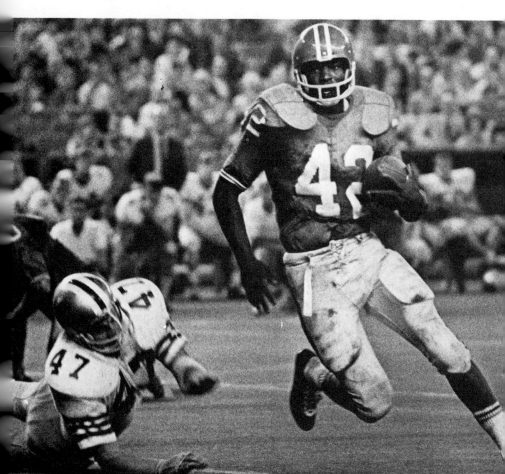

I sneaked out of the dorm and drove home to see the doctor I had when I tore a muscle in high school. I had about 120 yards at the half, but I could hardly walk. After the Michigan State game, Tom Wilson started wrapping it up real tight, but I didn't always keep up the heat treatments."

McVea recalls the disastrous start of his varsity career against Tulsa, the first game in the Astrodome: "I thought I could go out and take the ball and score when I got ready, like when I was a freshman. I just didn't take it seriously.

"I drove the family car to school when I was in high school (at Brackenridge). We were never poor. I never had it tough. I never needed a lot of clothes. I knew I needed three suits to alternate wearing to church. I knew I HAD to go to church. I never worried about records. I look back and think what could have happened if I'd been well my senior year. When we'd be winning, coach would ask me, 'Have you had enough?' Look at O. J. (Simpson) They could be winning, 50-0, and he'd still be in there."

McVea acknowledges his share of superstitions, on the field and off: "I always carried my own football shoes (size 8½-double E). I always had a room to myself at home. My sisters would come in and straighten up. I couldn't find anything, so I'd place things in a certain way in case they came in and messed with anything. Like passing bags out the window. I'd hear things on the street and believe it (he always went around the equipment room door for his basket, rather than have it passed through the window).

"I did so well in high school, I figured, why change? I got in the habit of leaving the belt unbuckled on my uniform pants. Once my high school coach cut it off before a game. Hank Stram (his coach with the Kansas City Chiefs) would get on me about it, and I'd tell him, 'Hank, you'll have to cut it off.' When I'd take clothes to the cleaner and have a good game, I'd always take them back to the same one."

McVea has no more success than anyone else at explaining his running style: "The more you think about it, the worse off you get. I was just blessed and born with it. It's just a talent. I never wanted to be better than anybody, I wanted to be me. I admired Gale Sayers and Jim Brown. Gale tried to recruit me for Kansas. He wrote me after the Tulsa game and told me,

211

'Don't worry, you'll have a lot of great games.'"

A couple of McVea's biggest thrills were visits from two well-known professional athletes. "Mike Garrett was in Houston for a dinner after he'd won the Heisman Trophy. He came out to the dorm to see me, but I was out somewhere. And Muhammad Ali came to the Astrodome to see me play one game."

McVea details a prelude to the Michigan State game, "Bubba and Tody Smith and four or five others on their team from Texas were at the Texas Southern University Relays that spring, and they were telling me what they were going to do to us at East Lansing. I went to see coach, and he said, 'You're going to be surprised. They're not all that fast.'

"The first play of the game, I went 25 or 30 (actually it was 48) and I said, 'Everything coach said is true.' What made me mad afterwards, all those writers are asking, 'Has he always been that good?' I'd made two All-American teams my junior year, and I go up there and they've never heard of me. It took a victory like that to get the school a little recognition. After that, we never had trouble getting anybody on All-America.

"Biggest thrill I ever had in college," says McVea, "O. J. (Simpson) played at East Lansing, and Leroy Keyes for Purdue, and the Michigan State guys said I was the best that had ever played there. What really got me was those guys up there talking about how good I was. I only played three quarters, and I was hurting. A coach from the Detroit Lions said I was good enough to start for them that Sunday."

McVea averaged 6.7 yards per carry on total offense during his career and 8.8 per play in 1966, records that still stand in the all-time UH list. In 1965-66-67 he averaged nearly 10 yards every time he touched the ball while running, receiving passes or returning kicks.

Ken Hebert,
Violent Competitor

Back home in good ole Pampa, Ken Hebert never played on a winning high school football team. "We'd kid each other that we should have four quarters of band and a halftime of football, because everybody left after the band played," he remembers.

Yet there was never any question that Hebert was a "winner," just like his boyhood neighbor, Randy Matson. Hebert used to retrieve Matson's shot as they played on the vacant lot in the days before Matson became an Olympic shot put champion and world record-holder.

Before leading the nation in scoring as a junior, then rewriting every school pass receiving record during his career, Hebert began to make his mark early. He scored UH's first touchdown in the Astrodome his sophomore year, on a 23-yard pass from quarterback Dick Woodall against Cincinnati, after the Cougars had been blanked by Tulsa and Mississippi State.

But it was against Kentucky in 1965, one of the pivotal games in UH football history, that Hebert pulled off the play that old grads will toast through the years.

The Cougars trailed the team that was being considered for the Cotton Bowl's visiting role. Hebert, the team's punter and place kicker for three years, was awaiting a fourth and 13 snap from center in punt formation deep in the Cougar end of the field.

When the ball sailed back, Hebert looked up, and, to the amazement of everyone in the Dome (especially Coach Bill

Yeoman) Hebert began running. He was finally caught 61 yards later to set up a touchdown shortly before halftime, and the Cougars came back to win a 38-21 stunner.

Hebert explains, "I got the snap, looked up, and on the right side absolutely no one was rushing. Everybody had turned their back and was going downfield.

"I was 15 yards behind the line. I started running and passing people. I'll never forget the look on their faces, their guys and ours."

And Yeoman? "He didn't say a word; then on Sunday he told me never to do it again."

The week before, the Cougars had upset Ole Miss, 17-3, their first victory ever over their old tormentor. "One of the finest games the school has ever played," says Hebert. "It was a real bloodletting, and they shed most of it. We started a trend in 1966, the Houston offense, that led the nation. We had nearly 20 seniors left off the 1964 freshmen, remember.

"The big factor was when Coach Yeoman made a total commitment to Bo (Burris). We were going to live and die with him at quarterback. We had no reservations about the veer being able to work. It gave us a total capacity to use the talent we had."

As the national scoring champion in 1966, Hebert, a 5-foot-11, 195-pounder, tallied 113 points including 11 touchdown passes, caught 38 passes for 800 yards and punted for a 41.3 average.

Kentucky again played a big role in Hebert's memory when the Cougars visited Lexington in 1966. "On Friday when we went to the stadium to loosen up, some of their students would drive by and cuss at us when we got on our bus," he remembers. "At the half the next day, people were throwing empty whiskey bottles at us when we went to our dressing room."

The Cougars were ahead at the time, 36-6, thanks to two touchdowns in the final 15 seconds of the half after Hebert applied the final block on Dick Post's 40-yard sprint. UH won, 56-18. Hebert caught a 60-yard scoring pass that day from Burris.

Two weeks before, Hebert caught four Burris scoring passes and kicked six points after touchdown in a 30-point performance against Tampa.

Said Yeoman, "Herbie is just a violent competitor and a great athlete."

Paul Gipson, who was to gain countless yards after downfield blocks by Hebert, said, "You can count on Hebert. If he sees a chance to cut down a man, he never misses."

Chosen to the football writers All-American in 1967, Hebert feels, "Michigan State was the one game that got us more national recognition than any we'd played. They must have carried eight or nine of their guys off the field. Before the game, they made us wait in the tunnel before we could come on the field while they introduced them, and their team ran through us, knocking us out of the way."

That type of incident was sure to stir Hebert's blood. There was a unique shoving incident with his teammate, Warren McVea, in full view of more than 35,000 witnesses during the 1967 game with Wake Forest. They both later shrugged it off.

Hebert wrapped up the scoring title against Utah in the final game of 1966 and gives Yeoman a big assist: "I'd just kicked a couple of extra points and in the last few minutes caught a touchdown pass. One official ruled it good and the other said I was out of the end zone, so it didn't count. Coach called another pass, and I was wide open. We didn't need that touchdown, but I was always grateful he gave me another chance, because there was no way of knowing whether I'd have won it or not without it."

Another Hebert clutch play was his 57-yard touchdown pass from Woodall with four and a half minutes to play that helped the Cougars overtake Georgia, 15-14, in 1967. "The play before, their cornerback had to stop Gipson and had taken a pretty good shot," Hebert reconstructs the play. "Coming back to the huddle I motioned to coach Yeoman that the guy might be shaken. But he wasn't dazed at all. On the film you could see he was with me step for step. It was just a 'streak' pattern, and Woody made one helluva throw."

Like other Cougars of his era, Hebert considers the 1965 game at Tennessee the start to prominence of Yeoman's veer offense. "I always considered that the turning point," Hebert says. "We'd had plane trouble and sat on the runway for two hours in Houston. We got to Knoxville too late to work out; it was dark and there were no stadium lights.

"Coach called a team meeting at the stadium instead. He made the statement that Bo was his quarterback. He went down the line and told everybody that we could do the job. That we had the talent and to do it for ourselves, to prove it to ourselves, not for the coaches or the university."

Because of the NCAA probation, Hebert and his classmates were barred from bowl games. "The probation had a very adverse effect," he admits. "All we had left to play for was self-pride. We had to go out and beat people for the sake of winning. We weren't running up the scores; we were playing everybody we could. I have a special place in my memory for the 1966 and 1967 teams.

"We were fortunate enough to assemble a group that was conducive to getting the job done, and coach took us through an era. We weren't all goody-goody types, but we had a common purpose."

Hebert did not mind his additional duties as the kicking specialist. "Punting was no strain at all," he explains, "but place kicking is a different type of leg action. It was a source of a lot of satisfaction and disappointment. At Ole Miss (in the 14-13 loss in 1967) I missed a field goal from the 10 and an extra point. I hit both as good as I could.

"If they go through, they're great, and if they don't, nobody talks to you."

Hebert also has special memories of the 1976 Cotton Bowl season: "After the Tech game I had a cowboy hat made up of red wool with a white band and a big white UH on each side. I wore it to the Cotton Bowl with Rich Stotter, Bo and Woody.

"I had a feeling of envy that these guys had the opportunity to play in the Southwest Conference. When we were in school, we'd have given our eyeteeth to play any SWC school. I'm just glad we made a contribution, no matter how big or small."

At the end of his UH career, when he had been voted to the football writers All-American, Hebert had scored 246 points, caught 90 passes for 1,785 yards and 22 touchdowns, kicked 89 of 103 points after touchdown, averaged 41.6 yards per punt.

"I've never coached or played with an athlete like Kenny," said Bill Yeoman, "and this school may never see another like him." Offensive line coach Billy Willingham called him "195 pounds of pure malice."

A .345 hitter while playing first base on the UH team which finished second in the 1967 College World Series, Hebert at times was overly enthusiastic. He was ejected from several games, and after one incident, Coach Lovette Hill advised, "Mistah Hebert, if you want to act tough, how about hitting that little ball over that big fence out there?"

On his next time up to bat, Hebert smashed a home run.

Finally,
Meeting The Big Orange

Over the spring and summer the excitement mounted among UH followers, ever since the announcement that the Cougars would again meet the University of Texas in football. Their September 21 game at Austin would be the first between the state's two largest universities since 1953, and it would have immense significance for both schools.

As early as May, tickets obviously were going to be in short supply.

Longhorn defense coordinator Mike Campbell, on hand at the Cougars' final spring game, said, "Houston is a basic football team. They don't do a lot of things, but they do them well. It's like a man with one pair of shoes. If he shines them every day, they're going to look better than six pairs of shoes some other guy owns." First, however, there was the problem of rebuilding the offensive line, where tackle Bill Cloud and center Pat Pryor were the only veterans. Ken Bailey was counted upon to step in at quarterback since Dick Woodall's departure. Chances were good for a strong defense, since eight starters returned, including end Jerry Drones; tackles Cliff Larson and Jerry Gardner; and cornerbacks Johnny Peacock and Mike Simpson. Another prominent returnee was defensive end Royce Berry after extensive rehabilitation for his injured knee.

After his great junior year, halfback Paul Gipson spent part of his class time taking ballet lessons, and confided, "Watch the people on the dance floor next time you go out. You can bet the ones that quit first are the ones who don't do much

Ken Bailey quarterbacked the 1968 Cougars.

dancing. Their legs got tired."

A sophomore split end named Elmo Wright drew some attention. Said receiver coach Joe Arenas, "Wright could be a great one, but it's all up to him. He's a terrific kid to coach because you can show him a new technique, and he can go out and execute it to near perfection the first time."

Gardner conceded that Cougar fans were talking almost exclusively about the Longhorns. "That's all we've heard about for a year," he said.

Coach Bill Yeoman pointed out, time after time, "Tulane comes ahead of Texas. It says so right there on the schedule."

Ahead of Tulane only 14-7 at the half, thanks to Gipson's 57-yard journey in which he twice reversed his field, the Cougars racked the Greenies, 54-7. Wright's first varsity reception was a 50-yard scoring catch from Bailey, and he later caught an 81-yarder. Simpson returned an interception 64 yards, and Gipson and Jim Strong each rushed for over 100 yards.

Noting UH's 40-point second half explosion, Longhorn assistant Fred Akers told UH aide Billy Willingham, "You guys made that scoreboard light up like a pinball machine."

Watching from the press box, Texas Coach Darrell Royal said, "We think the same thing now as when we came down here. They're a fine football team with a potent offensive machine."

Yeoman told his troops, "Now we're ready for the game we've been waiting for."

En route to Austin on the Cougars' chartered team plane, Harry Kalas, a member of their radio announcing crew, visited as usual with the coaches for a scouting report.

Defensive coordinator Melvin Robertson and line coach Ben Hurt diagrammed the Longhorn offense for Kalas. Royal reportedly had had his team working offensively with a full-T in the backfield with halfbacks Chris Gilbert and Ted Koy and fullback Steve Worster.

But the offense drawn up by Robertson and Hurt somehow looked like a "Y" alignment to Kalas. That night at a social gathering, Kalas drew up the offense and walked up to ask Royal about it.

"Say, coach, what do you call this?" Kalas asked Royal in

all innocence.

"Darrell turned white as a sheet," Kalas recalls, "and asked me, 'Where did you hear about this?'"

Then Royal, obviously highly disturbed, asked Athletic Director Harry Fouke, "Who is that young blond fellow over there?"

Fouke told him, "He's one of the announcers for the Houston Astros and is on our broadcast crew."

With an overflow crowd of 66,397 in Memorial Stadium the next night, the Longhorns lined up for the first time in their new offense. Assistant Melvin Brown relates, "I turned around and looked at Texas, and I'd never seen anything like it. I thought we'd had the course. I go running up to Melvin Robertson. I say, 'You see that?' He tells me, 'Yeah, yeah, I know, I know.'"

The crackling, bone-jarring 20-20 tie the teams played left lasting impressions on those who witnessed it and played in it. It remains as one of the most stirring, brutally physical games in their experience, outlined by the superb running of Gipson and Gilbert. Each scored all three of his team's touchdowns.

"I still dream about that game," Ronnie Herman, a UH offensive guard that night, said years later. "I dreamt about it all that summer, and I dream about it now."

"That was the first game I started," said Elmo Wright, "but I didn't really think about it being Texas until we got to the stadium, and there were all those kids waiting to get in the stands. It was mind-boggling."

Gary Mullins, a redshirt quarterback that year behind Bailey and Rusty Clark, recalled, "I was the backup place kicker. I wanted to play so bad. I asked Coach Yeoman the week before, if I kicked so many in a row in practice, could I get in? Then, during the game, we were driving at the end, and coach asked me if I had my kicking shoe with me. I felt like I had a cannon on my foot."

"Here we were, finally getting the chance to prove we could play with the Longhorns," said offensive guard Bill Bridges. "I remember the whole ordeal working up to it, the pressure. And how emotional the crowd was. The buildup before the game was like the whole season was riding on it.

"Then there was the viciousness of the hitting. Gipson hit

221

Mack McKinney so hard one play he knocked McKinney's helmet several feet straight up in the air. Carlos Bell (fullback) got his bell rung and was swaying back and forth in the huddle with his hands on his knees. He said, 'Let's go, let's go,' and he called the play we had just run. Bill Cloud sent him off the field."

Only three minutes into the game, Gipson lunged across from the one to complete a 59-yard push on UH's first series. Then Gilbert slashed off tackle and went 57 yards, and the half ended, 7-7.

After an interception at the Texas 18, Gilbert and Koy got in gear. Gilbert swept for 24, Koy for 40, and Gilbert gained the final 8. Two plays and 18 seconds later, Gipson uncoiled for 66 yards, and UH gained a 14-14 tie.

Then Gardner tipped a Longhorn pass that was intercepted by linebacker Charlie Hall, who lateraled to Berry, and UH was at the Texas 20. Gipson sailed the last five yards, but Terry Leiweke's conversion kick went wide, and it was 20-14.

Lloyd Wainscott jarred loose a fumble, and Bill Atessis recovered for Texas at the Cougar 20. Koy slammed over from the four with 14:21 to play; then Rob Layne missed the Longhorn extra point.

Although they controlled the ball for 30 plays to 12 by Texas in the fourth quarter, the Cougars could not score against the iron-willed Longhorn defense. A 73-yard thrust to the four ended when Leiweke's 19-yard field goal from a tough angle drifted wide. Taking over again on a punt at the Texas 46, the Coogs came down to fourth and inches at the one yard line with three minutes to play.

Gipson barged into a sea of orange jerseys; the ball was marked; and a measurement showed it inches short. Texas then allowed the final seconds to run out on fourth down without risking a punt from their end of the field.

Gipson tore out 173 yards on 28 carries, and Gilbert, starting his third straight 1,000-yard season, mounted 159 yards in 21 carries. Said Wainscott later, "I don't believe I've ever faced an offense as good as Houston's in the three years I've been here. I'll put Gipson with O. J. Simpson any day. No, I'd put Gipson over Simpson, because you don't knock Gipson down. You can stick him right in the mouth, butt him, but if

ALL-AMERICA FULLBACK PAUL GIPSON

Set an all-time UH rushing record
with 1550 yards in 1968...fifth
highest one-season total in the
history of college football...name
to All-America teams in both 1967
1968...also set UH career ground
gaining record of 2769 yards...
hometown: Conroe (Washington HS)

*Paul Gipson (46), shown here in the 20-20 tie with Texas in
1968 (with the state capitol in the background) posted two
1,000-yard rushing seasons for the Cougars (1967-68).*

you don't get your arms around him, he's gone."

Wainscott noted, "If you keep hitting a runner, he will
usually look for another place to run, but not Gipson. He would
just bring that head down and hit you right in the mouth, just
daring you to tackle him."

Royal made a rare trip to the visitors' dressing room. He
told the Cougars, "I've been in this locker room twice. Once

was after Arkansas beat us (in 1964) and tonight...You carried the fight to us, and we felt fortunate getting a tie out of it."

"That hurt me more than anything," Bridges revealed years later. "It was like him admitting we had kicked their tails, but he wouldn't admit it to anybody else. That was just my personal feeling."

"The biggest thing I remember," Bridges added, "was Gipson on the counter option at the goal over Cloud and me. We swear he made it. We were a foot and a half over the goal, and he was leaning over us."

Asked the best way to stop Gipson, Texas linebacker Corby Robertson replied, "With several others." The son of Corby Robertson, Sr., former chairman of UH's board of regents and athletic committee, helped pile up Gipson on that crucial play. "My feet weren't even on the ground," Corby, Jr., described it. "I got him about the middle and somebody else went over me and got him high."

At the end UH had margins of 22 first downs to 12 and 398 yards total offense to 314. The last half figures were 15 first downs to 4, and 259 yards offense to 121 in UH's favor, but they did not mean a single, solitary, additional point.

Late that night, Royal asked for suggestions on a name for the new Longhorn offense, and Mickey Herskowitz of the *Houston Post* labeled it the "wishbone." Besides the birth of the wishbone the game also signalled UH's potential at the ticket window in the SWC.

The Cougars and Cincinnati then strained the Astrodome's $2.5 million scoreboard to the fullest in a 71-33 UH victory. They combined for 35 points in the opening quarter and 41 points in the fourth period. Gipson returned the opening kickoff 91 yards to start the scoring orgy and retired late in the half with a strained back muscle after 131 yards and two touchdowns.

Wright caught eight passes for 244 yards, including a 75-yard TD. Cincinnati quarterback Greg Cook passed for 352 yards. The teams totaled an astounding 50 first downs and 1,074 yards total offense, 696 yards by the Cougars.

Ranked No. 10 nationally, the Cougars saved one of their worst performances for Oklahoma State and lost, 21-17. They fumbled 10 times, losing 4, and threw four interceptions before the Cowpokes scored with 56 seconds to play. The winning 70-yard drive began after a UH defender tried to lateral an interception and bobbled the ball.

Jim Strong, making his first start for the injured Gipson, rushed for 131 yards on 21 carries.

Nearly two weeks of rest and therapy did wonders for Gipson's injured back, and after a delicious afternoon at Jackson, Mississippi, Calvin McDougle, the UH film man, kept his lens aimed at Ole Miss Coach John Vaught taking the walk to the dressing room.

It was a signal occasion, for UH's 29-7 triumph was only its second win in 16 games with the Rebels and the first on enemy soil. Gipson cranked out 210 yards on 33 carries and scored on runs of 18 and 30 yards. Royce Berry, Jerry Drones, Charlie Hall, Glenn Graef, and Paul Shires stood out in the defense which sent Ole Miss quarterback Archie Manning out of the game with a cracked rib in the second quarter.

Ole Miss scored first after a UH fumble, one of five by the Cougars, before Bailey directed a 76-yard drive, overcoming a holding penalty and Wright's muff of a touchdown pass. Bailey completed 13 of 20 passes as the Cougars amassed 573 yards.

Wright and Bailey teamed up on a 79-yard TD pass to break the 7-7 halftime tie, but the Cougars fumbled at the Ole Miss two and were halted later at the three on fourth down. Carlos Bell nailed a punt returner for a safety and a 15-7 lead before Gipson's two fourth quarter scoring runs.

"They'd beaten us so many times, everybody wanted it in the worst way," said Bailey. "You could see it building for two weeks."

"Every time I looked up, there were six guys around me," Hall described the defensive effort. The Cougars retired to their motel and dunked the coaching staff in the swimming pool. McDougle relates, "In 1962, Bill's first year, Ole Miss beat us, 40-7, and had the first team in until 1:10 to play. Bill met Vaught on the field and shook his finger under his nose and said, 'You'll pay for that.'"

Georgia was ranked No. 7, and the largest crowd in Sanford Stadium history, 59,381, turned out at Athens. Several thousand more sat and clung to a railroad bridge and a trestle behind the end zones. It was a frustrating day "between the hedges" for the Cougars after their thrilling 15-14 comeback the year before.

Leiweke's 32-yard field goal and Wright's 80-yard scoring aerial from Bailey meant a 10-0 first period lead, but UH wasted several other chances. The Bulldogs, who had lost just twice at home in Vince Dooley's five seasons, converted a UH fumble into a touchdown, then began a 69-yard drive from their nine yard line with 1:59 to go. They kicked a tieing 38-yard field goal with 12 seconds remaining.

Gipson again was superb, rushing for 230 yards on 37 carries, both figures school records, through a defense featuring All-American Bill Stanfill. Wright caught six passes for 151 yards. "If O. J. Simpson is any better," said one of the game officials of Gipson, "I don't see how."

But the Cougars missed a 31-yard field goal and stalled at the 15, 35, and 17 before passing up a field goal after reaching the 19. From there the Dogs traveled to the tie.

Later, at UH's motel in Commerce, a Georgia alumnus approached Gipson and told him, "I'm in the class of '29, and I had to drive over here from Athens and shake your hand. You're the greatest football player I've ever seen in Sanford Stadium."

The temperature was in the thirties on a cold night in Memphis as Bailey kept handing the ball to Gipson and Strong, and the defense steadily provided opportunities. The result was a 27-7 victory over Memphis State, 140 yards on 31 carries for Gipson, and 117 on 10 for Strong. The defense intercepted five passes and recovered four fumbles, leading to three touchdowns. UH rushed for 430 yards and held Memphis State to 83.

Gipson became the first UH runner to produce two straight 1,000-yard seasons. Georgia's Dooley said, "I doubt that I've ever seen a running back to compare to Paul Gipson."

Memphis State's Spook Murphy added, "There are three super running backs today in college football—O. J. Simpson, Leroy Keyes, and Gipson. The other two have gotten more headlines than Gipson, but it is hard for me to believe that anyone is better than Gipson."

With Wright catching four touchdowns and 249 yards, the Cougars bundled up 793 yards and a 77-3 rout of Idaho. There was more to come.

226

One For The Record Book, Or Blowing The Computer

Revenge is a mighty motive, and the Cougars had plenty for their November 23 game with Tulsa, their final home appearance of 1968.

"They'd humiliated us and the veer offense up there the year before," offensive guard Bill Bridges referred to the 22-13 loss at Tulsa.

Down through the years the Hurricane also had planted other thorns in the Cougars' hide. And UH was inflamed by the realization there would, after all, be no chance for a postseason bowl game. The NCAA turned down the school's request that the three-year probation be lifted a month before its decreed termination in mid-January.

The stunning, improbable tale was headlined in the *Houston Chronicle*, "UH Wins Game of Century (100-6)." Read the *Houston Post*," "Wow! UH Tallies 100."

The 100-6 torching of Tulsa was the most one-sided score in NCAA history since Wyoming's 103-0 conquest of Colorado State College in 1949. It also caused problems for the computer in the office of the NCAA statistical service in New York City. Programmed for scores through 99 points, the computer had to be force-fed two cards for its electronic brain to digest the information.

The Cougars scored NCAA records of 76 points in the second half and 49 in the final quarter. Terry Leiweke, trying to ignore the cramp in his leg from all the activity, tied the NCAA record with his 13 points after touchdown.

227

Coach Bill Yeoman was embarrassed. He played everyone but the redshirts, and there were no uniforms for the student managers. When the carnage ended, Yeoman could say, "I'm embarrassed we could beat a team like Tulsa that bad."

With 22 seconds to play after Mike Simpson's 59-yard punt return, Leiweke toed the 100th point. He returned to the exultant Cougar bench, looked at the "100" on the Astrodome scoreboard and said of the point from which he kicked his points-after, "There's a pool of blood out there on the seven yard line."

Center Pat Pryor said, "Have we been thinking about this one very long? About a year, I'd say."

Compiling statistics of the game was likened to computing the accident toll for the Labor Day weekend, or the head count at the French Revolution, or what the lions had for lunch at the Colosseum.

UH scored 15 touchdowns, 37 first downs, 555 yards rushing, and 762 yards total offense. On and on the figures mounted, never seeming to stop. "I'm getting cramps in my legs from kicking so much," Leiweke had confided, moments before being summoned for the final point-after and then, blessedly, the final kickoff.

Leiweke was a transfer from New Mexico Military Institute, where, as a quarterback, he broke passing and total offense records set by an alumnus named Roger Staubach. "I was very nervous," he said of point 100, "but I couldn't let the other guys down after they got it up that high. I was on the spot."

"He told us later," said Bridges, "that it felt like all 35,000 people were sitting on his helmet. After we scored that last one, we all wanted that 100. At the half it was still anybody's game. It wasn't out of reach. Then it seemed like every time we got our hands on the ball, we scored. You can't tell guys who have been out there all year in those Monday scrimmages not to try to score."

UH's 24-0 halftime lead was cut to 24-6 in the third quarter before Carlos Bell turned end for 21 yards and began the last half UH scoring deluge. Paul Gipson, despite a broken nose suffered the week before, carried the ball for a UH one-game record 282 yards.

Gipson ran 35, 17, and 14 yards for TDs; Elmo Wright

*With clear sailing ahead, Paul Gipson (46) gains a chunk of his
school record 282 yards in 100-6 rout of Tulsa in 1968.*

caught a 60-yard pass from Ken Bailey and ran 66 for another
on an end-around; Clark passed for three scores and ran for
another, and on and on.

A 5-foot-8 reserve split end named Larry Gatlin caught a

ALL-AMERICA CORNERBACK JOHNNY

Winner of the Charles Saunders
as the University's outstandi
athlete...1968 All-America...
both the Hula Bowl and Senior
all-star games...also an acad
All-America choice...hometown
Goliad, Texas.

Johnny Peacock (37), 1968 Saunders Award winner as the school's outstanding scholar-athlete, also was an All-America cornerback.

25-yard pass from Rusty Clark for the next-to-last touchdown. That was the only touchdown of Gatlin's career. Almost a decade later, Gatlin, then a nationally known country and western singer, finally got to his bowl game. He entertained at Cotton Bowl parties before the Cougars played Maryland.

In fact, the Cougars even had two touchdowns nullified by penalties.

Pat Pryor decided, "The basketball team is going to have a heckuva time trying to match this."

The spark was gone at Jacksonville, Florida, however, where Florida State's Bill Cappleman—Ron Sellers aerial duo riddled the Cougars, 40-20. Once again, UH's Top Ten aspirations tumbled.

Cappleman completed 25 of 34 for 351 yards and four touchdowns. Sellers caught 14 for 214. Clark, quarterbacking the second half after a 25-0 deficit, connected on 14 of 20 for 226 yards, and Gipson rushed for 164 yards in his final game.

The Cougars swept the final NCAA offense list, setting a record of 562 yards per game in total offense and leading in rushing (361.7) and scoring (42.5). Gipson, chosen on the football coaches All-American, finished with UH running records of 1,550 yards in a season and 2,769 in a career.

The Brezinas,
A Family Of Cougars

Few families have contributed as much to the athletic tradition of a single university as the Brezinas gave to the Cougars.

Beginning with Bobby, the starting fullback on the 1962 Tangerine Bowl outfit, and continuing to Gus, Bernard, Greg, "Butch," and Steve, the six Brezina brothers compiled an unusual story of fidelity to one school.

Bobby (1960-61-62) co-captained the 1962 Cougars, led them in rushing and was voted their most valuable player.

Gus (1962-63-64), an offensive lineman, was one of the more talented players on Bill Yeoman's first teams.

Greg (1965-66-67), like Bobby, was a co-captain, receiving some All-American recognition in 1967, and is a linebacker on the all-time UH team selected before the 1976 season. He has linebacked for the Atlanta Falcons for nine years.

"Butch," whose real name is Mark, completed the Brezina clan in 1970-71 as a defensive end and a leading performer on the team which played in the Astro Bluebonnet Bowl.

Bernard, a back who left school for military duty, and Steve, a defensive lineman, also helped build the family's UH legacy.

They all came from Louise, about 50 miles down U.S. Highway 59 from Houston toward the Rio Grande Valley. Their mother, Mrs. Gertrude Brezina, raised her six sons and daughter, Nancy, by sticking to the old, time-tested family traditions.

After the death of their father when they were very young,

the Brezina youths, directed by their mother, all chipped in and helped out.

Butch once recounted those days: "I had to mow the yard and burn the trash. Those were usually my duties. I slopped the pigs, too, sometimes. Greg and I were hardheaded. We didn't always do what we were supposed to. Ma always had to keep after us."

After the death of Mr. Brezina, the family moved into the town, where Mrs. Brezina ran the school cafeteria for years. "She's tough," Butch paid her tribute. "It's hard to realize what she's done. If she wanted to, she could probably take me over her knee right now."

Of Czech and German ancestry, the Brezinas stage regular family reunions, and Butch recalls one when 400 to 500 relatives gathered at Shiner, in central Texas.

The Brezinas started playing football in the pasture beside their home. Usually Bobby, Bernard and Butch teamed against Greg, Gus and Steve. Nancy, their sister, was often the referee. If there was an absentee, she played, too.

When Butch failed to perform up to family standards at UH, he could count on a phone call from an older brother, usually Greg or Gus. "I get a feeling of inferiority if I don't whip the rear of the guy in front of me," Butch said. "When you don't perform to 100 percent, when you let your teammates down because of it, that's what gives you a feeling of insecurity."

Butch spoke feelingly of his small-town, family-oriented background: "You respect authority. You know that you have things you have to do that no one else will do if you don't. You learn to scratch and get after everything, just like our coaches. It's the same way outside of football when you get out of school. You have to get after it, because none of it comes free."

Greg, only seven when his father died, worked in the neighborhood grocery store or at the filling station two and a half blocks away. He took trombone and trumpet lessons in the sixth grade, a sometimes painful experience: "Every time I missed a note, my teacher hit me on the head with his baton."

A three-year starter at quarterback in high school, Greg gives much of the credit to his coach then, Gene Stogner. "He was like a father to me. I remember during a game, sometimes

233

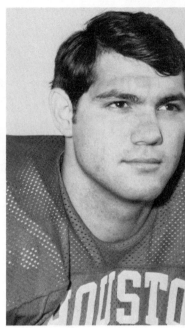

Greg (left) and Butch Brezina, two of four brothers (with Bobby and Gus) who lettered for the Cougars.

he'd be getting ready to send in a play, then he'd tell me afterward that I'd already called the play in the huddle. When I came to UH there were about 11 quarterbacks on the squad, so I sort of gave up on playing quarterback."

Greg had no doubt about his choice of college: "I never really considered going anywhere else. Gus told me there was going to be some 'static' around home if I didn't come here."

Bill Yeoman,
Father Of The Veer

The most ingenious inventions often are born of necessity. So it was for Bill Yeoman and his veer offense.

In midseason of 1965 Yeoman's necessity was obvious: his teams had won only 5 of their last 20 games, and Yeoman and his staff were about to get fired.

Already, Yeoman and Athletic Director Harry Fouke had been hung in effigy on campus. Yeoman recalls those troubled days, "Harry always said, 'We've got to hang together, or we'll hang separately.' And sure enough, there we were, hanging together—separately."

Nearly always one to look on the bright side, however, Yeoman told his secretary, "Thank God there's somebody out there who cares. Now there's hope."

Several weeks before, Yeoman apparently reached the limits of even his boundless confidence. The Cougars looked terrible in a 44-12 loss at Miami. Melvin Brown, lone remaining member of Yeoman's original 1962 staff, relates, "When we got back to the hotel from the stadium, Bill told Harry, 'Well, you've got your black suit on. This is as good a time as any.'

"Bill wanted to resign, but Harry wouldn't let him. He told Bill, 'Young man, you've got too much talent to do that.'"

Fouke says only that, "I never remembered that. I wasn't going to listen to it anyway."

So Yeoman decided the time was now for the veer. "We ran the outside veer with Billy Roland in 1962 from a wingback set," he explains. "It was the same play, then called 44 veer,

Dr. Philip G. Hoffman (right), University of Houston president, visits with football coach Bill Yeoman. Under Dr. Hoffman's direction, the university has grown to its present size of 38,000 students on four campuses.

Colonel Blaik used at Army. Then we ran some veer at the end of the 1963 season and started using the outside veer in 1964.

"We put the whole offense in in the spring of 1965 and averaged about seven yards per play; then I lost my guts until the middle of the season."

Brown says, "When people were hollering for Bill's scalp,

he made up his mind, 'I might get fired, so I'm going to use the veer.'"

Yeoman agrees, "We knew we were on our way out, and I wanted a chance to see if the darned thing worked."

Bo Burris, the first to quarterback the new offense, tells this version of its origin: "In the spring of 1964 we were having a half-line scrimmage one day. We were running the old belly series with the play called in the huddle. There was no option to it.

"One play I stuck the ball in (fullback) Mickey Don Thompson's stomach, and as I was riding with him and looked into the line, I could see he wasn't going anywhere, so I took the ball out of his stomach and pulled around him.

"Coach asked me why I did it. I told him and he said, 'Do it again.' Then he told Dick Post and Warren McVea, the halfback, to go wide, and that was the option pitch. The summer of 1965, my junior year, we went to the unbalanced line with the same offense. It was a high-risk offense, and I didn't have all the confidence in the world anyway."

Yeoman explains his reasoning behind the new offense, "For so many years, we didn't feel that we'd have the players that looked like the great Ole Miss and Alabama teams except at the skilled positions. We felt we had to finesse to a degree on offense and throw the ball."

Like his players on the 1965 team Yeoman calls that year's Tennessee game a critical one. "By then, it was obvious that if we're ever going to an option offense, Burris had to be the quarterback." Thus, with Yeoman's confidence placed in him, Burris became the regular.

The Cougars won three and tied one of their final four games that autumn, including their first victory over Ole Miss and the upset of Cotton Bowl-bound Kentucky.

Warren McVea, one of the first of the stable of runners who have made the veer so popular, admits his early misgivings: "I hated that offense. We had a heck of an argument in his office one day. I told him, 'You don't even have a sweep for me. I just run off-tackle and get killed.'"

By the next season, however, McVea was quickly convinced, "I was sold when I'd look up at the board and we'd have 40 and 50 points up there."

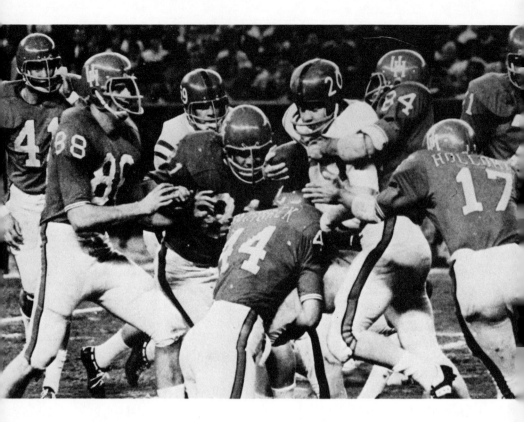

Cougar defenders surround Ole Miss ballcarrier in the 1965 upset of the Rebels, Houston's first victory in the series.

Yeoman said of the veer's evolution, "In 1964 it was a play. In 1965 it was the offense."

By that 1966 season the veer and its triple option attack took the Cougars to an 8-2 record, the school's best since 1952, and the first of three straight major college total offense titles. They also led the nation in rushing in 1967 and scored a rare statistical "triple crown" in 1968, setting a NCAA total offense record of 566.5 yards per game and also leading the nation in rushing and scoring.

Gary Mullins, another of UH's gifted quarterbacks, notes the concept of the offense is "taking advantage of defensive people by not blocking certain people. To me, it puts defensive players in the position of whatever decision they make is wrong. It creates confusion and tears down the defense."

Since the offense also utilizes two wide receivers and a "split" backfield as in the "pro set," opposing defenses cannot stack against the running game. Yeoman has always stressed a balance between running and throwing to wide receivers, like Elmo Wright and Ken Hebert, and tight ends, like Tom Beer, Earl Thomas, Riley Odoms, and Eddie Foster.

The Cougars' offensive explosion with Yeoman's innovation also coincided with the arrival of Billy Willingham as offensive line coach. The tutor of two All-American offensive guards, Rich Stotter and Bill Bridges, at UH, Willingham also designed the complex system of blocking for the veer.

Says Bridges, "The Houston Offense was refined in 1968. After so many repetitions (in practice) it finally jelled. Coach Willingham had to mastermind all the blocking techniques. We had three or four different blocking patterns for each play, according to the defense."

Stotter describes 1966 as the year "we were refining the veer and developing the passing game which helped to open up the running game. Also, when you consider that 13 out of the 22 starters on the 1966 team went into pro ball, we had a tremendous collection of athletes."

One problem of those early days of tinkering with the veer, Yeoman notes, was that "we didn't know exactly what we were doing, and there was no place we could call for past experience with it." Thus, like Edison and the light bulb, Yeoman and his staff had to provide their own illumination.

Requirements for the veer offense? "It takes quick, sturdy backs and a quick quarterback, the quicker the better," says Melvin Brown. "All the cuts for the backs are to the outside instead of against the grain. Mullins reduced the fumbles to practically nothing; he wouldn't pitch unless he had a clear pitch. Burris got us started. He had a sixth sense for knowing when to pull out and pitch the ball."

While the Cougar offense was gaining national acclaim, the defensive unit, called the "Mad Dogs," also gained prominence. O. A. "Bum" Phillips, now the Houston Oilers' head coach, retooled the defense after his arrival in 1965. He was succeeded as defensive coordinator by Melvin Robertson, and the "Mad Dogs" proved a constant pain to opposing offenses. They frequently came up with interceptions and fumble recoveries, a trend continued after Robertson went to Texas A&M in 1972.

The 1976 Cotton Bowl champions, for example, ranked No. 8 nationally in total offense while scoring 28.5 points per game, while the defense intercepted 29 passes and recovered 13 fumbles.

Brown recalls the dark days of 1963 (2-8) and 1964 (2-6-1), "I felt like we were making progress, and Bill would say, 'Keep the chewing gum in the middle of your mouth.' In other words, don't talk too much."

The successful recruiting of Warren McVea in the summer of 1964 also signaled an important milestone, says Yeoman: "It symbolized a different situation, the fact that we were

Houston's 1976 coaching staff included, (left to right, front): Clarence Daniel, Melvin Brown, Head Coach Bill Yeoman, Bill Willingham, and Gary Mullins. Back: Joe Arenas, Ronny Peacock, Barry Sides, Elmer Redd, and Don Todd.

attractive to the best, so-called 'blue-chip' players."

Yeoman once described that event, "I thought my chances of selling the boy were zilch, one in a thousand. I only visited him two or three times. All I did then was sit down with Mama, and Warren would pass through the living room."

But Yeoman quickly discerned something that many recruiters did not—that Warren, one of nine children, was essentially a homebody. "He wasn't going very far away," Yeoman observed.

Two events suggest the impact McVea's arrival at UH made upon the consciousness of the state's sporting folk. After McVea's stunning performance against Kentucky in 1966, two San Antonio sportswriters borrowed the UH game film for a showing in a brewery auditorium. With the public invited on a first-come, first-served basis, the 350-seat theatre was jammed two hours before showtime; about 1,000 were turned away. Another legendary event was McVea's six-touchdown performance in a 55-48 high school playoff win. Copies were made of the original game film, and so many high school coaches and booster clubs watched them, the films soon resembled an old Al Jolson movie.

UH's recruiting approach, says Yeoman, is based on two simple principles: "We tell a youngster he can expect a ton of hard work, plus we do everything possible to make certain that the best player is playing. If he doesn't want to come here, we don't want him. Just let us know so he can go somewhere else and we can go somewhere else."

Yeoman neither smokes nor drinks, though he takes no issue with those who do. Advised at a social function one evening that a high school youth named Albert Davis had elected to attend Tennessee instead of UH, Yeoman agitatedly stormed up to the bar. "Give me another soda water!" he ordered.

A center at West Point and captain of the 1948 team, Yeoman snapped the ball for the great backfield of Arnold Tucker, Glenn Davis and Doc Blanchard and also played line-backer. Later a graduate assistant to Colonel Earl Blaik for two years, Yeoman's time also was spent with other Blaik staff members like Murray Warmath, Vince Lombardi, and Eddie Crowder. After two years of Army duty in Europe, he joined

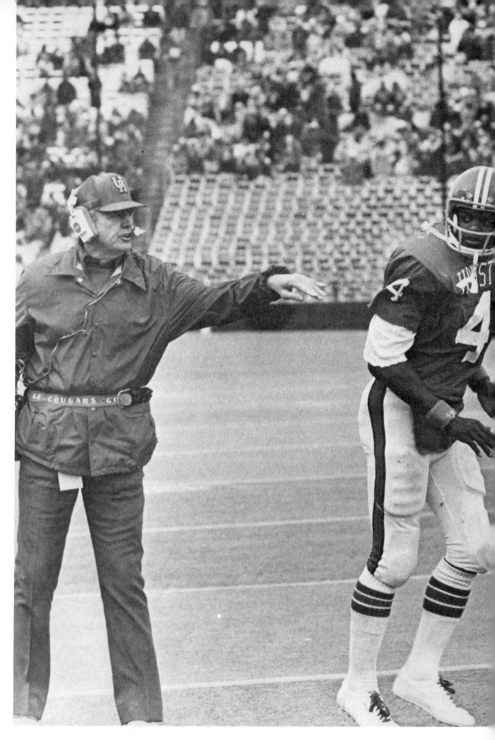

Danny Davis gets his instructions from Bill Yeoman in the fourth period of the 1977 Cotton Bowl.

Duffy Daugherty's staff at Michigan State in 1954. Yeoman was Daugherty's top aide when he accepted the UH position, his first as a head coach.

"Colonel Blaik was very Spartan, very disciplined and stressed the need for complete dedication," Yeoman contrasts the two major influences in his coaching career. "Duffy was equally as successful with a different approach, more of the life-can-be-beautiful routine. Blaik was totally consumed with the mechanics of football. Of course, in the situation at West Point he didn't have to worry about the alumni. It was such a pleasure to watch Davis and Blanchard and Tucker function in those days. It was like watching a clock."

In their home, Bill and Alma Jean Yeoman retain a framed letter from then-President Harry Truman. The message from one Army man to another praises Yeoman's sportsmanship as captain of the 1948 Cadets for granting the game ball to Navy after the Middies' upset tie with Army.

"There was a good deal of hesitancy on my part about liberating that football," Yeoman admits, "but the Colonel (Blaik) said he thought it would be a nice gesture."

Another memorable incident occurred during the team's 1948 football banquet at the Waldorf-Astoria, when General and Mrs. Dwight Eisenhower sat at the same table.

Born in Elnora, Indiana, and raised in Glendale, Arizona, Yeoman, 49, met his wife at her high school graduation dance in Bryan, Texas, while Yeoman was a freshman at Texas A&M. His father-in-law was head of the school's petroleum engineering department for 18 years.

Starting at Michigan State as defensive backfield coach, Yeoman applied for several head coaching jobs before UH. "Then Sonny Grandelius and a couple of our other coaches went to Colorado," he recalls, "and Duffy asked me to stay on a couple of more years. I didn't apply anywhere else after that. Then Duffy asked me if I'd be interested in the Houston job."

Corbin Robertson, then chairman of the athletic committee, relates, "I talked with Colonel Blaik for 45 minutes on the phone, and he made the same statement Duffy had made—I had talked to Duffy for an hour and a half about various coaches. They both said that Bill promised to become one of the great innovators in the game. When discussing Bill later, I had a certain reluctance for hiring an assistant, but he caught the whole committee's imagination. He obviously was a four-square guy with a sense of imagination.

"The thing I found impressive about Bill, not only did he have great ideas, but first he constantly built a solid foundation."

The Yeomans were eager to escape the Michigan winters, and, Yeoman recalls, "I'd visited the in-laws in Houston and had an inkling of what the school could become. I don't think I ever went on campus before I took the job. I'd visited with Harry and Corby in their homes."

Yeoman's arrival in December, 1961, to begin his task was anything but the sunny, warm climate he expected. "We landed in weather so bad they told me we wouldn't have come down if all the people hadn't been there waiting on me. It was just a very dark, cold night. I went to Oberholtzer Hall to meet the press, and I stayed in a room at the dorm that first night.

"I remember putting my head down on the pillow, looking at the ceiling, and saying, 'Yeoman, what in hell have you done?' I was 32 and felt like 80."

Yeoman began by asking questions. "It was obvious the school's image in the state was not what it had to be," he says. "I asked my father-in-law, 'Where are we better than other schools?'

"He said that students here could walk into class after having been out working in their profession and say, 'This doesn't work' or 'This is the right way.' The education was a great deal more relevant and up-to-date than at some of the older universities.

"At Michigan State, like here, one of the big pluses was night classes, so that there weren't restrictions on athletes' class scheduling during the season."

Houston's biggest advantage was geographical, in Yeoman's opinion. "The school was located in the best place in the state and maybe in the U.S. and there was a great feeling among the faculty. They were all for the Cougars, no matter what their department."

Yeoman recalls his first squad in 1962 "had 38 to 48 players. There were a few, total quality athletes like Bobby Brezina, Billy Roland, Milton Perkins, Ken Chancellor, Bill Van

Osdel, and Byron Beaver."

As for the immense job ahead, Yeoman notes, "When you're young, you don't know any better. It's like dying. The Good Lord never lets you know the moment he takes you. I like it that way; I'd never want to know. If everything was peachy-keen, there wouldn't be any coaching changes."

Demaree Jones, a 1963 co-captain, remembers the Cougars' first squad meeting with Yeoman: "He came walking in and told us, 'We're going to be No. 1 in the nation.' That was the first thing out of his mouth. He said, 'If anybody thinks different, then get gone.'

"He'd never cuss in front of us. Worst thing you ever heard him say was, 'Gee whiz' or 'Gosh darned.' He was always telling us, 'It's imperative you take a serious attitude to this upcoming game.' We were used to hearing, 'Get out and beat the hell out of them.' He came across light-hearted. We were floored by his ability to speak spontaneously. It was like yanking on a buzzsaw and getting it started."

Calvin McDougle, head of the men's PE department and the football movie-taker, refers to "the greatest bit of psychology I ever saw a coach use. We were getting ready to play at Florida State in Bill's first season. That Monday the boys were all dragging, and he tells them, 'You're not ready to play football. Go on in.' That night they're supposed to have a meeting after dinner, and they all come slinking into the dining room. 'Go on home, you're still not ready,' he tells them. He gave them Tuesday off, too, and they didn't practice until Wednesday."

Losers of four straight at the time, the Cougars won, 7-0, the first of four straight victories that took them to the Tangerine Bowl.

Despite his breezy air, Yeoman has shown he expects compliance with his rules. In past years he has suspended players of the quality of Paul Gipson, the school's No. 2 career rusher; Royce Berry, one of its greatest defensive ends; and Riley Odoms, an All-American tight end, for curfew violations.

Then there is the matter of "Yeoman Time." His watch tends to run 15 minutes fast in tense or trying situations, like after the 10-10 with Georgia at Athens in 1968. Rushing by taxi from Athens to Commerce to meet the team bus, sports news director Ted Nance, David Fink of the *Houston Post*, Charles Miller, and the author careened into the motel parking lot 10 minutes before the agreed hour. But the Cougars then were on "Yeoman Time" and had already left. There ensued a tense 80-mile race to the Atlanta airport. Fortunately a mechanical problem had delayed the team charter's departure.

Melvin Brown, who played for Bud Wilkinson at Oklahoma, notes, "Both have the capacity to work, work, work. Bill puts a lot more into recruiting. He makes himself actually sick with his pace and schedule. You can be in West Texas and look up and there he'll be; then he'll have a plane to catch. Bill has a knack for judging talent in wide receivers and running backs. I can remember Bud saying that Jim Tatum could take 25 players, and Bud could take 40, and Tatum would beat him. Bill is like that, too."

Golf Coach Dave Williams, a recruiting aide in Yeoman's first year, apologized for a 2 a.m. phone call to Yeoman after signing a prized recruit. "Call me any hour you sign an All-American," was Yeoman's reply.

"Bill's greatest attribute is his toughness and ability to work hard," says Williams. "People know if you're a good coach or not, because your record is there in black and white. Nobody knows if you're a good CPA or not."

Yeoman recounts one of the low points: "Mississippi State in 1964 (an 18-13 loss). They kicked three or four field goals and returned a kickoff for their only touchdown. I'll never forget that game. After the Miami game in 1965 a (44-12 trouncing) I apologized to the team for jacking around with the offense. That was the low point. I thought it was a very large basin."

The 1965 Kentucky game "was one of the best we have ever played," says Yeoman. "Ken Herbert's run from punt formation put a real 'hitch' in my 'get-along.' Texas in 1968, I felt that; I had trouble breathing that night. You're talking about real talent on one football field."

One of Yeoman's vivid memories of the 37-7 triumph at Michigan State in 1967 was the way it affected his wife, A. J., "She cried for two hours after the game because she was so close to Duffy's wife, and Duf was kind enough to schedule us and help me get this job."

246

Val Belcher (left), Paul Humphreys, and Wilson Whitley join Bill Yeoman (back to camera) to accept Houston Touchdown Club's Bayou Bucket from Del Womack after the 1976 win over Rice. The trophy is emblematic of the city championship, and the Cougars clinched the Cotton Bowl bid with their victory.

Yeoman recalls, "Before the game, Bill Peterson called from Florida State and asked us not to send our film of the UH-Florida State game to Alabama, his next opponent. I said, 'Fine, don't send yours to Michigan State.' He agreed. Melvin Robertson and I had seen Michigan State's spring game, and it was obvious they didn't know what we were doing with the veer. I knew what that game meant to our program."

A. J. Yeoman once admitted to the UH student paper, "I was first attracted to my husband because he could talk like Donald Duck."

Yeoman replies, "Don't tell me I didn't dazzle that woman. When I was 10 or 12 years old, kids used to pay me a dollar an hour to teach them to talk like that."

Now in his 16th season as UH head coach, Yeoman has seen the Cougars compile an 81-32-3 regular season record since 1966. In the 10 seasons from 1966 through 1975 the Cougars led the nation in total offense (440 yards per game), were sixth in scoring (30.2 points per game), third in rushing (283 yards per game), and seventh in rushing defense.

The First Bluebonnet

Bill Yeoman dismissed *Playboy* magazine's preseason ranking of UH as the nation's No. 1 team. Said Yeoman, "I paid about as much attention to that as when people hanged me in effigy."

With Paul Gipson graduated and Carlos Bell a scholastic casualty, fifth-year senior Jim Strong was heir-apparent at halfback. Ken Bailey returned at quarterback, challenged by Rusty Clark and redshirt Gary Mullins; Elmo Wright at split end; Billy Bridges at guard; David Schneider at tackle (moved from guard); and Calvin Achey at flanker. But end Jerry Drones, linebackers Charlie Hall and Glenn Graef, and safety Richard Harrington were the only returnees on defense. Gone were 30-game starters Johnny Peacock and Mike Simpson at cornerbacks and linebacker Wade Phillips. Defensive tackles Jerry Gardner and Cliff Larson, both two-year regulars, also had departed.

Still, Strong noted one welcome difference—the chance at a bowl game with the termination of the three-year NCAA probation. "We had had to replace bowl games with statistics," Strong explained. "It's really hard to get up for some games unless you're shooting for something, unless there's something at stake."

Florida's Gators then proceeded to shell the reconstructed defense with the aerial combination of John Reaves to Carlos Alvarez, both sophomores. Reaves passed for 342 yards and five touchdowns, breaking Steve Spurrier's Gator records as the Florida Field audience of 53,807 reveled in the 59-34 triumph.

Linebacker Charlie Hall, a member of the Cougars' all-time defensive team.

A 70-yard pass to Alvarez on the game's third play started the debacle. UH trailed 17-0 after seven minutes and 38-6 at the half. In short, the game bore a remarkable similarity to the 1968 finale at Jacksonville. Alvarez, a refugee from the Castro revolution in Cuba, caught six passes for 182 yards and two, touchdowns. Bailey tied the UH record with five touchdown passes, three to Wright.

The errors continued the second week at Oklahoma State, where the Cougars gave away five interceptions and three fumbles, and were penalized 132 yards. They trailed, 24-0, at the half, and bowed, 24-18. Wright caught a school record 12 passes for 200 yards and one touchdown, but the quarterbacks could not pass consistently.

Two days before the Mississippi State game, Yeoman announced that Mullins, No. 3 in line behind Bailey and Clark, would start at quarterback.

As if injected with some secret vitamin, the UH offense began functioning smoothly and the defense turned tigerish. Mullins completed five of six passes in the first half, and three of them produced touchdowns from 54, 42, and 12 yards to Wright. At the end of the 74-0 runaway, UH had 33 first downs, 736 yards total offense, and sub fullback Robert Newhouse had 245 yards rushing. The perked-up defense collected 5 interceptions, 2 fumble recoveries and 12 quarterback sacks.

At Arizona Strong suddenly meshed the gears of his career, rushing for 230 yards on 22 carries and darting on TD runs of 47 and 40 yards. Mullins also scored three times, and the Cougars, leading just 21-17 at the half, won, 34-17.

Bridges also had a night to remember. "We lined up for the first extra point," he recalls, "and I saw the guy in front of me had his chin strap undone. I drove into him with my helmet and split his chin. We scored again, and same thing, and I figured I'd get him again.

"But he twisted my facemask to one side and hit me with his elbow across the nose. Blood spattered all over that white uniform. I got four or five feet from the sideline, and my eyes crossed, and I went to the ground. I heard Jack Littlefield yell to Tom Wilson, 'Hey, Tom, we got us a dead soldier over here.'"

A defense which hounded quarterback Archie Manning all night, and Mullins' heady direction carried the Cougars to a stirring 25-11 homecoming victory over Ole Miss.

A week after his 540-yard performance against Alabama, Manning was limited to 137 yards passing and 19 yards running on 13 carries. Strong, meanwhile, rushed for 219 yards on 23

251

Bill Bridges, 1969 All-American offensive guard and selected Texas player of the year by the Houston Chronicle.

carries, gaining repeatedly through the left side behind tackle Charlie Moore, a 17-year-old sophomore, and Bridges.

Mullins ran 12 yards for the first score, then picked up the mishandled extra point try and passed to tight end Riley Odoms for a two-point conversion. The Rebs closed to 15-11 in the third period; then the Coogs drove 77 yards. Strong burst for 41 and Odoms, between two defenders in the end zone, made a leaping catch of Mullins' five-yard pass.

With Mullins accounting for 226 yards, UH totaled 523 to 220 for Ole Miss in scoring back-to-back wins over the Rebels for the first time in their series. Linebacker Mike Johnston, going all the way despite a broken hand on the game's third play, said, "I saw the bone sticking through, but I just mashed it back down."

"Houston has more ability than any football team I've ever seen," said Manning. "When they lose a game, they must lose it in their minds. There's no reason for their bodies to get beat."

In their first television appearance since their NCAA ban, the Cougars staged a pulse-pounder with Miami, Florida, winning, 38-36, on Mullins' seven-yard fourth down pass to tight end Earl Thomas with 11 seconds to play.

Wilson, the UH trainer, was so overcome with emotion at Thomas' catch that he doubled over and fell to the ground on the sideline, victim of a minor stomach spasm. "That was as tough a team as I ever hope to play against," Mullins said. "I took a beating, but so did all our other guys."

"The only thing I made sure of," Thomas explained, "was that I got across the goal line in a hurry. I couldn't help but catch the ball. It was right there where you'd want it."

UH started the winning drive from the Miami 46 with 1:04 left after a punt. With no time-outs left, Mullins hit Wright for 24 and 6, and flanker Otis Stewart for 9 and a first down at the 7. Three incompletions preceded the game-winner to Thomas.

Miami's Kelley Cochrane completed 17 of 31 passes for 343 yards and four touchdowns, including a 75- and a 76-yarder to Joe Schmidt. The Hurricane had halted UH after a first down at the one, where Mullins had the ball kicked out of his hands on fourth down.

Despite squandering several scoring chances, the Cougars brushed off Tulsa, 47-14, and amassed 527 yards. Mullins passed for 179 yards and two touchdowns and scored after picking up a fumbled snap and running six yards. Strong gained 117 yards and fullback Ted Heiskell 118. The defense intercepted five passes, two of which set up touchdowns.

Within reach of a record sixth straight victory, the Cougars headed for North Carolina State, the team which had dealt them so much misery two years before. It proved to be a chilling experience with a warm afterglow.

As a 35-degree north wind swept Carter Stadium, UH taped up scoring drives of 67, 55, 56, 71, and 80 yards for a methodical 34-13 victory over the Wolfpack. Heiskell rammed for 136 yards and Strong for 100. Wright's six receptions raised his career total to a record 95. Again, the "Mad Dogs" were raging, intercepting four passes.

253

28 JIM STRONG

ALL-AMERICA RU

Co-captai
Bluebonnet Bou
the nation's r
with 1293 yard
season rushing
football's fir
most valuable
hometown: San

51 BILLY BRIDGES

ALL-AMERICA OFFENSIVE GUARD BILL BRIDGE

  Named Texas Football Player of the
Year in 1969 by the Houston Chronicle..
consensus All-America...key blocker in
UH offense that led the nation in 1968.
also named one of the outstanding colle
athletes in the nation for 1969...
hometown: Carrollton, Texas.

*All-American guard Bill Bridges (51) leads the way for Jim
Strong (28) at North Carolina State in 1969. Strong rushed for
1,293 yards and was ranked No. 4 nationally.*

Significantly, after their slow start into the season, the Cougars did not lose the ball once through an offensive mistake, and they received their reward the following Monday.

Athletic Director Harry Fouke accepted a bid from the Astro Bluebonnet Bowl to meet Auburn on New Year's eve in the Astrodome. "The coldest I've ever been was Saturday at NC State," Fouke smiled, "but I was shaking for another reason besides the temperature."

Lovette Hill, the UH baseball coach and a former football aide, noted, "I may have to stay up now New Year's eve. Usually I go to sleep at sundown to keep from gettin' run over."

Bill Bridges added, "We finally got our bowl bid, and we aren't Cougar High anymore."

Two regular season games remained—Wyoming and Florida State—and the Cougars won both to equal the 8-2 record of 1952 and 1966.

Wright caught seven passes from Mullins for 262 yards and TDs covering 45, 33, 20, and 80 yards in a 41-14 stampede past Wyoming.

Bridges helped open the way to 200 yards rushing and three scores by Strong, his third 200-yard game of the season, in a 41-13 win over Florida State.

Mullins escaped for a 51-yard scoring sprint behind Wright's two clearing blocks downfield, and safety L. D. Rowden returned his eighth interception for a 55-yard scoring play. The defense recorded 10 quarterback sacks, but the Cougars required a 21-point fourth quarter to break away from a slim 20-13 lead.

Strong compiled 1,293 yards rushing, which ranked him No. 4 nationally and second only to Paul Gipson in UH history. Strong finished as the school's No. 3 career rusher with 1,936 yards.

Bridges was chosen on the Assoc.ated Press, football writers, and football coaches All-American first teams; Strong and Wright were on the AP second team. Bridges also was voted Texas player of the year by the *Houston Chronicle*.

The Cougars placed second in NCAA total offense and rushing, fourth in scoring and tenth in rushing defense.

A sophomore named Pat Sullivan quarterbacked Auburn, which matched UH's 8-2 record and was ranked 12th and 15th in the wire service polls. But the future Heisman Trophy winner never had a chance. As Clark Nealon wrote in the *Houston Post*:

> So you wait 23 ambitious years for your shot at a major bowl, the last three grinding through the frustration of probation. In those three years you are often accused of blowing the big one.
>
> Then you get your chance against the most respected all-around team in the Southeastern Conference....Freely called your toughest test of a regular season that wound up in a blaze of touchdowns.
>
> And you bowl over mighty Auburn almost like wooden soldiers.

Shocking as the margin of their 36-7 victory was, the Cougars simply left no doubt from the opening kickoff. Charlie

Jim Strong rushed for 1,293 yards in 1969.

Hall, Frank Ditta, and Allen Sumerford applied the tackle that shook the ball loose, and Nick Holm recovered at the Auburn 29. Agreed Bill Yeoman, "It set the tone for the night."

Strong rushed to a Bluebonnet Bowl record 184 yards on 32 tries, scored from 12 yards out, and set up another with a 74-yard dash.

A regular golf companion of Bo Burris and Ken Bailey, Strong, called "Chi Chi," explained the nickname, "Bo was always Arnold Palmer, Bailey was Jack Nicklaus and I was Chi Chi Rodriguez." Strong won the game's most valuable offensive player award and Jerry Drones the outstanding defensive player award as Auburn netted a single yard rushing.

Auburn Coach Shug Jordan called the Cougars "the best team we played this year beyond a shadow of a doubt." He added, "We talked all week about the Houston offense and the Auburn offense, and maybe everybody overlooked the Houston defense. Well, they're pretty damn good."

A coach who looks on artificial grass with disfavor, Jordan concluded, "Houston would have beaten us tonight on our home field or on a foam rubber mattress."

Thus did the Cougars end the tumultuous decade of the sixties.

"Kneed" By Fate

Gary Mullins' spring practice injury struck Cougar fortunes like a knee to the mouth. Their leader, director of nine straight victories (including the 36-7 bowl game thrashing of Auburn), suffered a severe knee injury in the varsity-exes game concluding spring drills.

Even while Bill Yeoman was trying to prepare untested sophomores Terry Peel and Joel DeSpain for the season opener, surprising news surfaced: the University of Texas reportedly was ready to sponsor UH membership in the Southwest Conference at the league's winter meeting. "I think Houston could complement any conference," said Darrell Royal, refusing further comment on the sensitive discussions.

Eight defensive starters were on hand. So were offensive regulars like split end Elmo Wright, tight ends Earl Thomas and Riley Odoms, and fullback Ted Heiskell. But who would guide them?

Yeoman decided on Peel, whose older brother, Tommy, was a starting offensive guard across town for the Rice Owls. "It didn't really hit me until the pregame warmups," said Peel. "Then all of a sudden I got all weak in the knees."

With the Coogs ahead, 14-7, on Thomas' 62-yard end-around, Peel lined up the offense a foot from the UH goal with Yeoman's words still ringing in his ears:

"He told me to just to make sure I threw the ball in an arc, that I got it far enough, and that I wasn't caught in the end zone. The only thing I thought about was not getting it intercepted and not getting caught for the safety."

Flanker Robert Ford, a 5-foot-7 sophomore with sprinter speed, streaked down the sideline, outran his coverage, and turned the pass into a 99-yard scoring play. It duplicated the Bo Burris-to-Warren McVea 99-yarder in 1966 against Washington State and originated from the same end zone.

From there, the Cougars subdued Syracuse, 42-15, after a 35-7 halftime lead. Wright caught a 54-yarder from Peel (four-for-eight for 182 yards) and teamed with DeSpain on a 60-yard TD. Mullins entered the game in the fourth quarter and threw a five-yard scoring pass to Nat "Puddin" Jones.

For the third straight year Oklahoma State upended UH, snapping a 10-game winning streak, 26-17, at Stillwater. The Cougars suffered five turnovers and 152 yards in penalties.

In the week off before going to Mississippi State, Mullins

Linebacker Charlie Hall (85), shown here in the 1970 game at Oklahoma State, is on the Cougars' all-time defensive unit.

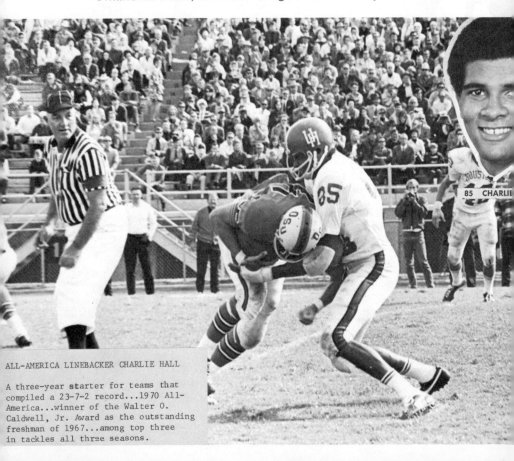

ALL-AMERICA LINEBACKER CHARLIE HALL

A three-year starter for teams that compiled a 23-7-2 record...1970 All-America...winner of the Walter O. Caldwell, Jr. Award as the outstanding freshman of 1967...among top three in tackles all three seasons.

Linebacker Frank Ditta (59), escorted by Charlie Hall (85), returns a blocked punt for touchdown against Oregon State in 1970.

explained, "I had a kind of misconception that I might re-injure the ligaments in the knee. But I've found out that was wrong. So I have a changed attitude. I'm pushing it as hard as I can. I've probably pushed it more this week than any week yet."

When UH got to Starkville Mullins told Yeoman he was ready to start again. Then Mullins threw 11 completions in 16 attempts for 173 yards; Heiskell and Tommy Mozisek ran well; and Wright caught six passes for 130 yards in the 31-14 victory.

Fortune smiled on the Cougars in a harrowing 19-16 win over Oregon State. Peel passed 22 yards to Wright in the end zone with 1:17 to play for the game-winner. Peel guided the winning drive from the UH 26 with only 3:06 to play to overcome a 16-12 deficit.

Linebacker Frank Ditta's 52-yard return of a blocked punt and Mozisek's 62-yard sprint accounted for TDs, but the defense played 45 minutes.

Mullins and State's Mark Dippel were ejected for fighting early in the fourth quarter.

Another great pass-catching show by Wright was not enough as the Cougars bowed to Alabama, 30-21. Wright caught nine passes for 112 yards and two touchdowns, all but one catch coming in the first half. After Elmo made a leaping TD catch at the side of the end zone in the final seconds of the half, NFL scout Harry Buffington exclaimed, "He's the greatest I've ever seen. He's unbelievable; how do you cover him?"

When the Tide regained the lead, 23-21, Bama's Steve Higginbotham intercepted a Mullins pass with 1:51 to play.

Halfback Johnny Musso ripped off a Crimson Tide record 156 yards rushing, threw a 15-yard touchdown pass, and caught five passes himself.

Sputtering offensively in the game between those against Alabama and Ole Miss, UH overcame a 9-0 deficit to overtake Tulsa, 21-9, after driving 84, 59, and 95 yards. Mozisek rushed for 114 yards and scored twice; Charles Ford intercepted two passes; and the defense gave up just 102 yards.

Neither Wright nor Archie Manning, Ole Miss's brilliant quarterback, was around for the finish of what proved to be the final game of the Cougar-Rebel series.

Manning suffered a broken arm early in the third quarter when tackled by linebacker Charlie Hall, and Wright hurt a knee several minutes later. Ole Miss won, 24-13.

Manning passed for 188 yards and two touchdowns in the first half, which ended in the Rebels' favor, 14-7. Mullins, unable to evade a heavy rush, threw four interceptions. Mozisek, suffering a bruised shoulder in the first half, was replaced by Robert Newhouse, who gained 148 yards.

Wright sat out the 28-0 victory over Wyoming in which Newhouse made his first start and rushed for 149 yards and a 41-yard TD. UH was unimpressive. Wyoming missed three field goals before the Cougars made their initial first down. Mullins pegged a 65-yard TD pass to Thomas while directing scoring drives of 80 and 83 yards.

The 26-2 win over Atlantic Coast Conference champion Wake Forest was distinguished by Wright's 31st career TD catch, one short of the NCAA record. "I thought we moved the ball better than any time this year," said Yeoman, "and the defense played extremely well." With two games still to play—both on the road—and Mullins getting quicker by the day after his surgery, the Cougars (6-3) were improving fast, but the bowl games were filling up.

Wright caught two touchdown passes and UH scored 41 points in the second half of their nationally televised Thanksgiving night game with Florida State at Tampa. The Cougars came back from a 21-12 halftime deficit for a 53-21 triumph as Wright's 32nd and 33rd career TD broke Howard Twilley's NCAA record.

Ford and Frank Ditta teamed up on a 70-yard interception return from the Cougars' 30 in the third quarter. Ditta ran the final 30 with Ford's lateral.

Another oddity was FSU's Dan Whitehurst coming off the Seminole bench to trip Nick Holm after an interception. FSU was assessed a 15-yard penalty.

Wright's 47-yard scoring catch from Thomas on a fake end-around put the finishing touch on his fabulous career as the Cougars thumped Miami of Florida, 36-3. Houston finished 8-3 for the season.

A week later, at the annual SWC winter meeting in Dallas, a committee was formed to study UH admission to the conference.

Elmo Wright, The Dancer

Elmo Wright used to sit in his school band, play his saxophone and watch his older brother perform on the football field. Thanks to a split lip that kept him from band practice one day, Wright became one of the greatest pass receivers in collegiate history. He also introduced the first of a now endless stream of show business antics after scoring, like "spiking" the ball and the end zone dance.

Wright set three national collegiate receiving records—including 34 career scoring passes in his three seasons (1968-70), and finished second on the all-time NCAA list with 3,347 yards receiving, surpassed only by Florida State's Ron Sellers. He also set NCAA records for average yards per catch in a career (21.9) and one season (20.2).

Now, whenever a player scores a touchdown and slams the ball down in the end zone or performs his own dancing exhibition, he unknowingly continues the trend started by Wright. He got credit for it later when he joined the National Football League, where his nickname was "Dancer."

Wright details the start of his post-TD exhibitions:

"If you want to be noticed, do something different. If you're walking down the street and want to be noticed, take your clothes off. I can remember purposely marching out of step in the band so I'd be noticed.

"The first pass I caught on the varsity was a 50- or 60-yard touchdown against Tulane. As I crossed the goal, I threw the ball on the field. People didn't know if I'd scored or not, but I

264

Elmo Wright (23), All-American split end, set three NCAA pass-catching records for the Cougars.

knew I had because I'd crossed the goal. That was my first act, and it didn't go over too well with Coach Yeoman, but I started the game against Texas. The rest of my sophomore year I spiked the ball in the end zone; then the NCAA cut it out and I thought, 'There went my whole act.'"

Wright continues, "The summer of my junior year, I'd met Steve Tannen (cornerback from Florida) at the Playboy All-American party in Chicago. He told me I wasn't going to catch any passes on him when we opened the season against Florida. Ken Bailey threw an 18- or 20-yarder, and I shook off Tannen when he tried to make the tackle. I just pranced all the way to the end zone, and I kept it up when I got in the end zone.

"They were booing me, and I was thinking, 'They really love me.' It was something people had never seen. The purpose was to get attention. Guys would tell me, 'You dance on me and I'll tackle you in the end zone or clip you.' I got letters telling me what kind of hot dog I was. I'd tell them, 'I'm going to make you famous, I'm going to dance on you.' I didn't think I was any hotshot. It gave me added incentive to score."

For years, Wright's musical career was mixed with football. "I looked at football from the third grade," he says, "when I first started playing the horn in the band, until the 11th grade. I was on the team in the tenth grade, but I just sat on the bench; then I'd be in the band at the half. It was embarrassing to my older brother, L. C., Jr., for him to be on the team and have a brother in the band.

"The band members would always throw a football around after practice, and one day the ball hit me in the mouth and split my lip. The bandmaster whipped me for getting my lip busted, and that ended my musical career. He had tutored me from the third grade to the tenth."

Wright started as a punter, "I'd sit on the bench with my fingers crossed, hoping my team wouldn't make a first down so I'd get to come in and kick. I had so much football knowledge from watching the games from the band, I was like a Monday morning quarterback. And it gave me the ability to concentrate. I could watch that ball all the way to the end of my fingertips."

As a high school senior, Wright caught 17 touchdowns among his 33 receptions as Sweeny High School won its division championship, and Wright was an all-stater.

"Seventeen players on our team got scholarships," he recalls, "but the way I really thought I'd make it out of Brazoria was by playing my saxophone.

"My older brother told me, 'Hey, you're not good enough to play college ball'; so it became a challenge to me. Then, two days before my first freshman game at UH, he was killed in a car wreck. It was an eerie feeling that game. It seemed like my head wasn't there, but I knew I had to do something for him. I caught two touchdowns and could have had a couple more. Any time after that when I was in a pressure situation, I always had that ability to concentrate, so I can say my brother helped me."

Wright had attracted the notice of Southwest Conference schools, which were then in early stages of recruiting black players. "Texas was recruiting me and another guy as their first blacks," Wright says. "He couldn't make it for some reason, and I didn't want to be the first black player alone at Texas. I visited SMU and Jerry LeVias showed me around.

"The concept of an indoor stadium like the Astrodome intrigued me about Houston. I remember back then, they had the idea of making its roof to open in good weather and close in bad weather, and I'd always wanted to play baseball in the Dome because I was on my high school team."

Still, there were hazards when Wright arrived at UH. "In practice one day before my freshman season, I almost had the ring finger on my left hand torn off. When you really concentrate, things appear in slow motion and you magnify what's happening. Rusty Clark drilled a pass; then I got hit and turned a somersault, and the ball hit my hand. When I got up, I could only see three fingers. The other one was bent back on top of my hand. The one thing that ran through my mind was, 'I can't play the horn any more.' I had no knowledge then of pass routes; I just caught the ball and ran to the end zone.

"I said, 'The masquerade is over. I'm on my way back to Brazoria.'"

But Wright went home with renewed determination: "I was going to make the team. My mother's first cousin lived two or three miles away down an asphalt road. She always had milk and cookies or cake whenever I showed up. I started running all the way from our house to hers and back. I was scared to death. I could see the opportunity of a lifetime falling on my face. I came back in superb shape because I knew I had to show what I could do."

What Wright did as a sophomore was to rewrite school records with 43 catches for 1,198 yards and 11 touchdowns. He placed second nationally in receiving yardage and touchdown catches.

Wright remembers catching an 80-yard scoring pass from Ken Bailey in the 29-7 triumph over Ole Miss in 1968 at Jackson, Mississippi: "I said later that I could tell from Ken's eyes that he knew I was going to break the pattern. And Ken

Elmo Wright (23) pulls in a touchdown pass from quarterback Gary Mullins (11) in the 1969 game with Wyoming.

said, 'You're damn right you could see it in my eyes, because they were as big as saucers when I looked up and you weren't where you were supposed to be.'"

Another memorable pass from Bailey was a long distance strike in the 10-10 tie with Georgia at Athens. "It seemed like it took forever for that ball to come down. When I'm running for the end zone I'm thinking I can fake throwing the ball down on the five and really throw it in the end zone.

"Little did I know Coach Yeoman was almost having a heart attack on the sideline when I faked it. At the same second I threw the ball down in the end zone, they shot off a cannon, and I thought they were actually shooting at me. When I came back to our bench, nobody wanted to be around me because they all thought the same thing."

Besides his natural speed and the supple hands he developed from his musical days, Wright had another attribute, "When I went in a game I was almost in a trance because of the ability I had to concentrate."

Wright, whose cousin, George Woodard, was an All-Southwest Conference fullback in 1976 at Texas A&M, retains bittersweet memories of the 1970 Ole Miss game at Oxford:

"Archie Manning (the outstanding Ole Miss quarterback) had got put out of the game earlier. I was thinking, 'In just a few games I'll be playing pro ball.' When Archie went off the field, people all stood and cheered him."

Then a few minutes later, Wright suffered a knee injury after catching a pass. "While I was lying there, I saw everything I'd worked for, my whole career, going up in smoke. Coach Yeoman ran over and stood over me, yelling at me, 'Get up! Get up and walk off this field.'

"I felt like I had to get up. I did, and walked clear around one end of the stadium to the dressing room, and I remember the people getting up and cheering me as I walked past. To this day, when I feel I just can't make it, I think of that day."

Wright missed one game, then returned to the lineup. His two touchdown catches in the season-ending 36-3 victory at Miami enabled him to break Howard Twilley's NCAA career touchdown record. Wright caught a shortie from Gary Mullins, then ended his UH career with a flair, a 47-yarder from tight end Earl Thomas on a fake end-around.

270

Besides his All-American football selections, Wright, the first round draft choice of the Kansas City Chiefs, also earned Academic All-American recognition in electrical engineering.

The Door Swings Open

May 3, 1971, is the day the Southwest Conference unlocked the gate and invited the Cougars to step through the front door. Dr. Alan Chapman of Rice made the motion to admit UH at the spring SWC meeting in College Station, and J. Neils Thompson of Texas seconded it. After nearly 20 years of often aggravating campaigning, the Cougars at last joined the club which had for so long ignored them.

After membership in the Lone Star (1946-47), Gulf Coast (1948-49) and Missouri Valley (1950-59) conferences, UH joined what is likely to be its last athletic conference, since this one was comprised of its logical neighbors and competitors.

Headlines read: "THE Marriage Benefits All"; "It's official now: UH joins SWC"; "SWC, UH both gain."

The inevitable finally happened, and logic (and economics) prevailed, even though the Cougars would not compete for the football championship until 1976.

For the eagerly-awaited first meeting with Rice, the Cougars fielded a veteran backfield—quarterback Gary Mullins, fullback Robert Newhouse, and halfback Tommy Mozisek. Tight end Riley Odoms seemed ready to reach his potential after being suspended for a curfew violation in late 1969. Charlie Moore, David Bourquin, and Steve Cloud were offensive line regulars. Other veterans were linebacker Frank Ditta, cornerback Ronny Peacock, defensive ends Bob Kyle and Kent Branstetter, and defensive tackle Mike Bolin.

At the end of the tense 23-21 UH victory over the Owls,

Morris Frank, the late *Houston Chronicle* and *Houston Post* columnist, headed for the exit and asked, "Didn't hear of anyone asking for their money back, did you?"

A two-touchdown underdog, the Owls surprised the crowd of 62,000 as they broke on top, 7-0. Bruce Gadd threw a 45-yard pass to Ed Collins, and Mike Phillips plunged the final yard 40 seconds before halftime. Mullins quickly got it back after intermission, hooking up with flanker Del Stanley for a 73-yard scoring pass on the first play. Stanley was a transfer from West Texas State and a walk-on. His first Cougar reception paid off handsomely.

Mullins then threw a flat zone pass to Robert Ford, who darted 11 yards to score behind Odoms' block to end a 77-yard advance. A Rice deep back stepped out of bounds at the one with the kickoff, and Butch Brezina caused a fumble that brought two points when Rice recovered in the end zone for a safety.

A roughing the passer penalty and another for pass interference that nullified Nick Holm's interception preceded Stahle Vincent's three-yard plunge, and Rice cut the UH lead to 16-14 with 12:45 to play.

Mullins' off-balance pass was intercepted by Bruce Henley and returned 30 yards to the UH 16. Mullins then saved his team from enduring embarrassment. He whacked Henley solidly, and Moore recovered Henley's fumble. "It was do-or-die," Mullins recalled. "I said, 'I've got to make the tackle.' I had to call on my old linebacker days."

From there Mullins took the Cougars 84 yards to the clincher. Newhouse broke for 21, then, driving through several tacklers, churned for 20 to the two. Mullins sneaked over for the touchdown and a 23-14 lead with 2:04 left. Gadd's final 20-yard pass to Collins closed the margin with 55 seconds remaining.

Afterwards, Cougars and Owls, once sworn enemies, walked up the ramp off the field together. "Hey, Bruce Gadd," UH assistant Ben Hurt put his arm around Gadd's back, "you guys did a hell of a job."

Said Brezina, "I wanted this one so bad. Four of my brothers played at UH before I did, and they always wanted the chance to play Rice and never got it. I got the chance, and I didn't want it to slip away."

Sophomore Woody Green and a 28-year-old army veteran, Dan Ekstrand, came off the Arizona State bench to deal the Cougars a painful 18-17 defeat at Tempe. Ekstrand rammed a 46-yard field goal with 19 seconds left for the Sun Devils' 18th straight victory, and Green rushed for 117 yards on 21 carries.

Newhouse's eighth straight 100-yard rushing game helped the Cougars struggle past Cincinnati, 12-3. Despite the wet Astroturf at Nippert Stadium, Newhouse still ground out 237 yards on 31 carries, and Leonard Parker nudged out 149 on 31 tries. UH lost five turnovers and 123 yards in penalties.

Ditta, son of a 1946 co-captain, hauled an intercepted pass

Frank Ditta, 1971 co-captain, followed in the footsteps of his father, Tony, who was co-captain of first Houston team in 1946.

100 yards in the third quarter to bring the Cougars from a 13-12 deficit against San Jose State and trigger a 34-20 victory. Ditta actually caught the ball a yard deep in the end zone.

"If it had been 10 yards more, I would have had to crawl over the goal," Ditta admitted. "I didn't slow down; I just ran out of gas." His third career TD (following a blocked pass and another interception) may have resulted because he was only 5-foot-10. Ditta reasoned: "If I'd been 6-4 or 6-5, he might have seen me. I don't think he'd ever have thrown that pass if he'd known I was there."

Later, Deryl McGallion, who replaced the tired Ditta, returned another interception 40 yards for a touchdown. Odoms caught 40- and 66-yard scores from Mullins.

Four touchdowns in a five-minute stretch of the first quarter quickly settled the issue in a 42-9 strapping of Villanova. Mullins ran for two touchdowns, passed for another, and broke Burris's career total offense record by bringing his total to 3,674 yards. Newhouse rushed for 139 yards, and sophomore quarterback D. C. Nobles accounted for 218 yards.

A three-touchdown underdog to Alabama, the nation's No. 4 ranked team, the Cougars moved the ball well offensively at Tuscaloosa, Alabama, but could not solve the Tide's wishbone offense. Houston lost 34-20. The game featured two superb running backs, UH's Newhouse, who rushed for 182 yards, and Bama's Johnny Musso, who gained 123. Both carried the ball 23 times. David Bailey's two scoring passes from Terry Davis were a big factor, while Odoms caught two short TD passes and had a third nullified by a penalty.

The assignment was a complete opposite the next week. Houston's opponent was Florida State, led by quarterback Gary Huff, the nation's No. 1 passer. UH managed a 14-7 victory before Gator and Bluebonnet Bowl scouts. The defense intercepted two of Huff's passes on the goal and another in the end zone. He completed 17 of 31 for 286 yards but double coverage on Rhett Dawson and Barry Smith prevented the deep pass.

Newhouse pounded for 192 yards on 34 carries against another Top 20 team.

Dividing their 472 yards almost evenly between running and passing, the Cougars dispatched Memphis State, 35-7. Newhouse rushed for more than 100 yards for the 12th time in 13

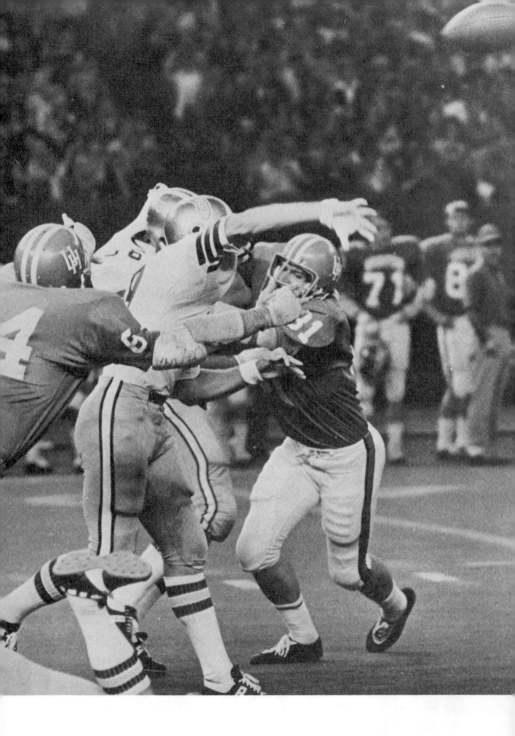

Defensive ends Butch Brezina (64) and Bill Stohler (81) pressure Florida State quarterback Gary Huff in the 1971 game.

games.

Newhouse (201) and Mozisek (195) staged a two-man running exhibit, combining for 396 yards rushing, in a 56-29 rout of Virginia Tech. Newhouse scored three times. Mullins passed for 3 touchdowns and set a school record with 36 TD passes in a career.

The pass rush, improved by the insertion of Bill Stohler at end and Thomas Ward at linebacker, sacked Tech's Don Strock, the national leader in passing and total offense, five times.

A few hours before the kickoff with Miami, of Florida, the Cougars accepted a New Year's Eve date in the Bluebonnet Bowl against Colorado. Houston had problems getting back to the business at hand. They led only 6-0 at the half before subduing the Hurricane, 27-6. Chuck Foreman rushed for 148 yards.

Soaring over teammate Craig Robinson (52), Robert Newhouse scores a Houston touchdown.

"I was glad to escape that one," said Yeoman.

"It took us the whole first quarter to get the bowl talk out of our systems," admitted split end Pat Orchin.

Once again, Newhouse churned out his 100 yards rushing (30 for 145) and broke Paul Gipson's one-season record of 1,500 yards.

Four touchdowns in the last half carried the Cougars to a 42-16 decision over Utah and a 9-2 regular season record. It was not easy, for UH trailed at the half, 16-14, before Newhouse stomped out 204 yards and two touchdowns, Mullins passed for one and ran for two. "I knew we couldn't hold them forever," said Utah Coach Bill Meek, former head coach of the Cougars.

Newhouse ended the season with 1,757 yards rushing, a school record and second in collegiate history. He increased his career total to another UH record of 2,961 yards and fumbled just seven times in 277 carries.

Odoms' 45 catches had been exceeded in a season only by Elmo Wright.

Riley Odoms, All-American tight end in 1971, pulls in pass.

RILEY ODOMS

Colorado, 9-2 like UH and ranked No. 7 nationally, scored a 29-17 victory over the Cougars in the Astro Bluebonnet Bowl, thanks largely to the running of a Texan. Halfback Charlie Davis of West Columbia gained 202 yards on 37 carries to win the outstanding offensive player award. Butch Brezina was voted the top defensive player, and Newhouse gained 168 yards on 35 tries.

Butch Brezina (right) receives an award as the most valuable lineman of the 1971 Astro Bluebonnet Bowl from Lloyd Gregory of the bowl committee.

Loser only to No. 1 Nebraska and No. 2 Oklahoma, the Buffs used a heads-up play by punter John Stearns in the fourth quarter to hold off the Cougars. With Colorado ahead only 23-17 late in the fourth quarter, Stearns was back to punt on fourth and nine at his 10.

After he fielded a low snap from center, he looked up and noticed no one was rushing him. Stearns raced 12 yards for a first down.

From there the Buffs drove to the touchdown that put them out of reach with 3:48 to play. A 32-yard interference penalty on a pass to Cliff Branch kept the drive going for the big, physical Buffs.

Stearns made another vital play before his fourth down run. He slapped down an end zone pass to a wide-open Odoms.

"The biggest I've seen," Mullins described the victors. "Size, speed, strength—they had it all."

Defensive coordinator Melvin Robertson and defensive line coach Ben Hurt departed to take similar positions on Emory Bellard's Texas A&M staff. Yeoman concluded the year by saying, "Let's go out and get some recruits."

Gary Mullins,
The Little Leader

Nearsighted, short (5-foot-9½), and stocky (195 pounds), Gary Mullins was hardly the picture of a classic football quarterback. Yet he became the first quarterback to direct the Cougars to two bowl games, and his passing and total offense figures when he left surpassed those of all-time Southwest Conference greats like Don Meredith, Bobby Layne, Fred Benners, and Sammy Baugh.

What Mullins did best, however, is shown by the Cougars' won-loss record under his stewardship—25-5, including one of the school's greatest nights, the 36-7 thrashing of Auburn in the 1969 Astro Bluebonnet Bowl.

A flock of great receivers, most notably All-Americans Elmo Wright and Riley Odoms and tight end Earl Thomas, contributed to Mullins' passing success.

But there was another factor, just as important. "I wasn't going to outrun them but I'll outbrain them," was Mullins' philosophy.

Mullins was an all-state quarterback for San Angelo Central's Class 4A state champions. His high school coach was Emory Bellard, now the head coach at Texas A&M, who called Mullins, "The greatest leader I ever saw on a football field."

Gary's father, Fagan (also called "Moon," like Gary) was a widely-known football coach in West Texas, where he coached at Anson, Crane, Cisco Junior College, and San Angelo Lakeview.

Billy Joe, and Larry Jack, Gary's older brothers, also had

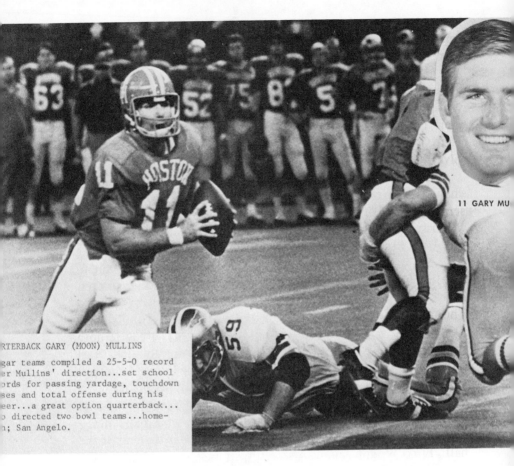

11 GARY MU

*Gary Mullins directed the Cougars to two bowl games and a
25-5 record as a starting quarterback.*

been high school quarterbacks. Larry played for Coach Bellard.
Raymond, a linebacker, played at UH with Gary.

"First game I ever saw UH play was Tulsa on national TV
in 1965, the first game in the Dome," Gary says. "I'd made up
my mind I wanted to play quarterback in college. Melvin
Robertson (then a UH assistant) was a good friend of my father.
I visited Texas, SMU and A&M, but UH was the only school
that didn't involve defense (he had also been a standout high
school linebacker).

"Under Coach Bellard we ran the option offense with a
wing T and full T. I felt well adjusted to the veer because of my

high school experience in the option. The veer fascinated me. It can frustrate opposing coaches, and then it frustrates their players. When we beat Ole Miss in 1969, we'd call plays at the line and their rover got to where he was jumping back and forth because wherever he lined up, we were going the other way."

Mullins watched from the sidelines as the Cougars began their 1969 season with a loss to Florida in the opener, 59-34. The Gator passing combination of John Reaves to Carlos Alvarez, then as unknown as Mullins, devastated UH.

After a 24-18 loss at Oklahoma State, Bill Yeoman changed quarterbacks. He elevated Mullins to No. 1 ahead of senior starter Ken Bailey. Mullins' first start was the 74-0 rout of Mississippi State, the first of nine straight victories leading to the Astro Bluebonnet Bowl.

No. 4 in the victory string was the 38-36 scrape past Miami of Florida. The victory kept the Cougars in the running for their first major bowl appearance. Mullins' touchdown pass to Thomas in the final minute of play brought them from behind.

"There were 11 seconds left," Mullins says. "I made a note of that mentally because that was my uniform number. Earl said he'd be there in the end zone, I just had to get the ball there.

"I was floored as I threw it, and I was sticking my head up from the ground, like an ostrich, trying to see what happened."

Mullins recalls, "I'd been knocked out near the end of the half. Elmo Wright caught a screen pass and looked like he was going to break loose. I was in the middle of things and saw this linebacker looking off downfield. I thought I'd just put a shot on him, and he caught me with his knee in the head and kept on going. He probably never even felt me."

After that Miami game, Mullins' father gave him a bit of advice, "Son, when you go over to the bench to talk to Coach Yeoman, hustle more, don't slouch."

Mullins praises the support he got from the man he supplanted, Ken Bailey, and from Rusty Clark, another senior quarterback. "Ken kept a light air about things. He always had the ability to keep things 'loose.' He kept the tempo going and gave a lot of encouragement, so did Rusty."

Significantly, after the season Bailey won the school's Charles Saunders Award as the outstanding senior athlete. The honor is based on scholarship, leadership, and sportsmanship.

The next spring, the situation changed traumatically for Mullins. In the final spring game, which matched the varsity against the exes, Mullins suffered a severe knee injury which left his football future—and the Cougars'—in doubt.

"We'd run 18 veer, the option to the left," Mullins recalls, "and Jerry Drones was the defensive end. I'd handed off the first time, and the play got about two yards. This time I kept the ball, and darned if Drones wasn't outside this time. So I cut inside and the pursuit got me."

Mullins took a hard hit on the knee while his leg was twisted—"to me it sounded like a 30.06 going off in my head," he says. "Tom Wilson (Houston's athletic trainer) gave up his whole summer. I was determined to play, but he told me it would be hard for me to play at all next year, if ever. I remember while I was in the hospital Tom telling me that he didn't know if I'd be able to ever play, even knowing how hard I'd work, but he'd hang with me. It was a very emotional time for both of us."

After the surgery for ligament damage, Mullins began the long hours of rehabilitation, supervised by Wilson. By the third game of the 1970 season, Mullins was back at quarterback— starting again against Mississippi State.

Even after directing UH to another Astro Bluebonnet Bowl appearance, in 1971 against Colorado, Mullins says, "After the injury I didn't feel I was back to where I was before. Sometimes I'd think maybe I didn't pay the dues I was supposed to be paying."

After the injury to Mullins, Yeoman began withholding the starting quarterback from the final spring game.

At the end of his career Mullins ranked first in career total offense at UH with 4,698 yards and No. 1 in career passing yardage (4,095), records he still holds. His 245 completions are a UH career record, so are his 37 touchdown passes.

"I had small hands so I worked at squeezing a rubber ball, doing curls to strengthen my grip," Mullins says. "I was fortunate to have great receivers like Elmo, Riley, Earl, Pat Orchin, Robert Ford, and Del Stanley."

Mullins describes the 1969 bowl game with Auburn as "a super high for me. I came while the school was on probation,

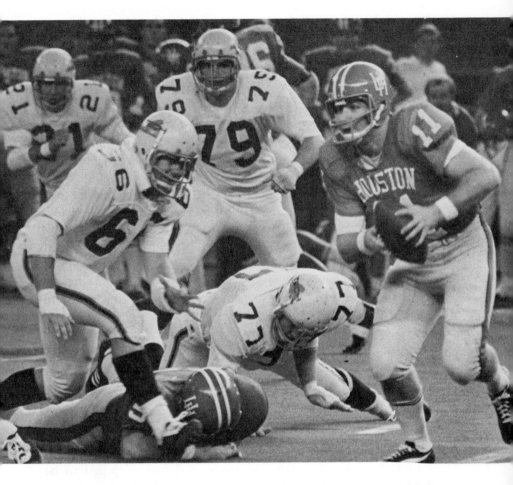

*Gary Mullins (11), who quarterbacked the Cougars to a 25-5
record as a starter, goes along the line on an option play against
Virginia Tech in 1971.*

and those teams were super. The 1969 team to me was special, a
close-knit bunch. We were always together. It was a perfect
challenge for me, because Auburn had Pat Sullivan at quarterback, and I enjoyed playing against quarterbacks with reputa-
tions. Once we came back and won the Miami game, it convinced us, 'We're not going to get beat unless we beat ourselves.' We heard those 'War Eagle' yells late at night from their
fans at the hotel next to us.

"Ole Miss was a grudge game for me. I'd played against

285

Jack Mildren and Bill Montgomery in high school, and now Archie Manning. Plus I'd thought about maybe going to Ole Miss and Alabama. It meant a lot when Bear Bryant said the nice things about me that he said after our Alabama game in 1970."

Now a UH assistant coach, Mullins believes, "Coach Yeoman has a tremendous amount of confidence in what he believes, a great drive, and faith in his staff. The others feel his confidence. Without a doubt, because of the veer he will have made one of the greatest impacts on college football."

Though Yeoman sent in plays from the bench, Mullins at times would come to the sideline to discuss a difference of opinion. "Those were just consultations," he explains. "I never overruled Coach Yeoman."

The game-week routine was always the same for Mullins: "Starting on Wednesday I was so keyed up I couldn't eat. All I could get down was coffee. I wasn't ready until I threw up before the game. In high school, Coach Bellard wouldn't take us out on the field until then. At UH, if I didn't get sick before, they'd tell me, 'You're not up for the game.'"

And how does a stumpy, not very fast, nearsighted quarterback succeed? "Have the constitution of a bulldog," Mullins replies. "Keep biting."

Robert Newhouse, Churning "Gator"

After sitting on the bench for his first two varsity games, Robert "Gator" Newhouse took the direct approach to get into the Cougar lineup. He walked out on the Astroturf the night UH was playing Mississippi State in 1969 and told fullback Ted Heiskell, "I'm coming in for you."

At the end of the 74-0 rout, Newhouse had churned out 245 yards on 23 carries, including 71- and 1-yard scoring runs. That was also Gary Mullins' first appearance at quarterback, and it seemed the Cougars suddenly had two new stars.

But Newhouse, despite his ingenuity, had to wait his turn. His chance was delayed by an almost fatal auto accident the next summer. But Newhouse already had shown his ruggedness. He recalls the car crash which he survived: "About two weeks before the season opener my junior year, my wife's father passed away, and I was going to the funeral. After our workout that day, Elmo Wright and I and several others went over to a prof's house for dinner, and I started driving home late.

"Up near Lufkin there was a car driving without lights on the side of the road. There was a wreck, and when I woke up, I was in the ditch with blood all over me. I'd been thrown out the right side of my VW, and had knocked off the door."

Bruised and sore, Newhouse returned to campus, but several weeks passed before he shook off the effects. Newhouse relates another chapter which occurred in 1976, his fifth season with the Dallas Cowboys.

"I had some X-rays taken because of a leg injury, and they

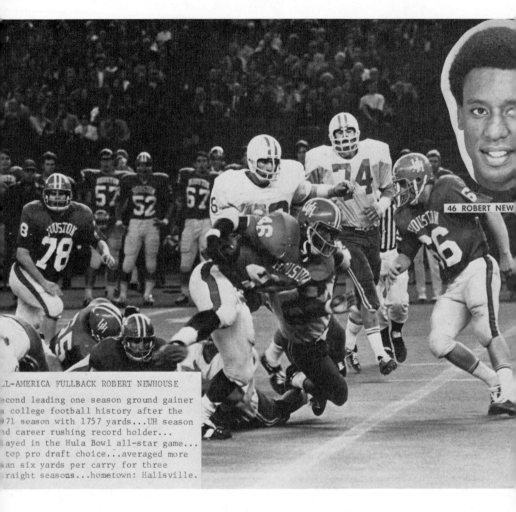

.L-AMERICA FULLBACK ROBERT NEWHOUSE
cond leading one season ground gainer
college football history after the
971 season with 1757 yards...UH season
d career rushing record holder...
ayed in the Hula Bowl all-star game...
top pro draft choice...averaged more
an six yards per carry for three
raight seasons...hometown: Hallsville.

Robert Newhouse rushed for 1,757 yards in 1971, second highest in NCAA history.

showed I'd had a cracked pelvis which had healed by itself. I'd spent the night of that wreck in the hospital but never had X rays."

By 1971, however, Newhouse was primed, and his senior season stands as one of the finest running performances in NCAA history.

Newhouse rushed for 1,757 yards that season, second best in NCAA annals. Cornell's Ed Marinaro set a collegiate record with his 1,881 yards, but Newhouse carried 79 less times, and his 6.34 average per carry exceeded Marinaro's 5.28.

The 2,961 yards rushing that Newhouse compiled in 1969-70-71 stands as a UH career record, and he played only one year as a full-time starter!

"My senior year, it seemed to me that I could do nothing wrong," he recalls. "Everything just went right."

Equipment manager Jack Littlefield ran into peculiar problems when he tried to outfit Newhouse.

Newhouse said, "I never had a pair of shoes fit me all through high school or my first two years at UH." Another problem was his football pants. "Only thing I really disliked about football was having to wear those baggy pants to get them to fit. In high school we just had one pair to practice in and also to play in."

Littlefield had the size 10½-quadruple-E football shoes Newhouse needed made by a Houston sporting goods dealer. "He's like an upside-down pyramid," Littlefield described Newhouse, who was barely 5-foot-9 and weighed 200. "His shoes are five and a quarter inches wide across the bottom of the ball of the foot."

Newhouse had to wear a size 36 waist, about six inches too large, then have them cut down to accommodate his massive legs and 26-inch thighs.

By season's end he'd also battered five or six helmets. "He'd flatten the padding inside them so much, he could nearly spin them around on his finger," Littlefield noted.

"Gator," Newhouse's nickname at UH, did not stem from his physique, running style, or toughness. Instead, a roommate thought of it after noting his lengthy sleeping habits.

Like many outstanding UH players, including Bo Burris, Cotton Guerrant, Dick Post, Charlie Hall, Jerry Drones, Rich Stotter, and Jim Strong, Newhouse was practically unnoticed in high school.

He lived on a farm about 20 miles from Galilee High School in Hallsville, a sleepy east Texas town five miles from Longview. "There were 26 in my senior class, and 18 to 22 on the football team," Newhouse says. "For excitement, we'd run up and down those black-top roads, steal watermelons, and go fishing."

Bobby Baldwin, then a UH assistant and a former UH player himself, heard tales of Newhouse from the bread delivery-man at the athletic dorm. The deliveryman's brother coached in the same district. The school was too poor to film its games, so Baldwin, impressed by what he heard, went to see Newhouse in person.

"The first I knew about UH was the day Coach Baldwin showed up at the school with a big, red jacket on and said he'd heard of me," Newhouse says. "If I hadn't gone there, I proba-bly would have gone to East Texas State on an academic grant." A cousin, Fred Newhouse, was a world-class quarter-miler at Prairie View A&M and won a gold medal at the Montreal Olympics as a member of the victorious U.S. 1600 meter relay.

Assistant Coach Melvin Brown described Robert's running style, "We talk about the Gator Walk. You knock his legs side-ways or out from under him, and he finds some way to get his feet back underneath. When you hit Gator, you know you've hit something. Like a brick wall."

A Brief Slump,
Then Another Bonnet

No way could Bill Yeoman be optimistic about the prospects for 1972. Contemplating the loss of quarterback Gary Mullins, runners Robert Newhouse and Tommy Mozisek, tight end Riley Odoms (a first round NFL draftee) and eight defensive starters, Yeoman figured, "We have not fielded a team as young in 10 years."

Quarterback D. C. Nobles had logged 29 minutes of experience. Flanker Del Stanley, the walk-on who caught the 73-yard TD against Rice, had been added to the scholarship list.

Yeoman's pessimism was proved correct when Rice defeated the Cougars, 14-13, in the season opener. The Owls fought off UH at their one on the game's final play.

"This city belongs to you now," an exultant Al Conover told the Owls after his first game as Rice's head coach.

With 2:17 remaining, Nobles directed the Cougars from their 23. They used their final time-out en route, and on the final play Nobles' swing pass to "Puddin" Jones carried 12 yards to the 1. "I thought it was a touchdown," Nobles said later.

"I thought I was over the line," Jones added, "but the official marked it on the one, so I just don't know."

"There are people who get paid for that (marking the ball's progress), and it's not my job," Yeoman added. "I'm just not going to say."

Mark Williams kicked both Rice extra points, but a fouled-up placement ruined UH's second conversion try. Bruce

Gadd passed to Ed Collins for both Rice touchdowns.

Several days before, UH safety Burl Fuller noted he had phoned Gadd the previous year, after the Cougars' 23-21 victory: "I called him up just before we got on the bus to go to the airport and leave for Arizona State. I just wanted to wish him a lot of luck that Saturday and the rest of the year."

In their televised rematch with Arizona State the next week, UH trailed, 20-0, in the first quarter and 33-21 with six minutes left before the situation became exciting. Linebacker Harold Evans blocked a Sun Devil field goal, and Nobles followed with a 46-yard scoring pass to Marshall Johnson. Evans, voted the game's outstanding defensive player, earlier had returned an interception 17 yards for a touchdown.

With the score, 33-28 (the way it ended), Nobles flung another 46-yard scoring pass to Johnson with four minutes left, but a clipping penalty nullified it. Still, the Cougars drove to a first down at the four, where Nobles lost a fumble.

Once again, Woody Green bedeviled the UH defense, this time gaining 195 yards on 36 tries. Brent McClanahan added 121 on 21 carries.

The Cougars defeated Tulsa, 21-0, for their first victory, then rallied from 21-7 and 27-14 deficits for a 27-27 tie at Virginia Tech. Nobles ended a 90-yard fourth quarter drive with a 6-yard pass to Miller Bassler; then Nobles connected from the 20 to Bryan Willingham. With 72 seconds left, the potentially winning extra point went wide.

VPI's Don Strock completed 34 passes for 527 yards, including 20 for 27 and 301 yards in the first half. Jones ran for 162 yards for UH.

For the second time in three years, Terry Peel and Robert Ford repeated their 99-yard touchdown act, this time against San Diego State. The Cougars burned the unbeaten Aztecs, 49-14. Ford caught seven passes for 231 yards and three touchdowns.

Peel, substituting in the third quarter for Nobles, thought the only 99-yard repeat in college history was "...spooky. It was like when you dream something, and wake up, and feel you've been there before. It was the same end of the field and the same play. Robert caught the one against Syracuse (in 1970) on the 33 and this one on the 35. He told me, 'When you got in the

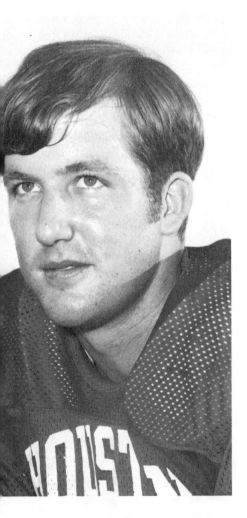

Quarterback Terry Peel (left) and flanker Robert Ford, who combined for two 99-yard scoring passes, in 1970 and 1972.

huddle and told them to give you three seconds, and you looked down the line at me, I knew what was coming.'"

After a 33-13 whipping at Miami, the Cougars permitted three touchdowns in the final six minutes and lost at Mississippi State, 27-13. In the next game the Cougars handed Florida State its second loss in eight starts, 31-27.

A three-man defensive line helped defend against Gary Huff, the nation's No. 2 passer. Huff completed 27 of 51 for 409 yards. Johnson debuted at halfback with a 120-yard day.

UH followed a 48-13 sacking of winless Colorado State with a 33-14 decision over New Mexico. In that game Jones broke the 1,000-yard rushing figure for the year with a 184-yard performance.

A fourth straight triumph, 49-0 over Cincinnati, brought a final 6-4-1 record. Jones' 145-yard night brought his season rushing total to 1,216 yards, No. 4 in UH history. Nobles completed a record 101st pass.

"A year makes a tremendous difference," said Yeoman before the first kickoff for 1973, and it was obvious.

For starters, D. C. Nobles had a full season of experience under his belt, and tank-like fullback Leonard Parker was

"Puddin" Jones evades tacklers at Florida State in 1972.

healthy again and ready to increase the list of 1,000-yard rushers. Nine defensive starters awaited the opener with Rice, including the entire front four and the three linebackers.

Reggie Cherry recovered his fumble in the end zone for the go-ahead touchdown. Later he waded through tacklers from 18 yards out in the fourth quarter to seal a 24-6 victory.

Assistant Melvin Brown described Cherry's sprint, "That was unreal; it was a super run. Once he jumped over one guy who had come in to tackle him and when he did, he landed in the middle of two others. Somehow he got away from both of them. Cherry has real cutting ability and he knows when to make the cut. That comes from experience. Now Marshall Johnson has more speed than Cherry. Not just a little more, a whole lot more. Parker gives you the solid toughness and strength. He's not very fast, but he's one tough son of a gun."

Nobles passed for 118 yards and ran for 96.

Parker (135) and Cherry (102) each gained 100 yards and the Cougars bested South Carolina and its version of the veer, 27-19. Ken Baugh, 240, and 280-pound Everett Little steadily pounded holes in the left side of the Gamecock defense for the backs, and Nobles operated deftly.

Carolina's Jay Lynn Hodgin's 93-yard kickoff return closed the gap to 17-13 before Parker poured the coals to a 70-yard scoring march. The Cougars offset a final South Carolina score with a field goal.

"It's been a while since I saw a finer team," said Paul Dietzel. "They manhandled us up front."

Nobles, a protege of UH assistant Elmer Redd at Lufkin Dunbar, fought a constant weight problem. He began the season with less than 170 pounds on his 6-foot-1 frame. He also had to remember not to throw off his back foot and overthrow.

The habit began when D. C. (his real name) played fireman back in Lufkin. Visiting his girl friend, he smelled smoke, ran outside, and noticed a neighbor's house ablaze. He broke a window and helped bring out the furniture, but lodged a hunk of glass in his left heel.

"It wasn't just a sliver but a hunk," Redd explained. "That's where that habit started. When he doesn't rush, he's a picture thrower with the quickest arm and wrist around."

Nobles' 23-yard pass to Miller Bassler, Bassler's first catch

D. C. Nobles (3) quarterbacked the 1973 Cougars to an 11-1 record.

of the season, broke a 14-14 tie with 13 seconds left in the first half at Memphis State. D. C. then guided an 80-yard thrust with the second half kickoff and the Cougars won, 35-21. Parker hung up 133 yards.

Thanks to Cherry, Johnson, and Parker the Cougars compiled an unusual "triple" in an impressive 14-9 victory at San Diego State. Each of the trio gained over 100 yards. Parker gained 152, Johnson 126, and Cherry 103 as the Cougars rushed for 442 yards, the most ever surrendered by the Aztecs. Cherry's 84-yard run was UH's longest ever from scrimmage.

San Diego quarterback Jesse Freitas completed 21 of 38 passes for 265 yards but suffered four interceptions, and his team could rush for just 52 yards.

UH staged an 85-yard drive, all on the ground, after Howard Ebow's interception in the second quarter. Cherry's long dash at the right corner led to the second touchdown early in the third period. Ebow made a second diving interception at the 20 and Jeff Bouche another at the 39 in the last quarter.

"Leonard is so consistent and persistent," Brown said. "They get tired of tackling Leonard. Baugh, Little, and Max Vater did excellent jobs in the offensive line. We've been using an unbalanced line against a 5-2 defense so that Little can go against the nose guard. He's just so big and strong. He's coming fast. You couldn't miss the linebackers, especially Howard Evans. He's so quick. He had two big fourth down stops."

The Cougars required a 40-point second half to get past Virginia Tech, 54-27. Larry Jefferson returned the second half kickoff 95 yards to put UH ahead, 21-17, and Ebow's interception and 25-yard return three plays later led to Nobles' five-yard keeper.

Parker rushed for 119 yards and Nobles for 100. Frank Scalise caught a 43-yard TD pass from Nobles.

Nobles' passing form was exceptional at Miami, where the Cougars scored three touchdowns and a field goal in the second half to wrap up their sixth straight victory, 30-7.

Nobles completed 13 of 22 for 223 yards and one touchdown. Cherry rushed for 104 yards, including a 66-yard scoring run, and caught an 8-yard TD pass from Nobles.

Then Auburn brought the Cougars to a screeching halt, 7-0. UH did not commit a single turnover on offense, gained a substantial 310 yards to Auburn's 192, yet failed to score for the first time in 81 games.

Auburn staged a 51-yard drive midway through the first quarter; then the Cougars missed field goals of 32 and 31 yards.

In the last four minutes, Houston stalled after reaching the 12.

Parker blasted out 155 yards and two touchdowns; Donnie McGraw got 94 yards and one touchdown; and the Cougars scorched Florida State, 34-3. Nobles contributed to the 606-yard performance by passing for 189 yards and slithering for 56 on just four carries. He threw an 83-yard TD to Bryan Willingham, who caught four passes for 134 yards.

Troublesome Colorado State fell, 28-20, at Fort Collins as Parker tunneled for 200 yards and two scores on 35 carries. He also became UH's seventh 1,000-yard rusher, joining Gene Shannon, Dick Post, Paul Gipson (who did it twice), Jim Strong, Robert Newhouse and "Puddin" Jones. Robert Giblin's interception at the 19 and Nobles' three-yard pass to Marty Watts in the third period widened the dangerously thin 20-14 halftime lead.

The next week was Nobles' turn to put on a great running show. He gained 126 yards on 13 carries and scored the first 14 points in a 35-0 romp over Wyoming. McGraw (14 for 114) also joined in the century act.

Leonard Parker, one of seven Cougar 1,000-yard rushers.

Assured of their third Bluebonnet Bowl in five years, the Cougars trailed Tulsa, 16-0, at the half before regrouping for a 35-16 win and a 10-1 regular season record, their most successful ever.

Within a three and a half minute span of the fourth quarter, Johnson darted 42 yards for one score and passed 34 yards to Frank Scalise for the decisive points. McGraw gained 129 yards on 17 carries, Johnson 120 on 18.

Parker finished the year with 1,123 yards. UH ranked fourth nationally in total offense, fifth in rushing defense, seventh in rushing offense, and tenth in total defense.

Then the Cougars "played like a team on a crusade," ambushing Tulane, 47-7, in the Astro Bluebonnet bowl and gaining their first finish ever in the Top 10. The AP ranked them ninth in its final poll.

Nobles was superb and so were the "Mad Dogs." The defense held Tulane to four first downs in the second half. Said Yeoman, "This is the best football team I've had at the University of Houston."

Linebacker Deryl Ray McGallion, voted the game's outstanding defensive player, added, "People have looked down on us, but when we play someone to compare with and we win big, it should prove something."

A Top 20 team before the game and 9-2 in regular season,

Linebacker Deryl McGallion (left) and defensive end Mack Mitchell, key defensive players on the 11-1 team of 1973.

Receiving a free ride is Bill Yeoman after Houston's 1973 Astro Bluebonnet Bowl triumph over Tulane.

Tulane suffered its worst defeat in 66 games, dating back to the 54-7 loss in 1968 to UH. Of their 655 yards total offense, the Cougars compiled 288 on seven long yardage plays. Among them was Johnson's 75-yard dash in the first quarter. Nobles also passed 60 yards to Bassler to set up one touchdown and 61 yards to Willingham for another TD. McGraw shook loose from 32 yards away. Johnson (5 for 114) and McGraw (13 for 108) were the leading runners. Nobles, chosen the outstanding offensive player, completed 8 of 13 passes for 201 yards.

"I really felt terrible before this game," D. C. admitted. "I've had a bad cold. Deep down inside I didn't feel we were ready, and I was worried. The fellas just played great."

Ahead only 21-7 at the half, the Cougars were backed up to their three-yard line. But Nobles, throwing from his end zone, connected with Willingham for 60. Four plays later, four tacklers ganged up on McGraw only to discover Nobles had the ball, and he scored easily from the two.

Roger Mayes then plucked a Tulane fumble out of midair on the kickoff, and the Cougars were camped on the Greenies' 20. McGraw carried three straight times for the second touchdown in 74 seconds.

"I know this team has had a certain amount of recognition," Yeoman said, "but not nearly what it deserves. This team can play football, and they can play football with anybody in the United States. I mean anybody."

A Tough Act To Follow

Ranked in most of the preseason top 10 lists, the Cougars seemed to face bright prospects for 1974. Among 16 returning starters were the defensive front four of Larry Keller, Wilson Whitley, Lee Canalito, and Mack Mitchell. There were runners like Marshall Johnson, Donnie McGraw, and Reggie Cherry behind an experienced offensive line.

But then came the crunch. "Any time you lose your trigger man, you're in a little bit of a bind," said Bill Yeoman, who had signed a new five-year contract the preceding spring. "D. C. Nobles was as good a college quarterback as there was in the country last year."

David Husmann, Nobles' successor, played the final quarter of the 47-7 bowl game lacing of Tulane but just 26 minutes of the regular season. The Cougars left town for three of their first five games, including the season opener at Arizona State.

Freddie Williams' 69-yard bolt in the first quarter started a long evening for the Cougars at Tempe, Arizona, where they bowed, 30-9. Houston suffered six turnovers and allowed Williams 178 rushing yards.

Then the computer printout went wrong. Donnie "Quick Draw" McGraw journeyed 91 yards with Husmann's pitchout off an option play and the Cougars stunningly reversed the momentum, defeating Rice, 21-0.

The Cougars fumbled on the game's first play, and Rice recovered at the UH 13. Then, on first down at the UH one,

Tommy Kramer fumbled, and Mark Mohr recovered for Houston. Three plays later it was third and two when McGraw, a 9.4 high school sprinter, streaked around left end for the longest run from scrimmage in UH history.

Afterwards, Rice Coach Al Conover noted, "Our computer told us it was a thousand to one shot they'd do that at that time. We were pinching them in. Our defensive end was supposed to smack the quarterback, and that's just what he did...It was a calculated risk that didn't work. They really fooled us."

McGraw got his fitting nickname in elementary school: "We were running and I hadn't raced the fastest cat in the class yet. So I raced him and beat him, and he wanted to race again, and I beat him again. They started calling me Quick Draw, and it stuck."

Miami, of Florida, gained revenge with a 21-3 televised thumping of the Cougars in the third game as Woody Thompson rushed for 85 yards, and middle guard Rubin Carter helped clamp down the UH offense.

"With them double and triple teaming me I knew our tackles would give them hell," said Carter. "Last year they put it on us pretty good, and we came out to get revenge."

Four first half touchdowns provided the spark for a 49-12 victory at Virginia Tech. Roger Mayes blocked a Tech punt that Mark Mohr returned for the second score, and Guy Brown's fumble recovery set up the third. Reserve fullback John Housman rushed for 117 yards and two touchdowns.

With Housman starting for the first time, and Bubba McGallion taking over at quarterback in the fourth quarter, the Cougars overhauled South Carolina, 24-14, at Columbia, South Carolina.

McGallion raced for 23 on his first carry and sent Johnson across from the 11 to tie the score. Joe Rust's fumble recovery on the Gamecocks' first play led to another Johnson touchdown, and Lennard Coplin booted a 43-yard field goal. Housman rushed for 153 yards and Johnson for 101.

Housman (31 for 141), Cherry (17-116) and Johnson (16-102) compiled a 100-yard rushing triple in a 27-6 victory over Cincinnati in which linemen like Everett Little, 6-foot-5 and 270 pounds, and David Brooks, 6-foot-5 and 288 pounds, opened the holes. "The way our backs are running," Little

303

explained, "all you have to do is give them some kind of opening, and they're gone. I think we're more excited about playing now. Winning has a lot to do with that."

Brooks added, "When you've got as many quick backs as we have, you give them two-tenths of a second of blocking, and they're right by you. You've just got to bust a gut blocking for people like that."

Both had heard some gibes over their size. Little recalled, "Some Arizona State guys were saying to me and Brooks, 'If you'd lose some weight, you might be able to play football.' We couldn't say too much about it at the time, but we opened some holes."

Brooks noted, "I hear people from the stands a lot of times yelling, 'No. 71 you're too fat' or something like that."

At Georgia, the Cougars jumped out to a 13-0 lead in the first six minutes and held off the 'Dogs, 31-24, in an offensive show. McGallion's 76-yard pass to Johnson on the game's second play led to the first score and Bubba Broussard's intercepted pass set up the second one. Georgia donated UH's third TD after fumbling an interception at its eight. UH mashed out 75 yards on the ground for its fourth touchdown, and Coplin followed Mohr's interception with a 38-yard field goal.

UH had to overcome 10 fumbles—5 of them lost—to edge out Memphis State, 13-10. Johnson traveled seven yards for the winning touchdown in the fourth quarter. Roger Mayes' interception at midfield provided the opportunity, then the visitors missed a tieing 48-yard field goal on the game's final play.

In a much smoother operation, the Cougars decisively defeated Florida State, 23-8. Houston collected 466 yards rushing. Cherry (26-170), Housman (29-159), and McGallion (13-93) led the seventh straight victory.

Yeoman felt that McGallion might have been even more of a discovery than was Gary Mullins in 1969. Mullins had played briefly in the first two games that year before taking over to quarterback nine straight wins. McGallion had even less experience than Mullins when the latter directed his first collegiate team to the Bluebonnet Bowl. McGallion, like Gary Mullins, was the son of a high school coach. A 5-foot-10 sophomore, he was due to be redshirted and had not played a single minute in the first four games before entering in the fourth quarter at

South Carolina.

Yeoman recalled, "We wanted to call a play and sent it in with Frank Scalise. Bubba wasn't familiar with the play, so the others drew it up for him in the huddle right out there on the field."

Bubba's father, Ray, the head coach at Silsbee, Texas, said, "He started off when he was old enough to walk with a football in his hands." An older brother, Deryl Ray, an outstanding linebacker for the 1973 Cougars, had helped pave the way in the ticklish situation of the coach's son being the quarterback.

"I can remember what my brother went through in his sophomore year," Bubba noted. "He really caught some hell. If your father is the coach and you don't perform well, there are always going to be a few people who try to make something out of it. You've got to perform your best every week."

In the regular season's final game, the winning streak quickly went down the drain on a bitingly cold day at Tulsa. The Hurricane recovered UH's fumble of the opening kickoff in the end zone and thumped the Cougars, 30-14.

The nation's fourth best rushing team and No. 9 in total defense, UH headed for its Astro Bluebonnet Bowl date with North Carolina State.

Lou Holtz, the Wolfpack coach, liked to perform magic tricks, and he apparently taught some to his players. With Dave Buckey guiding Holtz's form of the veer, State scored twice in the last eight minutes after trailing, 31-17, to gain a 31-31 tie.

Tommy London's nine-yard scoring run with 3:38 left closed UH's lead to 31-23; then the Pack recovered their onside kick at the Cougar 47. After Buckey passed 27 yards to Pat Hovance, he sneaked the final yard with 2:17 left, but NC State still trailed, 31-29.

Stan Fritts then fought through the middle for the two-point conversion that tied the game and finished a 35-point fourth quarter scoring burst by the two teams.

Housman gained 134 yards on 21 rushes. Buckey passed for 200 yards on an 18-for-28 log.

The Cougars thus headed for their final year as an independent on a half-win, half-tie, sort of a "jump ball situation," but things got worse.

Oh, the start was all right and the finish was decent, but

305

the other eight games were something else. In 1975 the Cougars learned how a "lame duck" feels. They slipped to the depths of a 2-8 season, bedeviled by injuries and all manner of inconsistencies as they prepared—finally—for Southwest Conference competition. The only wins were 20-3 over Lamar in the opener and 42-30 over Tulsa in the last game. From alumni and students alike, the talk centered around the SWC, so how do you get excited over North Texas, Virginia Tech, Cincinnati, etc? To make matters worse, they lost to their only two SWC opponents (Rice, 24-7, and SMU, 26-16) and really hit the skids in a 28-0 trouncing at North Texas. Following that were kickoff returns of 100 yards in a 24-20 loss at Miami, Florida, and 99 yards in a 28-23 defeat by Cincinnati.

No wonder Bubba McGallion looked back on the wreckage and noted, "You'd get up in the mornings and wonder whether it was safe to go to class. There were all those streets to cross."

Tom Wilson, "Camp Fun" Director

Tom Wilson, athletic trainer for University of Houston football teams since 1953, has always been convinced the Cougars were destined for something extraordinary. But even Wilson could not have forecast the Cougars' rags to riches saga of 1976.

"Something good has always happened in the destiny of this university," says Wilson who was voted national trainer of the year in 1976 by the College Athletic Trainers Association of America.

Wilson lost his leg when he was 15 as the result of a football injury in Lufkin, Texas. An exceptional athlete at the time, he finally resolved not to permit the loss of the limb to ruin his life.

He continued his amateur boxing career for several years afterwards. "When I was a little boy," he recalls, "I never missed a newsreel of a Joe Louis or Ray Robinson fight at the Pines Theater. I'd study them by the hours."

As a college student at Stephen F. Austin in Nacogdoches, Texas, Wilson competed in the Sunday rodeos in east Texas hamlets like Tenaha, Timpson and Huntington. "I used to ride wild bulls and bareback broncos," he said. "You could pick up $5 or $10 and that was pretty good money in those days. Then one day a boy who lived down the hall at SFA got killed when a bull fell on him, and I decided to give it up."

Wilson's first ambition was to become a coach "but nobody was going to hire a one-legged coach." Then came the incident that was to eventually join Wilson and the Cougars.

On a visit to his uncle's prosthetics firm in Oklahoma City to get a new artificial leg, he met Byron Byrd, the athletic trainer at Oklahoma A&M. Byrd had lost a leg at Iwo Jima in World War II. "I started talking to him and it was like a giant light switch going on in my head," Wilson said. "He advised me to either go to the University of Texas and work with Frank Medina or to Rice and Eddie Wojecki. I had some friends playing football at UT, and I told them I wanted to meet Frank. He could have run me off if my mind had not been fixed on it."

Wilson served as Medina's top assistant at Texas before joining the Cougars. "Now," he says, "I've been here at UH from the crawling to the running."

He has infused his drive and dedication into countless Cougar football players, notably through "Camp Fun," the ironically-named off-season training program through which Wilson and his student assistants prepare Bill Yeoman's squads for the rigors of the upcoming season.

Wilson recalls wearing his four Astro Bluebonnet Bowl rings to the 1975 Texas high school coaching school in Fort Worth. He was asked, "Are you a ring salesman?"

He replied, "That's not just a ring; that's a life."

He explains, "I spent a long time getting them and an awful lot of young men bled for them. I'll always feel bad for those men from the teams that were on probation. Every young man who wore that Cougar jersey made a contribution. There's been some great warriors.

"Kenny Bolin (halfback, 1959-61) was a hell of a man to be as skinny as he was and do the job he did. Kenny Stegall (1953-55, deceased) always had a special place in my heart. There were so many of them; it seems like they were just here yesterday.

"I've never known a tougher son of a gun than Leonard Parker (fullback, 1971-73).

"Some things don't have a price tag. Just watching these young men perform, I wouldn't trade knowing any of them. What we shared you can't buy. I remember one game at Rice Stadium, Bill Howell (1961-63) took a shot in the kidney. He told me he was passing blood. I took a look and it was pure red. He was ready to go back out again, but he was on his way to the

Tom Wilson, Houston's athletic trainer since 1953.

hospital in five minutes.

"Cotton Guerrant (1964-65), he was an hombre. He just totally annihilated somebody from Ole Miss who weighed 240 or 235 (about 45 pounds more than Guerrant).

"Dickie Post (1964-66) was a very intense warrior. He'd go right to the death; he was a born warrior. God, he was tough."

Wilson explains, "To the public, football is a game. Football is physical warfare. You're not trying to break somebody's nose or tear up a knee joint, but the velocity and the physical impact is such you have to be prepared for it.

"Not everybody should play football. The reward is the satisfaction of attaining something no one else can do. If you choose to play football, you have to be willing to sacrifice. I'm not saying that's right or wrong; I just know that is the way it is.

"That's one of the blessings I have from God, knowing how

long to drive them and when to let up. I do know how to handle young men. You can't prevent all injuries. You have to prevent them by preparation. It's hateful for me to have one of these men injured.

"It's just the basic nature of man to compete, and football fulfills that need. It has great lessons of life, the ups and downs and frustrations and successes.

"I absolutely will not tolerate goldbricking or slacking of duty. He doesn't have to be a first-stringer as long as he's doing all he can.

"It never ceases to amaze me, the size and strength of these men. Some of them could grab me around the chest and bear-hug me and break every bone in there."

Long ago Wilson concluded, "There are no rich trainers, and there never will be." But there are other rewards. "My satisfaction is all of us being together and laughing and talking about Camp Fun and laughing about how those other people (teams)

Waving trainer Tom Wilson's sword after Houston's SWC home debut, Bill Yeoman celebrates the Cougars' 1976 triumph over the Texas Aggies.

died at the end."

Wilson's philosophy of playing the game to the hilt is epitomized in the phrase he uses, "Put them to the sword and take no prisoners." One day after practice in 1969, Jerry Gardner, a former defensive tackle and co-captain, then a graduate assistant, presented Wilson with a used U. S. Army Cavalry sword purchased for $12.95 at an army-navy surplus store. Since then Wilson brings out the sword at what he deems are ripe psychological moments.

Wilson says, "To me, a 'game' is Ping-Pong or tennis or golf. We're going into combat. Losing is hateful to me. You feel like everything was wasted, that you could have lost by just doing nothing. Winning never comes cheap. I'm talking about blood and sweat and tears.

"The night we beat Tulsa, 100-6, we had 'Kill' signs pasted up in the locker rooms. On the opening kickoff Charley Ford and a couple of others hit one of their players and knocked him out. It looked for awhile like he was hurt bad. We took him to our dressing room. 'Kill' is not the word for it, 'Win' is the word. We've never been cheap-shot artists.

"At Florida State a couple of weeks after that (the Cougars lost, 40-20) a couple of them were giving me a bad time. 'Where's your 100 points now?' I just told them, 'We live by the sword and we die by the sword.'"

Wilson recalled his most memorable games at UH:

The 100-6 Tulsa game: "I loved doing it. Poor Coach Yeoman, I felt sorry for him; he got so much criticism and did everything he could not to score. We were so emotional, and he tried to shut it off. Everybody wanted 100 but the coach. You don't deliberately set out to beat somebody that bad. What can you do? Your army is on the march. You can't just stop and turn it off and pick it up again."

The 20-20 tie with Texas in 1968: "It was two magnificent squads doing physical combat."

The 37-7 victory at Michigan State in 1967: "We didn't really need the plane to fly home afterward. The reception at the airport will be something I'll remember the rest of my life. After we'd worked out up there the day before, we came down the tunnel to our dressing room and some of their players were standing there. They started to snicker when we walked by.

311

They were looking at us like we were a bunch of farmers. Everything went perfectly for us that day."

The 1969 Miami, of Florida, game, when tight end Earl Thomas caught a last-minute touchdown pass from Gary Mullins for a 38-36 victory: " One of the magnificent drives I've ever seen. We weren't going to be denied. They gave me the game ball."

The 16-6 defeat by North Carolina State two weeks after the Michigan State game: "That's the kind that's going to test your real moral fibre. You're got to bow your neck and come back. You have to analyze what happened and get ready for the next battle, because it's coming quick. I never have been whipped enough to stay on the canvas and take the count."

Wilson admits, "I take getting beat a little calmer now. In my younger days I was known to put a fist through a door, but that was too rough on my hand."

Former All-American Ken Hebert sums up Wilson's profound effect on hundreds of Cougars: "Tom gave us so much. When you gauge the success of the program, you've got to put it into direct proportion to Tom's efforts. You seek his approval. He's the toughest critic out there. I love him. I can't say enough about him. It's easier to coach when you're already mentally tough, and Tom made us that way."

1976:
Year Of The Turnaround

The odds were astronomical, so who can blame the "experts"? Who in his right mind could have prophesied this 61st Southwest Conference campaign, the Cougars' first after the five-year wait decreed by the terms of their admission?

UH was picked to finish sixth in the poll of 30 sportswriters participating in Dave Campbell's *Texas Football Magazine* vote. The Cougars were picked behind Texas, A&M, Arkansas, Baylor, and Texas Tech, in that order. And, after a 2-8 season, with an inexperienced quarterback named Danny Davis, and a suspect defense and offensive line, how could anyone have picked them much higher?

One who could was Joe McLaughlin of the *Houston Chronicle*. He actually ranked the Cougars No. 1 on his ballot, "because the Cougars have waited a long time to prove they belong in the SWC." The author's ballot had Texas Tech first.

The Cougars made their SWC debut in their September 11 opener at Waco, Texas. A rich vein of history was attached, for UH had been the Bears' first opponent when they opened Baylor Stadium in 1950.

The pregame invocation that day concluded, "We welcome the University of Houston into our Southwest Conference family. Lord, help us make their visit as memorable as possible." It was indeed memorable.

Held to 66 yards total offense and trailing by a weird 5-0 count at the half, UH came back to score a convincing 23-5 triumph. Ecstatic defensive tackle Wilson Whitley exclaimed,

313

"You just don't know how much abuse we've taken over the last year. I want everybody to read the papers. That should shut some people up."

Davis, making his first varsity start, was a virtual unknown. A sophomore, he had been redshirted in 1975 to recover from knee surgery after a freshman injury. He had also changed his name from Jones to Davis after being legally adopted by his stepfather, a Dallas minister.

A faulty center snap by Houston on a fourth down punt handed Baylor a first quarter safety; then the Bears followed

Coach Bill Yeoman and Alois Blackwell signal the Cougars' first Southwest Conference touchdown in their 1976 opener with Baylor.

the ensuing free kick with a 36-yard field goal. They didn't score again.

Early in the third quarter Houston's Mark Mohr recovered a fumble at the Baylor 45, and Davis struggled through three defenders from the 4 for UH's first SWC touchdown. A pass for a two-point conversion failed, and the Cougars led, 6-5.

Cornerback Anthony Francis then made the first of a string of big interceptions during the season, this one at UH's 13, and the offense rolled 87 yards. Davis threw for 22 to split end Don Bass and ran for 11 more, and on fourth down Dyral Thomas took Davis' pitchout and lunged over from the 1.

In the fourth quarter, Ken Perry applied a hard rush to the Baylor passer, Whitley deflected the ball, and linebacker David Hodge intercepted to set up Lennard Coplin's 22-yard field goal

Scoring Houston's first SWC touchdown, Danny Davis (4) eludes Baylor's Mike Nelms to reach the end zone in the 1976 opener.

Preparing to send Dyral Thomas in with a play, Bill Yeoman watches action in the 1976 Baylor game, Houston's Southwest Conference debut.

and a 16-5 lead. Forced to gamble on fourth down deep in their own territory, the Bears turned the ball over, and Thomas scored from the five in the final seconds.

Fullback John Housman rushed for 85 yards on 13 carries.

Significantly, the Cougars did not lose the ball a single time under Davis' cool direction. "I wasn't really nervous," Davis said. "I felt okay once they shot the opening gun, and the announcer started talking, and the bands were playing. It just took us awhile to show what we can do."

"Obviously," added Coach Bill Yeoman, "the kids took this one a lot more seriously than they would playing Virginia Tech or Cincinnati. They did it without any prodding, too."

After the season had ended, Whitley described the feelings this day of the team that had waited so long, its nose pressed against the SWC's door:

"The Friday before the game, when we walked out on the field, you could feel something electrifying. The moment was here; we've got something to take care of. It's showtime.

"About 3 p.m. the next day, we were in the tunnel waiting to go on the field, and it seemed like everybody's head was as high as they could get them. It's the first time I've been that frenzied. You could feel that air of confidence. You could just see it over Coach Yeoman, and you could look all the way up the tunnel and see that same look in everybody's eyes."

Caught between euphoria and their eagerly-awaited home SWC debut with Texas A&M, the Cougars went to Florida. Just as in 1969, they were bombed by a red-hot offense. The Gators stacked up a quick 28-0 lead, rang up 615 yards and an easy 49-14 victory.

The next week, a rare Rice Stadium sellout crowd of 70,001, largest to ever see the Cougars play at home, filed in to watch UH play A&M. UH's game plan was pegged to Davis'

Randy Love (22) turns the corner in Houston's 1976 game with Texas A&M.

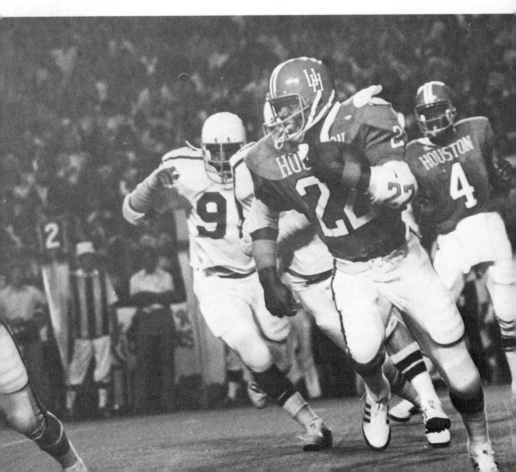

passing arm, and the Cougars quickly found holes in the Aggie secondary.

But first David Hodge tipped an Aggie pitchout, Mohr intercepted and raced 12 yards to A&M's 25. A few plays later, Davis hit tight end Eddie Foster with a 32-yard scoring strike.

Minutes later a 50-yard connection to flanker Robert Lavergne sent the score to 14-0 in the first quarter.

An 18-yard touchdown pass to Foster offset an Aggie field goal for a 21-3 halftime lead, and the defense took over in the second half. Davis, completing 11 of 19 passes for 173 yards and three touchdowns, was chosen national back of the week by *Sports Illustrated* and was the Associated Press back of the week in the conference.

West Texas State, nonconference foe, followed, and the Cougars had trouble getting started before amassing a 50-7 victory. Alois Blackwell's 57-yard sprint and Coplin's 22-yard, last-play field goal provided a slim 10-7 halftime lead before UH rolled up 548 yards rushing, including 200 by Blackwell. Francis had two of the four interceptions made by the defensive unit.

The Cougars then made their first trip to the Cotton Bowl—to meet Southern Methodist University. Yeoman called their 29-6 victory "a very workmanlike win." Cougar fans hung up a sign reading, "UH will be back New Year's Day," and, with their third straight conference victory, their followers began to stir.

For the second straight game, Francis nabbed two interceptions and was the nation's leader with seven. Hodge also had two and Mohr a fifth as Whitley and his friends applied a fearsome pass rush.

A safety and Davis' 45-yard pass to Foster provided a 9-0 first quarter lead; then Randy Love, Thomas, and Charlie Lynch ran for touchdowns.

"I want to come back," announced trainer Tom Wilson.

But Arkansas put a crimp in those hopes with its 14-7 victory the next week in Rice Stadium, making notably big defensive plays as UH's offense was plagued with mistakes.

The Razorbacks took over the SWC lead by scoring twice in the first half. An interception at the Arkansas 41 and a pair of penalties costing 20 yards preceded Hog quarterback Ron

Anthony Francis led the nation with 10 intercepted passes in 1976.

Calcagni's eight-yard keeper which ended a 59-yard move in the first quarter. Then speedy Ben Cowins broke up the middle and dashed 89 yards in the second quarter for a 14-0 halftime lead.

Davis whipped the Cougars 64 yards to the four in the third quarter, but a fumble killed that threat. Thomas' 6-yard run ended an 80-yard advance, and UH trailed just 14-7 with nearly 10 minutes remaining.

A fumble at the Arkansas 11 with 3:07 to go and an interception at the 32 killed off the Cougars, who committed six offensive turnovers. It was a time to regroup, and hope that someone else down the line would take care of the Razorbacks.

Despite losing five of their 10 fumbles, the Cougars did not need their running game in a 49-21 thrashing of TCU, attended by the 30-year reunion of the 1946 UH team.

Bass caught four TD passes, a SWC record. Davis and Bubba McGallion threw for 443 yards, another SWC record, completing 18 of 24 passes. Meanwhile, the Cougar defense intercepted four TCU passes and held the Frogs to 64 yards rushing.

Bass caught scoring aerials of 72, 32, and 54 yards from Davis and an 11 yarder from McGallion. McGallion passed 9 yards to Lavergne for UH's fifth TD pass of the game.

Then came the trek to the "Orange Mountain," Memorial Stadium in Austin, Texas where the Texas Longhorns had not been beaten in 43 games. "Cougars rout Horns, 30-0," headlined the November 7 *Houston Chronicle*. "UH usurps House of Orange, 30-0," informed the *Houston Post*.

The *Chronicle*'s Peebles called the contest "the best football game the Cougars have played in their 30 years." It's doubtful if any have been more satisfying.

Dealing the Longhorns their first shutout since their wishbone era began in 1968, the Cougars reluctantly handed out 24 yards rushing, the lowest total since Texas began keeping records, and pounded out the worst defeat in Darrell Royal's 20 years of coaching the Horns.

A Dad's Day audience of 77,809, the largest crowd to ever watch UH, was in the stands. "I guess there were a lot of sad dads," chortled Foster.

"And mothers," added Jones Ramsey, the Texas sports

Don Bass (84) leads the Cougars into Memorial Stadium at Austin, Texas, where Houston ended the Texas Longhorns' 42-game home field winning streak.

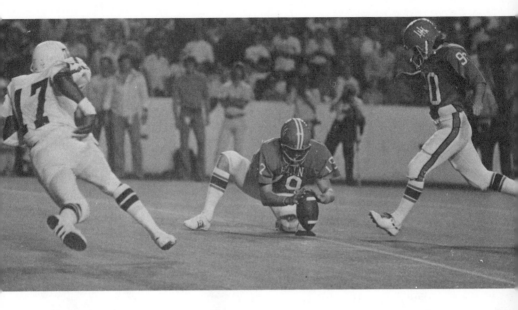

Lennard Coplin, Houston field goal record-holder, prepares to swing his leg during the 1976 season.

information director.

 Freshman Cougar Elvis Bradley, who had won a starting spot in the secondary against A&M, intercepted a pass at the UH 21 early in the game. A 79-yard drive into the wind followed. Davis pitched out to Blackwell for the last 7 yards.

 Late in the first half Hodge recovered one of five Texas turnovers and Coplin, the wind at his back, booted a 30-yard field goal 36 seconds before halftime.

 Another Texas fumble, this one on the first play of the second half, was recovered at the 22 by Robert Oglesby, and Coplin converted it into a 20-yard field goal.

 Leading, 13-0, UH traveled 75 yards to the Texas 15, where the stubborn Longhorn defense forced another field goal by Coplin, a 32-yarder. Lynch's l-yard plunge ended a 65-yard drive in the fourth period and sent the count to 23-0. Davis' 28-yard sprint to cap an 80-yard drive with 3:22 remaining was the dessert in Houston's scoring feast.

 Thomas (16 for 64), Lynch (6 for 61), Blackwell (17 for 52), Davis (13 for 46), and Randy Love (9 for 42) were the leading runners. Whitley and his roommate, Vincent Greenwood, shared the AP award for SWC defensive player of the

Wilson Whitley (78) sacks Texas quarterback Mike Cordaro, then recovers the fumble in Houston's 30-0 rout of Texas in 1976.

week.

"We were totally dominated," Royal said later, "I am embarrassed it was by that margin."

"We felt like we could beat them convincingly if we didn't fumble," said Whitley, "and their home winning streak was an added incentive."

Yeoman commented about that homefield aura, "We have played in most of the great mythical stadia. We've been between the hedges in Athens, Georgia. We've been in Oxford, Mississippi, and East Lansing, Michigan, and our players realize that no bleacher, no wall, no grandstand seat is going to come out and make a tackle. When you have this understanding, you just go out and play a football game."

That night Arkansas was tied by Baylor, 7-7, leaving Tech at 4-0, Arkansas 3-0-1 and UH 5-1 in the SWC standings.

After an off-week, the Cougars' next game was against Tech at Lubbock, Texas.

When the Cougars arrived at Lubbock, a Cotton Bowl berth was theirs to be taken, because the Aggies had dealt Arkansas a mortal blow the previous Saturday. Tech, 8-0 and ranked fifth nationally, also had much at stake. The Red Raiders were within reach of their first conference title since beginning SWC competition in 1960.

With an apparently safe 27-5 lead going into the game's final seven minutes, the Cougars were saved by Bradley's end zone interception in the final minute when the Raiders were only 10 yards away from a possible tie.

"After they scored and made it 27-19," Whitley recalled later, "I said, 'Hey, man, these guys are trying to take my dream away!' I knew we'd come up with something to stop them."

Davis, trying to pass from his end zone in the first quarter, was trapped for a safety but then directed an 81-yard march. He scrambled and passed for 26 to Bass. Thomas scored from the one.

Brian Hall's 37-yard field goal for Tech cut the margin to 7-5; then Davis passed 39 to Rickey Maddox for a touchdown. Later Coplin kicked a 39-yard field goal. Fighting the halftime clock, Davis passed to Lavergne for 20; then Tech drew a costly pass interference penalty at the seven. Davis hit Foster in the end zone with seven seconds left in the half.

Blackwell rushed for 59 yards on four carries in a drive ended by Coplin's 26-yard field goal. Those three points increased UH's lead to 27-5 before the heart-pumping finish.

Tech, which cracked the Cougar 10 four times in the game without scoring, began closing the margin. Defensive end Richard Arledge intercepted Davis' pass on first down at the UH four and returned it seven yards for Tech's first touchdown. On their next series, Allison passed the Raiders 93 yards. His pass to Billy Taylor netted the final 16. Sammy Williams caught a toss from Allison for the two-point conversion.

UH recovered Tech's attempted onside kick and drove to the Raider 19, but there the Cougars fumbled. Houston rooters had to suffer through the nail-biting final minutes. "There's no question," said Yeoman, "that I had a nervous pulse at the end of the game."

Tech quarterback Rodney Allison completed 20 of 31 passes for 327 yards and ran 19 times for another 41. Davis was 9 for 13 passing for 159 yards; Blackwell rushed 17 for 103.

Thus, while Maryland accepted the Cotton Bowl's invitation to oppose the SWC winner, UH moved a stride closer——a victory over Rice——to another trip to Dallas.

Rice's Tommy Kramer staged a sensational passing display the next Saturday, November 27, at Rice Stadium, but the Cougars unloaded too many guns. They amassed a 35-6 halftime lead, survived Kramer's 409 yards passing, and won, 42-20, to complete the road to the Cotton Bowl. "Cougars plant Rice, harvest Cotton" headlined the *Houston Chronicle*.

As Bob Galt wrote in the *Dallas Times Herald*, "What started out in September as an impossible dream ended in reality here Saturday as the Cougars, their diapers flapping in the breeze, took care of the Rice Owls, 42-20, to gain at least a share of the SWC championship and a spot in the Cotton Bowl opposite Maryland."

Amid the pandemonium of the Cougar locker room, Wilbur Evans, Executive Vice President of the Cotton Bowl, issued the formal invitation to Dr. Philip Hoffman, UH President, Fouke, and Yeoman.

Dr. Philip G. Hoffman (right), university president, and Coach Bill Yeoman accept the Cotton Bowl invitation from Wilbur Evans (left), executive vice president of the Cotton Bowl Athletic Association, after the Rice game.

Evans told the Cougars, "I remember 11 weeks ago after the Cougars beat Baylor, I read where you were called the 'upstart Cougars.' I'll tell you one thing, you didn't start anything you couldn't finish."

"Is there anything else we have to do to get up there?" Yeoman wanted to know.

"Just pack your bags," Evans replied.

"I haven't slept for two weeks," Yeoman admitted. "It'll reach me soon. This feeling probably tops any feeling I've had in coaching...I couldn't even have made up a dream like this season has been."

A red-eyed, smiling Val Belcher, one of the tri-captains with Whitley and Paul Humphreys, said, "You work all your life for something like this, and it's something that's indescribable."

Blackwell rushed for 153 yards and three touchdowns on 20 carries; Thomas had 110 yards and two TDs on 13 carries. Mohr, who blocked two punts and intercepted a pass, was *Sports Illustrated* defensive player of the week.

Jewell Wallace, the school's first football coach, listened to the radio broadcast at his Fort Worth home. "I knew some day they'd be big time," he said. "It took a long time, but they're there now. They had some big ideas even back in 1946. I told Fouke at our reunion this year that when I first went to work there——I thought of the song 'Something Big Could Come of This.' Now we can sing, 'Baby, You've Come A Long Way.'"

"As the years go by," added Jack Gwin, who shivered in

Val Belcher, 1976 tri-captain and All-Southwest Conference offensive lineman.

the stands with former co-captain Bill Cook, "you're more and more proud to be part of something like this."

Said Johnny Goyen, the Houston city councilman, former UH cheerleader and student president, "I still can't believe it. I guess it'll sink in tonight or tomorrow. Or on New Year's Day."

There remained, however, one bit of unfinished business, the final game of the regular season with Miami.

It was not an easy win, especially after the emotional end of the SWC schedule. Reserve linebacker Willis Williams' interception at the Cougars' goal line with 1:59 to play preserved the Cougars' 21-16 victory.

With first and goal at the UH two, Miami's quarterback tried to pass as Whitley was tugging on his body, and the Cougars nailed down their ninth win against two losses. Anthony Francis intercepted 2 passes to tie the SWC record of 10 in a season and win the national title in that category. Blackwell rushed for 170 yards and one TD in 24 tries, his fourth 100-yard game of the season, and Davis ran 4 and 25 yards for scores.

Playing its seventh bowl team of the year, Miami competed with much more emotion than UH. Miami's Coach Carl Selmer, attending a hockey game the night before, was paged for a long distance call from Miami and informed he had been fired.

Tech defeated Baylor, 24-21, the same day to gain a share of the SWC title with UH.

Wilson Whitley:
"Quicker Than Quick"

Minutes after Cougar defensive tackle Wilson Whitley received the Lombardi Award from former President Gerald Ford, Coach Bill Yeoman said, "Vince would have been proud. Wilson is his kind of player."

Whitley won the Lombardi Award in voting by a nation-wide panel of coaches and media for the American Cancer Society and Houston Rotary Club. He won over Notre Dame's Ross Browner, the Outland Award winner; Al Romano of Pittsburgh; and Robert Jackson, Texas A&M.

That night, flanked by Gerald and Betty Ford and toast-master Bob Hope, Whitley admitted that early in his UH career he thought of quitting, but his mother and older sister refused to allow him to stay home. Then Whitley added, "I have to give my deepest thanks to our trainer, Tom Wilson. After the Cotton Bowl, I realized why Tom worked us the way he did. It was all worth it."

The Lombardi Award, emblematic of the nation's best senior collegiate lineman, was one of the series of honors won after the 1976 season by UH's most decorated football player. Whitley, the bell cow of the Cougar defense, was on All-Americans selected by the Associated Press, football coaches, and football writers, and was United Press International's defensive player of the year in the Southwest Conference. He also was the Washington Touchdown Club choice as college line-man of the year.

Before the season Yeoman had predicted, "There won't be

Former President Gerald Ford (left) and Bob Hope flank Lombardi Award winner Wilson Whitley during the 1976 banquet in Houston.

a better defensive tackle in the country than Whitley."

Among the shower of accolades from Cougar opponents stands out the one voiced by Texas Tech Coach Steve Sloan,

"They better give the guy across from Whitley a shot of novocaine. He's the $6 million Bionic Man. We couldn't block him. He's one of the finest tackles I've seen."

Tech offensive lineman Mike Sears added, "Looking at films of Whitley makes me shudder."

Whitley described the Cougars' attitude entering their first SWC campaign after the 2-8 record of 1975. "The public said, 'After last year, nothing is expected of you.' We heard a lot of

Applying strong-arm tactics to Tommy Kramer, Rice's All-American quarterback, is Houston All-American Wilson Whitley (78).

predictions we wouldn't win three or four conference games. We felt we had a lot to prove. It wasn't a grudge, but it was disheartening they wanted to keep us out as long as they did."

A starter since his freshman year, Whitley was a high school all-stater at Brenham, Texas, which several years before had sent fullback Roosevelt Leaks to Texas. The Whitley farm near Washington-on-the-Brazos is 10 or 15 miles from the school. Wilson recalls, "I'd ride the bus to school in the morning, and my mother would have to pick me up after practice and drive me home. Then, starting my sophomore year, I started to drive."

Whitley's attitude during the season was, "If I don't get an award this year and we go to the Cotton Bowl, I'm going to be completely happy." Often double-teamed by offensive lines, he sometimes lined up anywhere from middle guard to the outside, as he did in the Rice game.

"It brightens my day when they run the other way and Ross Echols and Vincent Greenwood and Guy Brown make the tackle," Whitley told the *Houston Post*'s Ray Collins, "but that's why I have to go elsewhere to make plays."

A 6-foot-1, 222-pounder when he reported for his eighth grade team, Whitley firmed into a 6-foot-3, 268-pounder for UH. "He's a monster," quarterback Danny Davis describes him. "He just picks people up and throws 'em away." "He's quicker than quick," says UH defensive line coach Don Todd, "and he's got the size and the strength. But the thing that sets him apart is his ability to diagnose plays."

Yeoman concludes, "Wilson is as good as I have ever been exposed to. When you consider his all-around skills, such as quickness, speed, athletic ability and all, he's the very best I've been around."

Cotton Bowl 1977

Bill Yeoman was driving to his team's Dallas hotel head-quarters to join the Cougars after the Christmas holiday when the reason for this trip surged over him. Traveling on the free-way loop around the Cotton Bowl, Yeoman glanced out the car window: "I saw that big stadium sitting there, and that was the first time I ever felt like it was for real."

Later, in quieter moments, when Yeoman was asked for perhaps the hundredth time how such a "turn-around" could occur, he replied with a smile, "The Good Lord did it this year. I had nothing to do with it. He told me, 'I gave you everything you needed last year, and you went 2-8. I'm tired of your groping around.'"

Perhaps the first inkling came months before. Yeoman relates, "When the defensive coaches asked the players to list their goals, every one of them said, 'To be the best defense.' Not to lead the team in tackles or interceptions, because you can do that and still violate the team defense.

"I've never felt more in control than this year," Yeoman says, "and the players reflected it. Playing for a championship, we knew they all could be expected to play hard. I felt much calmer than before."

Trainer Tom Wilson points out, "That was the first time in a long time we'd gone 2-8 around here. It wasn't turning it around as much as going back to the way we'd been playing all the time. What did they expect—that we'd be 2-8 every year?"

Then Wilson noted an immensely relevant fact, "Each

Saturday, playing in a conference you're going for something. As an independent, you're just going. If it had been the year before, losing to Florida and Arkansas, there went our whole year."

"The Cotton Bowl was our goal from the time of the 1975 game," Wilson Whitley says. "We all thought the Cotton Bowl was the ultimate. We gave Arkansas 14 points the first half and got going the second half. They were the first place team and if that was the best the conference had to offer, we could handle the rest. We thought we could beat any of them."

Quarterback Danny Davis agrees, "It started right after that 2-8. A lot of guys made up their minds to work harder. We had a hard 'Camp Fun' and a real hard spring working against the No. 1 defense."

"Everybody did a little soul-searching, if they were really putting out 100 per cent, or just thought they were," adds halfback Alois Blackwell. "Everybody came closer together, we were going places together and that makes you work harder. You don't want to not do your job and let your friends down."

Davis decides, "We had a change in mental attitude, dedication to working, and we had a lot of help from Upstairs. We had no really bad injuries, and I had a knee that was operated on before.

"Before the season, I had a great deal of confidence in myself, but I wasn't ready to go out and accept making mistakes. Then, after I'd made about my seventh mistake and cost us the Arkansas game, I decided, 'If I'm going to go out and do the job, I have to be ready for whatever happens.'"

The Cougars also refer to an incident during spring drills. "It was a scrimmage out at Tully Stadium," Davis says, "and it was a hot, humid Saturday morning. We usually ran 60 plays on offense, and we had a habit of counting them off. When we hit 60, we started taking our pads off. Coach said, 'Who told you to take your pads off? Get back out there.'

"We went back out, and it got to be very physical. The defense was yelling at me, 'Kill him! Kill him!' even though they were all my friends. That's how intense it got. After the spring we felt our No. 1 defense was the best defense we'd face, they threw everything at us, and all that was left was to get into a game."

"That day checked everybody out," Blackwell agrees. "We saw what we were capable of doing."

"I've never seen coach like that, before or since," says Wilson Whitley.

"I didn't really care whether they liked me that day or not," Yeoman notes. "The head coach was disgruntled, too."

Before leaving the campus for Christmas, Davis had returned to the UH book store. His T-shirt with the *1976 SWC Champs* lettered on it was well-worn. "I wanted to buy one that said *1977 National Champs*," Davis says. "The same lady who sold me the first one said, 'Don't you think that's a little early?' I said, 'Yeah, I guess you're right,' and I didn't buy it."

The Cotton Bowl was a somewhat familiar scene for Davis. He had been on the field before, but in a different role. "When I was in junior high at Pearl C. Anderson, I worked there selling concessions on Saturdays and Sundays," Davis explains. "I never got to go much on Sundays because of church. I'd rip right out of Sunday School to the stadium. I sold mainly soft drinks. My best day I made about $30 selling hot Dr. Peppers.

Bill Yeoman confers with quarterback Danny Davis during the 1977 Cotton Bowl.

"I remember working one Texas-OU game," says Davis, "but my real inspiration came from SMU. I remember watching Jerry LeVias and Raymond Mapps and Chuck Hixson.

"When the game was over, we'd go down to the field and play football. We didn't have a ball, we'd roll up a sweater or get a cardboard box and roll that up."

Defensive back Mark Mohr had delayed his graduation in order to play one more season. He explains, "After last season I decided we had been a team that didn't ever show what it could really do. We shouldn't leave people with a bad taste in their mouths. It just didn't set right with me. We'd had a bunch of inexperienced people, and we'd fumbled quite a bit on offense and gave up the big play on defense. It just seemed we were always on the short end of the stick." Two days after the Cotton Bowl, Mohr went to work for an accounting firm.

The reality of what they had accomplished dawned on the Cougars in different ways. Mohr recalls, "I didn't get really excited about it until two nights before, when I was watching an in-depth TV program on the two teams."

"It really hit me the day before the game," says Davis, "driving to the stadium for the media to take pictures. I was thinking, 'I hope I don't get too excited, I just hope I can hold out one more day.'"

Blackwell says, "The whole week we were at Dallas, it didn't really dawn on me. Then, when I was coming down the tunnel to go out for the pregame with the first group, and I heard the bands, and I looked up and saw the stands. That's when it hit me."

Whitley compares his feelings as he waited to take the field, "It was just like a bronc waiting for the chute to open so we could raise some hell. I remember Rickey Maddox saying, 'Let my people go.' I felt I had something to prove. For three years the only note I got was when we'd get beat. I wanted to prove how good I was, how I went to UH to be a winner."

Rich Stotter, the former All-American offensive guard, was one of many ex-Cougars in the Cotton Bowl stands. "I'm 32-years-old and president of my own company, but I would have traded it all to have been suited up and playing in the greatest game for UH football," he said later.

Robert Newhouse also sat and watched and remembered,

"I can recall Tom Wilson, and how he used to run us. It dawned on me, 'Here it all of a sudden was, what we'd all been driving for.' I just wished I could have played in it."

Into the bitterly cold wind, whipping around the stadium in the 30-degree temperature, strode equipment manager Jack Littlefield. He was living up to his part of a bargain struck the week after the 49-14 thrashing at Florida. Littlefield insisted to Ray Collins of the *Houston Post,* "We'll still be in Dallas on New Year's Day. And I'll wear a tuxedo on the sideline."

"And I'll wear a tux in the press box," chimed in Ted Nance, UH's sports information director. The press box was enclosed and heated, but Littlefield shivered through the first half in his formal attire before changing to warmer clothes at the half.

Months before, Nance and his wife, Charlyn, were given a December trip to Hawaii with the basketball team in recognition of his 20 years service to the Cougars. "We'll give up Hawaii for Dallas when we're in the Cotton Bowl on January 1," Nance promised, and they did.

After the kickoff for the 41st annual Cotton Bowl, the Cougars went quickly to work. Maryland, ranked No. 4 nationally and one of only three major college teams unbeaten and untied in regular season, was justly proud of its defense. It had shut out the Terps' final three opponents and was ranked second nationally.

But UH's veer offense savaged that reputation with Davis, Blackwell, Dyral Thomas, and mates erecting a 21-0 first quarter lead over the Terps.

Then, after a remarkable play by Davis when Maryland determinedly pulled within striking distance in the fourth quarter, the Cougars finished the final chapter in their saga of 1976.

The score was UH 30, Maryland 21, and Yeoman termed it "the most satisfying season in the school's history. I don't know how anything could be more gratifying."

Harry Fouke was to say, "I don't know how to explain it, I just want to sit back and enjoy it."

UH finished fourth in the final wire service national rankings. Yeoman was runnerup to Pittsburgh's Johnny Majors in the football writers' coach of the year poll and was the Texas

Equipment manager Jack Littlefield shivers in tuxedo on a Cotton Bowl sideline as he lives up to his part of an early-season promise.

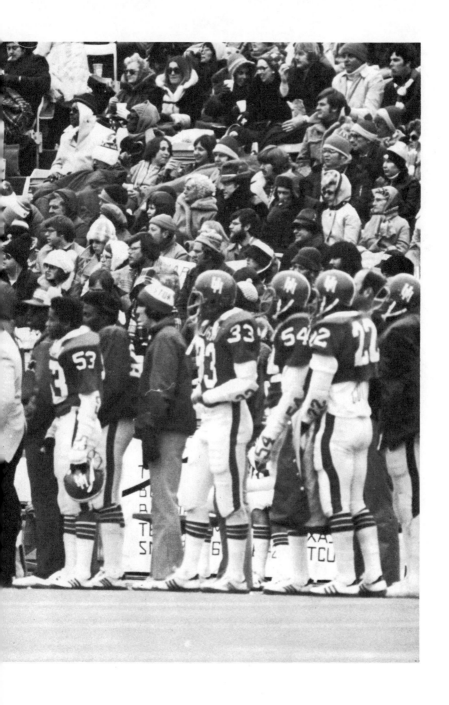

Guy Brown (8) wraps up Maryland fullback Tim Wilson (14) during the second quarter of 1977 Cotton Bowl action.

Sportswriters Association coach of the year.

Houston Chronicle sports editor Dick Peebles wrote, "Just winning a share of the Southwest Conference title and getting to the Cotton Bowl in their first year in the league was not all the University of Houston wanted. No, sir!"

Headlined the *Washington Post*, "An Eel Named Davis Put Out the Lights." Mike Jones described it in the *Dallas News*, "The victory polished off a peanuts-to-Washington year for UH."

Utilizing the speed of their backs, the Cougars ran much of the time at Joe Campbell, Maryland's All-American defensive tackle. They discerned that Campbell had the outside responsibility on Davis, so Blackwell and Thomas repeatedly slashed off tackle on the dive play. UH scored three times in less than six minutes during the critical opening quarter.

"They really took it to us that first quarter," said Maryland quarterback Mark Manges. "We haven't seen a team that quick or even close to it all year." The Terps had gone 22 quarters without allowing a touchdown by rushing before Thomas bolted 11 yards to end an 80-yard jaunt.

Mohr then blocked a Maryland punt out of bounds at its 38, and three plays later Blackwell raced 33 yards through Campbell's hole. Voted the game's outstanding defensive player, Mohr explained the blocked punt, "They lined up without a huddle so the defense doesn't have time to set up a good rush. I fell into the gap between the end and tackle, and no one touched me. I hit the protection man, and dove over him, and the punter was too close to him. I put my arms straight up, and he kicked the ball right into my arms."

On the first play after the kickoff, Whitley stripped the ball from Manges, and Mohr recovered at the Maryland 25. After Davis ran for 17, Blackwell thrust the final 11 yards through a hole opened by Val Belcher and Ramon Rosales. Blackwell, voted the offensive player of the game, rushed for 149 yards on 22 carries, and Thomas added 104 on 14.

In the final minute of the first period, Maryland, which allowed only 22 points in opening quarter all year, trailed 21-0. Manges' 6-yard keeper made it 21-7 in the second quarter, but Davis then passed the Cougars most of the way in a 97-yard scoring drive. He threw for 25 to Eddie Foster, then connected with Don Bass from 33 yards for UH's fourth touchdown and a 27-7 halftime lead.

After the UH defense stopped Maryland at the Cougar one foot line early in the third quarter, the Terps recovered a fumble at the victor's 35. Manges then passed 11 yards to Eric Sievers for a TD.

Another UH fumble at its 30 enabled Maryland to score again, and, suddenly, with six minutes to play, the Cougars led only 27-21. Their situation was indeed perilous after the kickoff. On third down and six they stood on their 11 yard line. A fourth down punt would be against the wind.

Then Davis made the play that UH fans will retell and embellish over the decades. Somehow eluding the grasp of four charging Terps, Davis miraculously got the pass away to flanker

Mark Mohr, voted outstanding defensive player of 1977 Cotton Bowl.

Robert Lavergne, who was dangerously close to the right sideline at the 24. The Cougars had the precious first down.

From there, winding down the clock, the Cougars trudged
into Maryland ground. Again, this time on a fourth and inches
play at the Terp 41, the Cougars had the answer. Instead of a
sneak or a line plunge, Davis pitched out wide to Thomas, who
darted 32 yards. Lennard Coplin's 28-yard field goal with 18

*Finding daylight, Alois Blackwell (32) sprints on a long-gainer
against Maryland in the 1977 Cotton Bowl.*

Wilson Whitley (78) puts his All-American grip on a Maryland ballcarrier in the 1977 Cotton Bowl.

seconds left closed out the day.

"I still don't see how he got out of there and got the pass away," said Campbell of Davis. "I was right on top of him and so were a lot of others."

Maryland linebacker Mike Miller noted, "We had everybody coming on the play. A bunch of them got good penetration, and it looked like they had him wrapped up. I thought, 'That's it; that's the ball game.' Then all of a sudden he broke out of there, and got the pass away. That was the best play I've ever seen."

Lavergne explained, "When I saw Danny in trouble back there, I said, 'Lord, please let him get loose. I turned back to give him a closer target. It was a must play because we had to have a first down right there."

Said Maryland Coach Jerry Claiborne, "That was a great play, and it took a great quarterback to make it."

Later in the UH locker room, Davis, emotionally spent, had tears in his eyes. He explained later that a cousin, Dwaine Staten, a tight end who had played with him at Dallas Carter, had died of meningitis at SMU during Davis' freshman year at UH. "Then another friend, Lee Gary Robinson, had been killed in Dallas," Davis related. "And then my older brother. We had all talked about watching each other play in the Cotton Bowl and being together. It seemed like everytime I called home, people I had told about the Cotton Bowl and that I wanted there, something bad had happened to them."

Davis soon regained his composure and folded away his prophetic T-shirt, the one that read, "1976 SWC Champs."

Back at the hotel, Jack Littlefield, still trying to get the cold out of his bones, went to sleep waiting for the Orange Bowl telecast to begin.

ATHLETIC DIRECTOR HARRY FOUKE

Harry Fouke has built an athletic department at the University of Houston that is second to none in the Southwest and ranks among the nation's elite.

A 1935 graduate of Rice University and holder of a master's degree from Columbia, Fouke became UH's first and only director of athletics in 1945. Since that time, he has guided the Cougar athletic program toward a steady course of excellence. His keen direction was recognized by the entire Houston sports community in 1968 when he was

HARRY FOUKE

named "Mr. Sportsman" for the city of Houston and honored at a city-wide banquet.

Fouke was also honored by the UH Alumni Organization in 1971. He was the recipient of the Alumni President's Award, which is given annually to an outstanding non-alumnus.

He was honored again in 1976 by Rice University when he was named the outstanding ex-letterman of that school.

Born in Texarkana, Ark., in 1913, just six blocks from the Texas border, Fouke graduated from Main High in San Antonio before enrolling at Rice. He also lived in Ft. Collins, Colo., briefly as a schoolboy.

He was a star halfback at Rice from 1932 to 1934, helping to lead that school to its first Southwest Conference championship in 1934. As a Rice senior, Fouke was the winner of the Bob Quin Award, the school's top athletic award presented annually for outstanding athletic accomplishment, leadership and scholarship.

His first position in the field of athletics was as head football and track coach at San Antonio Tech from 1935 to 1940. The following year he served in that same capacity at Thomas Jefferson High School, also of San Antonio.

He was then promoted to director of athletics for San Antonio public schools, where he served for a year before accepting that same post with the Houston public school system in 1942. Just three years later, the University of Houston announced plans to enter intercollegiate athletics, and immediately the board of regents sought Fouke's enthusiastic leadership.

Although, he is no longer active in teaching, he was a professor of physical education and chairman of the physical education department for 30 years.

He is a member of the University Council and a past member of the Administrative Cabinet of the College of Education. He is also a member of Phi Delta Kappa and Kappa Pi fraternities.

The Cougar AD is a past president of the National Association of Collegiate Directors of Athletics. He continues to participate in sports, playing tennis and golf. He is also an avid fisherman.

Fouke reached two of his long-time goals as UH athletic director in 1971. He signed the first contracts for football and basketball games between Houston and Rice and also accepted an invitation of membership to the Southwest Conference on behalf of the University of Houston.

SPORTS INFORMATION

A University of Houston graduate, Ted Nance has been the Sports Information Director since January 1960. He previously served three years as full-time assistant.

Nance spent one year as a reporter in the city room of the Houston Chronicle after his graduation from UH in 1956.

The 42-year-old Nance is a member of the U.S. Football Writers, U.S. Basketball Writers, Texas Sports Writers Association, College Sports Information Director of America, and is a past member of the board of directors of the National Football Foundation and Hall of Fame.

Nance is a native of Dearborn, Mich., and graduated from Dearborn High School. He has been a resident of Houston since 1956.

Ted Nance

Appendix

(Information In This Appendix Is From Material Compiled By The Department of Athletics, Office Of Sports Information, University of Houston.)

MASCOT SHASTA

Shasta IV arrived at the University of Houston in January 1977 to replace the retired Shasta III. She was born Dec. 8, 1976 in Centerhill, Fla.

Shasta lives on campus in a glass enclosed, air-conditioned cage. Her care is financed by the athletic department and the Student Association. The Cougar Guard, a student organization, is in charge of her care and display.

She is fed a special blend of horsemeat and vitamins each day and exercised regularly by the Guard. Shasta IV is de-clawed, but she will bite.

A spectator at all home athletic events, Shasta also makes most of the football and basketball road trips.

Shasta IV replaced Shasta III, an 11-year-old Cougar that was obtained from the Dallas Zoo as a cub.

Shasta I was a 17-year-old Cougar imported from Mexico by the Alpha Phi Omega fraternity. Shasta I, a 110-pound beauty, probably saw more UH athletic contests than any Cougar fan. She never missed a home game and made several trips with the team. She was obtained by Manuel King for $250.00 as a 75-pound cub in 1947. Shasta I was retired in 1963.

More than 225 names were submitted by students in a "Name the Cougar" contest, sponsored by the Cougar, the UH student newspaper. The three names that were judged in the finals and then voted upon by the student body were: "Shasta," "Spiritana," and "Raguoc."

Joe B. Randol submitted the winning entry. His entry was as follows:
Shasta have a cage.
Shasta have a keeper.
Shasta have a winning ball club.
Shasta have the best.

FIRST GAME ON ASTROTURF

The first football game ever played on Astroturf was the September 23, 1966, game between the University of Houston and Washington State University. The UH Cougars beat the WSU Cougars 21-7 in that one in the Astrodome.

RECORDS

LONGEST PLAYS AT UH

°Ties NCAA record.

Longest Runs From Scrimmage:
91—TD, Donnie McGraw, 1974, UH-21, Rice-0
84—Reggie Cherry, 1973, UH-14, San Diego St.-9
81—TD, Boyd Tingle, 1947, UH-14, McMurry-13
80—TD, Ken Bolin, 1961, UH-21, Boston College-0
80—TD, Ken Bolin, 1961, UH-13, Cincinnati-7
80—TD, Donn Hargrove, 1953, UH-25, Detroit-19
80—TD, Marshall Johnson, 1972, UH-31, Florida St.-27

Donnie McGraw

Longest Pass Play:
°99—TD, Bo Burris to Warren McVea, 1966, UH-21, Washington St.-7
°99—TD, Terry Peel to Robert Ford, 1970, UH-42, Syracuse-15
°99—TD, Terry Peel to Robert Ford, 1972, UH-49, San Diego St.-14
87—TD, D.C. Nobles to Willie Roberts, 1971, UH-42, Villanova-9
86—TD, Bo Burris to Ken Hebert, 1966, UH-48, Tampa-9

Frank Ditta

Longest Punt:
84—Alan Neveux, 1949, UH-23, North Texas-28
80—Ken Hebert, 1966, UH-28, Miss St.-0
78—Jackie Gwin, 1946, UH-16, S. F. Austin-7
75—Ken Pridgeon, 1951, UH-28, Louisville-35
73—Randy Owens, 1951, UH-14, Wichita-19
73—Hal Roberts, 1972, UH-49, San Diego St.-14

Longest Punt Returns:
82—TD, Dick Spratt, 1966, UH-21, Fla. St.-13
82—TD, Joe Lopasky, 1963, UH-14, Auburn-21
72—TD, Jolly Hartsell, 1949, UH-14, West Texas-13
71—TD, Ken Stegall, 1955, UH-54, Montana-12
70—TD, Max Clark, 1948, UH-14, Texas A&I-0

Terry Peel

Longest Kickoff Returns:
103—TD, Ronnie Powledge, 1963, UH-55, Detroit-18
95—TD, Larry Jefferson, 1973, UH-54, Virginia Tech-27
93—TD, Claude King, 1958, UH-37, Miami-26
92—TD, Warren McVea, 1965, UH-16, Fla. St.-16
91—TD, Paul Gipson, 1968, UH-71, Cincinnati-33

Longest Interception Returns:
°100—TD, Frank Ditta, 1971, UH-34, San Jose State-20
89—TD, Paul Sweeten, 1957, UH-7, Auburn-48
76—TD, Pat Studstill, 1958, UH-44, Wichita-0
76—TD, Carl Mittag, 1949, UH-27, Hardin-Simmons-27
70—TD, Charles Ford and Frank Ditta, 1970, UH-53, Fla. St.-21

Dick Spratt

Longest Field Goals:
40-yd line—Randy Owens, 1951, UH-31, Okla. A&M-7
35-yd line—Lennard Coplin, 1975, UH-22, Florida St.-33
35-yd line—Carlos Lopez, 1969, UH-34, No. Car. St.-13
34-yd line—Ken Hebert, 1967, UH-37, Mich. St.-7
33-yd line—Lennard Coplin, 1974, UH-24, South Carolina-14

Paul Sweeten

ALL-TIME CAREER LEADERS

Bo Burris

TOTAL OFFENSE 2500 YARD CLUB

PLAYERS AND YEARS	YARDS	YEAR-BY-YEAR
1) Gary Mullins, qb 69-71	4698	(1831-1103-1764)
2) D.C. Nobles, qb, 71-73	3697	(318-1640-1739)
3) Bo Burris, qb, 64-66	3663	(480-1337-1846)
4) Robert Newhouse, fb, 69-71	2961	(416-788-1757)
5) Paul Gipson, fb, 66-68	2883	(119-1100-1664)
6) Ken Bailey, qb, 67-69	2528	(513-1615-400)
7) Gene Shannon, hb, 49-51	2507	(498-798-1211)

RUSHING 1000 YARD CLUB

PLAYERS AND YEARS	YARDS	YEAR-BY-YEAR
1) Robert Newhouse, fb, 69-71	2961	(416-788-1757)
2) Paul Gipson, fb, 66-68	2769	(119-1100-1550)
3) Gene Shannon, rb, 49-51	2507	(498-798-1211)
4) Dick Post, hb-fb, 64-66	2219	(528-630-1061)
5) Jim Strong, rb, 67-69	1936	(105-538-1293)
6) Reggie Cherry, rb, 72-74	1811	(430-794-587)
7) John Housman, fb, 74-76	1788	(988-466-334)
8) Tommy Mozisek, rb, 69-71	1708	(81-935-692)
9) Ted Heiskell, fb, 68-70	1668	(309-870-489)
10) Marshall Johnson, rb, 72-74	1587	(295-447-845)
11) Max Clark, hb, 49-50	1580	(259-461-860)
12) Leonard Parker, fb, 71-73	1549	(301-125-1123)
13) Warren McVea, hb, 65-67	1461	(114-648-699)
14) Donnie McGraw, rb, 73-75	1369	(556-456-357)
15) Puddin Jones, fb, 70-72	1348	(26-106-1216)
16) Alois Blackwell, rb, 75-76	1298	(364-934)
17) Ken Bolin, rb, 59-61	1058	(160-542-356)

Vic Hampel

PASSING 1000 YARD CLUB

PLAYERS AND YEARS	YARDS	YEAR-BY-YEAR
1) Gary Mullins, qb, 69-71	4095	(1433-1046-1616)
2) Bo Burris, qb, 64-66	3248	(326-1256-1666)
3) D.C. Nobles, qb, 71-73	2706	(207-1351-1148)
4) Bobby Clatterbuck, qb, 51-53	2125	(1113-736-276)
5) Ken Bailey, qb, 67-69	2042	(346-1279-417)
6) Dick Woodall, qb, 65-67	1836	(326-286-1224)
7) Don Sessions, qb, 59-61	1680	(407-549-724)
8) Jack Skog, qb, 62-64	1531	(50-1045-436)
9) Alan Neveux, qb, 48-49	1488	(549-939)
10) Billy Roland, qb, 60-62	1396	(24-420-952)
11) Danny Davis, qb, 76	1348	(1348-)

Ken Bailey

PASS RECEIVING 600 YARD CLUB

PLAYERS AND YEARS	YARDS	YEAR-BY-YEAR
1) Elmo Wright, se, 68-70	3347	(1198-1275-874)
2) Ken Hebert, se, 65-67	1785	(359-800-626)
3) Don Bass, te-se, 74-76	1241	(198-646-397)
4) Vic Hampel, e, 50-52	967	(26-545-296)
5) Eddie Foster, te-se, 73-76	947	(63-163-197-524)
6) Riley Odoms, te, 69-71	877	(97-50-730)
7) Robert Ford, flk-se, 70-72	869	(230-101-538)
8) Warren McVea, flk-hb, 65-67	811	(341-414-86)
9) Mike Spratt, se, 63-65	728	(237-124-267)
10) Gene Shannon, hb, 49-51	658	(173-140-345)
11) Tom Beer, e, 65-66	653	(325-328)
12) Robert Lavergne, fk, 73-76	608	(27-184-151-246)

TOP FIVE
ALL-TIME STAT LEADERS
(ONE SEASON)

Bob Borah

Tom Beer

TOTAL OFFENSE	YARDS	YEAR
1) Bob Burris, qb	1846	1966
2) Gary Mullins, qb	1831	1969
3) Danny Davis, qb	1768	1976
4) Gary Mullins, qb	1764	1971
5) Robert Newhouse, fb	1757	1972

RUSHING	YARDS	YEAR
1) Robert Newhouse, fb	1757	1971
2) Paul Gipson, fb	1550	1968
3) Jim Strong, rb	1293	1969
4) Puddin Jones, fb	1216	1972
5) Gene Shannon, hb	1211	1957

Gene Shannon

Dick Post

PASSING	YARDS	YEAR
1) Bo Burris, qb	1666	1966
2) Gary Mullins, qb	1616	1971
3) Gary Mullins, qb	1433	1969
4) D.C. Nobles, qb	1351	1972
5) Danny Davis, qb	1348	1976

PASSES CAUGHT		YEAR
1) Elmo Wright, se	63	1969
2) Elmo Wright, se	47	1970
3) Riley Odoms, te	45	1971
4) Elmo Wright, se	43	1968
5) Ken Hebert, se	38	1966
Don Bass, te	38	1975

347

RECORDS BY INDIVIDUALS

Robert Newhouse

RUSHING

MOST CARRIES IN A GAME: 37
Paul Gipson, 1968, UH-10, Georgia-10
Gain: 238 Loss: 8 Net: 230 TD: 0
Paul Gipson, 1968, UH-27, Memphis St.-7
Gain: 141 Loss: 1 Net: 140 TD: 0
MOST CARRIES IN A SEASON: 297
Robert Newhouse, 1971, 11 games
Gain: 1776 Loss: 19 Net: 1757 TD: 12
MOST YARDAGE IN A GAME: 282
Paul Gipson, 1968, UH-100, Tulsa-6
Carries: 29 Gain: 282 Loss: 0 TD: 3
MOST CARRIES IN A CAREER: 461
Robert Newhouse, 1969, 1970, 1971 (30 games)
Gain: 3015 Loss: 54 Net: 2961 TD: 19
MOST YARDAGE IN A SEASON: 1757
Robert Newhouse, 1971, 11 games
Carries: 277 Gain: 1776 Loss: 19 TD: 12
MOST YARDAGE IN A CAREER: 2961
Robert Newhouse, 1969, 1970, 1971 (30 games)
Carries: 461 Gain: 3015 Loss: 54 TD: 19
BEST AVERAGE PER CARRY IN A SEASON
(Minimum 60 carries): 8:8
Warren McVea, 1966, 10 games
Carries: 74 Gain: 666 Loss: 18 Net: 648 TD: 5
BEST AVERAGE PER CARRY IN A CAREER
(Minimum 180 carries): 6.7
Warren McVea, 1965-66-67 (28 games)
Carries: 217 Gain: 1548 Loss: 87 Net: 1461 TD: 9

Gary Mullins

PASSING

MOST ATTEMPTS IN A GAME: 36
D.C. Nobles, 1972, UH-28, Ariz. St.-33
Comp: 15 Int: 1 Gain: 239 TD: 2
UH-27, Va. Tech-27
Comp: 17 Int: 0 Gain: 193 TD: 2
MOST ATTEMPTS IN A SEASON: 209
D.C. Nobles, 1972, 11 games
Comp: 101 Int: 7 Gain: 1351 TD: 15
MOST ATTEMPTS IN A CAREER: 509
Gary Mullins, 1969, 1970, 1971 (30 games)
Comp: 245 Int: 24 Gain: 4095 TD: 37
MOST COMPLETED IN A GAME: 22
Bo Burris, 1965, UH-38, Kentucky-21
Att: 30 Int: 0 Gain: 175 TD: 4
MOST COMPLETED IN A SEASON: 101
D.C. Nobles, 1972, 11 games
Att: 209 Int: 7 Gain: 1351 TD: 15
MOST COMPLETED IN A CAREER: 245
Gary Mullins, 1969, 1970, 1971 (30 games)
Att: 509 Int: 24 Gain: 4095 TD: 37
MOST YARDAGE IN A GAME: 284
Bo Burris, 1965, UH-17, Ole Miss-3
Att: 19 Comp: 9 Int: 21 TD: 2
MOST YARDAGE IN A SEASON: 1666
Bo Burris, 1966, 10 games
Att: 204 Comp: 98 Int: 21 TD: 22
MOST YARDAGE IN A CAREER: 4095
Gary Mullins, 1969, 1970, 1971 (30 games)
Att: 509 Comp: 245 Int: 24 TD: 37
MOST TD PASSES IN A GAME: 5 (Tie)
Bo Burris, 1966, UH-35, Okla. St.-9
Att: 23 Comp: 13 Int: 2 Gain: 213
Ken Bailey, 1969, UH-34, Fla.-59
Att: 28 Comp: 13 Int: 1 Gain: 213
MOST TD PASSES IN A SEASON: 22
Bo Burris, 1966, 10 games
Att: 204 Comp: 98 Int: 21 Gain: 1666
MOST TD PASSES IN A CAREER: 37
Gary Mullins, 1969, 1970, 1971 (30 games)
Att: 509 Comp: 245 Int: 24 Gain: 4095
BEST COMPLETION PERCENTAGE ONE GAME: 83.3
Jack Skog, 1963, UH-55, Detroit-18
Att: 12 Comp: 10 Int: 0 Gain: 140 TD: 0
BEST COMPLETION PERCENTAGE ONE SEASON
(Min. 60 Att.): 59.2
Lonnie Holland, 1959, 10 games
Att: 76 Comp: 45 Int: 9 Gain: 423 TD: 3
BEST COMPLETION PERCENTAGE IN CAREER
(Min. 180 Att.): 53.7
Billy Roland, 1960, 1961, 1962 (24 games)
Att: 212 Comp: 114 Int: 10 Gain: 1396 TD 12

Paul Gipson

Warren McVea

Jack Skog

(Continued on next page)

PASSING (Continued)

FEWEST INTERCEPTED IN A SEASON (Min. 60 Att.): 3
Bobby Clatterbuck, 1953, 8 games
Att: 61 Comp: 30 Gain: 276 TD: 0
FEWEST INTERCEPTED IN A CAREER (Min. 180 Att.): 10
Billy Roland, 1960, 1961, 1962 (24 games)
Att: 212 Comp: 114 Gain: 1396 TD: 12

Billy Roland

TOTAL OFFENSE

MOST PLAYS IN A GAME: 51
D.C. Nobles, 1972, UH-28, Ariz. St.-33
Rush: 15 for 41 Pass: 15 for 239
MOST PLAYS IN A SEASON: 303
Danny Davis, 1976, 11 games
Rush: 142 for 420 yds; Pass: 77 of 161 for 1348 yds.
MOST PLAYS IN A CAREER: 756
Gary Mullins, 1969, 1970, 1971 (30 games)
Rush: 603 Pass: 4095
MOST YARDS IN A GAME: 361
Dick Woodall, 1967, UH-50, Wake Forest-6
Rush: 95 Pass: 266
MOST YARDS IN A SEASON: 1846
Bo Burris, 1966, 10 games
Rush: 180 Pass: 1666
MOST YARDS IN A CAREER: 4698
Gary Mullins, 1969, 1970, 1971 (30 games)
Rush: 603 Pass: 4095
AVERAGE GAIN PER PLAY IN A SEASON (Min. 60 Plays): 8.8
Warren McVea, 1966, 10 games
Rush: 74 for 648 Pass: 0 for 0
AVERAGE GAIN PER PLAY IN A CAREER (Min. 180 Plays): 6.7
Warren McVea, 1965, 1966, 1967, 28 games
Rush: 217 for 1461 Pass: 0 for 0

Dick Woodall

PASS RECEIVING

MOST CAUGHT IN A GAME: 12
Elmo Wright, 1969, UH-18, Okla. St.-24
MOST CAUGHT IN A SEASON: 63
Elmo Wright, 1969, Yds: 1275 TD: 14
MOST CAUGHT IN A CAREER: 153
Elmo Wright, 1968-70, Yds: 3347 TD: 34
MOST YARDS RECEIVING IN A GAME: 262
Elmo Wright, 1969, UH-41, Wyoming-14
MOST YARDS RECEIVING IN A SEASON: 1275
Elmo Wright, 1969, No: 63 TD: 14
MOST YARDS RECEIVING IN A CAREER: 3347
Elmo Wright, 1968-70, No: 153 TD: 34
MOST TD PASSES CAUGHT IN A GAME: 4
Ken Hebert, 1966, UH-48, Tampa-9 (5-205-4)
Elmo Wright, 1968, UH-77, Idaho-3 (7-249-4)
Elmo Wright, 1969, UH-41, Wyoming-14 (7-262-4)
Don Bass, 1976, UH 49, TCU-21 (5-188-4)
MOST TD PASSES CAUGHT IN A SEASON: 14
Elmo Wright, 1969, Yds: 1275 No: 63
MOST TD PASSES CAUGHT IN A CAREER: 34
Elmo Wright, 1968-70, Yds: 3347 No: 153

Elmo Wright

PUNTING

BEST AVERAGE IN A SEASON (Minimum 30 punts): 43.6
Ken Hebert, 1967, 10 games
Punts: 42 Yds: 1380 Blkd: 0
BEST AVERAGE IN A CAREER (Minimum 60 punts): 41.6
Ken Hebert, 1965-67 (29 games)
Punts: 157 Yds: 6530 Blocked: 0
MOST PUNTING YARDAGE IN A SEASON: 3047
Ken Hebert, 1965, 10 games
Punts: 75 Blkd: 0 Avg: 40.6
MOST PUNTING YARDAGE IN A CAREER: 6530
Ken Hebert, 1965-67 (29 games)
Punts: 157 Yds: 6530 Blocked: 0 Avg: 41.6

Ken Hebert

PUNT RETURNS

MOST YARDAGE IN A GAME: 199
Don Bean, 1966, UH-73, Tulsa-14 (5-199-2)
MOST YARDAGE IN A SEASON: 522
Don Bean, 1967 (45-522-2)
MOST YARDAGE IN A CAREER: 906
Don Bean, 966-67 (64-906-5)
BEST AVERAGE IN A SEASON (Minimum 10 ret.): 20.2
Don Bean, 1966 (19-384-3)
BEST AVERAGE IN A CAREER (Minimum 15 ret.): 18.1
Ken Stegall, 1953-55 (19-343)

Don Bean

KICKOFF RETURNS

MOST YARDS ON KO RETURNS IN A GAME: 136
Willie Roberts, 1969, UH-34, Florida-59 (4-136-34.0)

MOST YARDS ON KO RETURNS IN A SEASON: 579
Willie Roberts, 1971, (25-579-23.2)

MOST YARDS ON KO RETURNS IN A CAREER: 1456
Willie Roberts, 1969-70-71 (63-1456-23.1)

BEST AVERAGE IN A SEASON (Minimum 6 returns): 30.4
Ronnie Powledge, 1963 (7-213-30.4)

BEST AVERAGE IN A CAREER (Minimum 15 returns): 27.3
Claude King, 1957-58-59 (16-436-27.3)

Claude King

PASS INTERCEPTION RETURNS

MOST INTERCEPTIONS IN A GAME: 5
Bryon Beaver, 1962, UH-19, Baylor-0 (5-18)

MOST INTERCEPTIONS IN A SEASON: 10
Bryon Beaver, 1962 (10-56)
Paul Shires, 1968 (10-45)
Anthony Francis, 1976 (10-118)

MOST INTERCEPTIONS IN A CAREER: 14
Gus Hollomon, 1965-67 (14-200)

MOST YARDS RETURNED IN A GAME: 100
Frank Ditta, 1971, UH-34, San Jose St.-20 (1-100)

MOST YARDS RETURNED IN A SEASON: 119
Red Purdum, 1949 (5-119)

MOST YARDS RETURNED IN A CAREER: 200
Gus Hollomon, 1965-67 (14-200)

Willie Roberts

Gus Hollomon

SCORING

MOST POINTS IN A GAME: 30
Ken Hebert, 1966, UH-48- Tampa-9
TD: 4 Ex-Pts: 6-7 FG: 0-0

MOST POINTS IN A SEASON: 113
Ken Hebert, 1966 (TD: 11 Ex-Pts: 4-46 FG: 2-7)

MOST POINTS IN A CAREER: 246
Ken Hebert, 1966-67 (TD: 22 Ex-Pts: 89-103 FG: 7-20)

MOST TD'S IN A GAME: 4 (Tie)
Ken Hebert, 1966, UH-48, Tampa-9
TD: 4 Ex-Pts: 6-7 FG: 0-0
Elmo Wright, 1968, UH-77, Idaho-3
TD: 4 Ex-Pts: 0-0 FG: 0-0
Elmo Wright, 1969, UH-41, Wyoming-14
TD: 4 Ex-Pts: 0-0 FG: 0-0
Don Bass, 1976, UH-49, TCU-21
TD: 4 Ex-Pts: 0-0 FG: 0-0

MOST TD'S IN A SEASON: 14
Elmo Wright, 1969 (TD: 14 Ex-Pts: 0-0 FG: 0-0)

MOST TD'S IN A CAREER: 35
Elmo Wright, 1968-70 (TD: 35 Ex-Pts: 3 FG: 0-0)

MOST FIELD GOALS IN A GAME: 3
Lennard Coplin, 1975, UH-22, Florida St.-33; 1976, UH-30, Texas-0

MOST FIELD GOALS IN A SEASON: 9
Lennard Coplin, 1976, Att: 15

MOST FIELD GOALS IN A CAREER: 19
Lennard Coplin, 1974-76, Att: 29

MOST EXTRA POINTS IN A GAME: 13
Terry Lieweke, 1968, UH-100, Tulsa-6 (Att: 14)

MOST EXTRA POINTS IN A SEASON: 52
Terry Lieweke, 1968 (Att: 57 Pct: 91.2)

MOST EXTRA POINTS IN A CAREER: 92
Ricky Terrell, 1971-72 (Att: 102, Pct: 90.2)

BEST EX-PT PERCENT IN A SEASON (Minimum 15 Att): 95.2
Ricky Terrell, 1971, Att: 21 Made: 20

BEST EX-PT PERCENT IN A CAREER (Minimum 60 Att): 90.2
Ricky Terrell, 1971-73, Att: 102 Made: 92

Byron Beaver

Ricky Terrell

TEAM ALL-TIME SEASON HIGHS AND LOWS

	Year-High	Year-Low
Yards Rushing	1973 - 3798	1965 - 1071
Yards Passing	1968 - 2003	1947 - 270
Total Offense	1968 - 5620	1947 - 1775
Total First Downs	1968 - 260	1946 & 1947 - 82
First Downs Rushing	1973 - 187	1965 - 65
First Downs Passing	1969 - 82	1950 - 16
First Downs by Penalty	1970 - 16	1954 - 3
Passes Attempted	1972 - 253	1946 - 82
Passes Completed	1972 - 117	1947 - 19
Own Passes Intercepted	1966 - 21	1953 - 5
Passing Percentage	1963 - 54.5	1947 - 17.8
Touchdowns Rushing	1968 - 36	1965 - 7
Touchdowns Passing	1966 - 23	1947 - 2
Touchdowns	1968 - 60	1947 - 14
Punting Average	1967 - 44.4	1958 - 31.0
Penalties	1971 - 91	1960 - 29
Yards Penalized	1971 - 828	1960 - 283
Fumbles	1974 - 61	1958 & 1959 - 23
Own Fumbles Recovered	1951 - 31	1961 - 7
Fumbles Lost	1954 & 1974 - 32	1958 - 9
Rushing Plays	1974 - 720	1964 - 362
Total Plays	1973 - 891 2	1947 - 486
Punts	1947 - 105	1955 & 1968 - 35
Yards Punting	1947 - 3369	1958 - 1198
Punt Returns	1967 - 49	1964 - 17
Punt Return Yards	1967 - 548	1975 - 65
Kickoff Returns	1969 - 40	1952 - 13
Kickoff Ret. Yards	1963 - 998	1952 - 226
Pass Int. Returns	1968 - 31	1975 - 7
Pass Int. Yards	1972 - 382	1975 - 71
Points	1968 - 425	1947 - 96

RUSHING

MOST PLAYS IN A GAME: 84, 1969, UH-14, Miss. St.-0; 1973, UH-14, San Diego St.-9
FEWEST PLAYS IN A GAME: 26, 1951, UH-20, No. Texas-14
MOST YARDS IN A GAME: 555, 1968, UH-100. Tulsa-6
FEWEST YARDS IN A GAME: -21, 1947, UH-0, S.W. Texas-2
BEST AVERAGE PER GAME: 361.7, 1968, 10 Games
LOWEST AVERAGE PER GAME: 107.1, 1965, 10 Games

PASSING

MOST ATTEMPTED IN A GAME: 46, 1969, UH-18, Okla. St.-24
FEWEST ATTEMPTED IN A GAME: 0, 1946, UH-14. S.W. Texas-12
MOST COMPLETED IN A GAME: 22, 1965, UH-38, Kentucky-21
FEWEST COMPLETED IN A GAME: 0
    1946, 2 games; 1947, 3 games; 1955, 1 game
MOST HAD INTERCEPTED IN A GAME: 7,
    1966, UH-6, Ole Miss-27
MOST YARDS IN A GAME: 443, 1976, UH-49, TCU-21
FEWEST YARDS IN A GAME: 0
    1946, 2 games; 1947, 3 games; 1955, 1 game
MOST TD PASSES IN A GAME: 5, 1966, UH-35, Okla. St.-9; 1968, UH-77, Idaho-3; 1976, UH-49, TCU-21
BEST COMPLETION PERCENTAGE IN A GAME: 75.0
    18 of 24, 1976, UH-49, TCU -21

TOTAL OFFENSE

MOST PLAYS IN A GAME: 96, 1968, UH-71, Cincinnati-33
FEWEST PLAYS IN A GAME: 41 (Tie)
    1951, UH-20, N. Texas-14; 1963, UH-6, Memphis St.-29
    1964; UH-0, Auburn-30
MOST YARDS IN A GAME: 733, 1968, UH-77, Idaho-3
FEWEST YARDS IN A GAME: -21, 1947, UH-0, S.W. Texas-2
MOST YARDS PER GAME IN A SEASON: *562.0, 1968, 10 Games
FEWEST YARDS PER GAME IN A SEASON: 161.4, 1947, 11 Games
*All-time NCAA record at that time.

PUNTING

MOST IN A GAME: 25, 1947, UH-0, S.W. Texas-2
MOST YARDS IN A GAME: 849, 1947, UH-0, S.W. Texas-2
MOST HAD BLOCKED IN A SEASON: 5, 1947, 11 Games
BEST AVERAGE IN A GAME: (Min. 6): 53.1
    1948, UH-13, W. Texas-28

PUNT RETURNS

MOST YARDS IN A GAME: 199, 1966, UH-73, Tulsa-14
BEST RETURN AVERAGE IN A SEASON: 16.05, 1955, 10 Games
LOWEST RETURN AVG. IN A SEASON: 2.8, 1975, 10 Games

KICKOFF RETURNS

MOST YARDS IN A GAME: 205, 1973, UH-54, Virginia Tech-27
BEST RETURN AVERAGE IN A SEASON: 26.3, 1963, 10 Games
LOWEST RETURN AVG. IN A SEASON: 13.5, 1976, 11 Games

PASS INTERCEPTION RETURNS

MOST IN A GAME: 6, 1952, UH-20, Texas Tech-7 and 1966, UH-48
Tampa-9
MOST YARDS RETURNED IN A GAME: 148, 1971, UH-34, San
Jose St.-20

——PENALTIES AGAINST

MOST IN A GAME: 14, 1971, UH-42, Villanova-9
MOST YARDS IN A GAME: 153, 1970, UH-17, Okla. St.-26
FEWEST YARDS IN A GAME: 0, 1951, UH-6, Texas Tech-0; 1960,
UH-7, Florida St.-6

FUMBLES BY UH

MOST IN A GAME: 11
1949, UH-26, Wichita-6; 1951, UH-33, Detroit-7
MOST LOST IN A GAME: 8, 1949, UH-26, Wichita-6

FIRST DOWNS

MOST IN A GAME: 37, 1968, UH-100, Tulsa-6
FEWEST IN A GAME: 1, 1947, UH-7, Hardin-Simmons-33
MOST IN A GAME BY RUSHING: 29, 1968, UH-100, Tulsa-6
FEWEST IN A GAME BY RUSHING: 1
1947, UH-7, Hardin-Simmons-33
1964, UH-0, Auburn-30
MOST IN A GAME BY PASS: 16
1976, UH-49, TCU-21
MOST IN A GAME BY PENALTY: 5, 1950, UH-14, St. Bona-29

SCORING

MOST POINTS IN A GAME: 100, 1968, UH-100, Tulsa-6
MOST TD'S IN A GAME: 14, 1968, UH-100, Tulsa-6
MOST EX-PTS IN A GAME: 13, 1968, UH-100, Tulsa-6
MOST EX-PTS IN A SEASON: 53, 1968, 10 Games
FEWEST EX-PTS IN A SEASON: 7, 1959, 10 Games
MOST FG'S IN A GAME: 3, 1975, UH-22, Florida St.-33; 1976,
UH-30, Texas-0
MOST FG'S IN A SEASON: 9, 1976

OPPOSITION RECORDS

(UH Team Defense)

OPPONENTS' SEASON HIGHS AND LOWS

	Year-High	Year-Low
Rushing Plays	1970 - 566	1958 - 334
Yards Rushing	1975 - 2131	1946 & 1967 - 943
Passes Attempted	1969 - 332	1948 - 111
Passes Completed	1972 - 150	1948 - 24
Touchdown Passes	1969 - 16	1952, 1956 &
		1957 - 3
Passing Percentage	1958 - 53.1	1948 - 21.6
Yards Passing	1972 - 1964	1957 - 574
Total Plays	1970 - 829	1953 - 523
Total Offense	1976 - 3666	1967 - 2076
Punts	1948 & 1967 - 86	1955 - 42
Yards Punting	1967 - 3401	1955 - 1464
Punt Returns	1970 - 38	1951 - 10
Punt Return Yards	1965 - 433	1968 - 71
Kickoff Returns	1968 & 1969 - 65	1960 - 23
Kickoff Ret. Yards	1973 - 1350	1954 - 444
Pass Int. Returns	1968 - 31	1953 - 5
Pass Int. Yards	1967 - 339	1953 - 45
Penalties	1947, 1950 &	1953 - 36
	1954 - 72	
Yards Penalized	1967 - 848	1953 - 301
Fumbles	1975 - 41	1964 - 11
Fumbles Lost	1953 - 22	1964 - 4
First Downs	1972 - 187	1947 - 91
First Downs Rushing	1963 - 120	1966 - 52
First Downs Passing	1962 - 90	1948 - 14
First Downs Penalty	1966 - 19; 1975 - 19	1949 - 3
Points	1975 - 244	1952 - 80
Touchdowns	1951 - 35	1952 - 12

OPPONENTS' RUSHING

MOST PLAYS IN A GAME: 71, 1963, Texas A&M; 1970, Ore. St.
FEWEST PLAYS IN A GAME: 19, 1958, Wichita
MOST YARDS IN A GAME: 440, 1951, Tulsa
FEWEST YARDS IN A GAME: -20, 1969, Miss. St.

OPPONENTS' PASSING

MOST ATTEMPTED IN A GAME: 53, 1972, Virginia Tech
FEWEST ATTEMPTED IN A GAME: 2, 1957, Texas A&M
MOST COMPLETED IN A GAME: 35, 1972, Virginia Tech
FEWEST COMP. IN A GAME: 0, S.W. Texas (47), Tenn. (53)
MOST YARDS IN A GAME: 527, 1972, Virginia Tech
FEWEST YARDS IN A GAME: 0, S.W. Texas (47), Tenn. (53)
MOST TD PASSES IN A GAME: 6, Mississippi (1960)
BEST COMPLETION PCT. IN A GAME: 76.2
Mississippi, 1961, 16 of 21

OPPONENTS' TOTAL OFFENSE

MOST PLAYS IN A GAME: 94, 1972, Virginia Tech
FEWEST PLAYS IN A GAME: 38, 1949, SLI
MOST YARDS IN A GAME: 605, 1972, Virginia Tech
FEWEST YARDS IN A GAME: 74, 1969, Miss. St.
MOST YARDS PER GAME IN A SEASON: 322.3, 1972, 11 games
FEWEST YARDS PER GAME IN A SEASON: 207.6,
1967, 10 games

OPPONENTS' PUNTING

MOST PUNTS IN A GAME: 20, 1947, S.W. Texas
MOST YARDS IN A GAME: 708, 1947, S.W. Texas
MOST HAD BLOCKED (BY UH) IN A SEASON: 6, 1952, 10 Games
BEST AVERAGE IN A GAME (Min. 6): 48.2,
1949, Trinity (11 for 530 yards)
BEST AVG. IN A SEASON: 41.6, 1965, 10 Games (72 for 2995)

OPPONENTS' PUNT RETURNS

MOST IN A GAME: 7, 1949, West Texas
MOST YARDS IN A GAME: 150, 1965, Miss. St.
BEST RETURN AVERAGE IN A SEASON: 16.3, 1955, 10 Games
LOWEST RETURN AVERAGE IN A SEASON: 4.7, 1975, 10 Games

OPPONENTS' KICKOFF RETURNS

MOST IN A GAME: 13, 1968, Tulsa
MOST YARDS IN A GAME: 296, 1968, Tulsa
BEST RETURN AVG. IN A SEASON: 24.4, 1975, (37 for 903)
LOWEST RETURN AVG. IN A SEASON: 15.0, 1949, 10 Games

OPPONENTS' PASS INTERCEPTIONS

MOST IN A GAME: 7, 1966, Ole Miss
MOST YARDS RETURNED IN A GAME: 111, 1971, Villanova

OPPONENTS' PENALTIES

MOST PENALTIES IN A GAME: 16, Baylor, 1960
MOST YARDS PEN. IN A GAME: 152, Oklahoma St., 1970

OPPONENTS' FUMBLES

MOST IN A GAME: 8, Wichita, 1956; Memphis St., 1975.
MOST LOST IN A GAME: 6, St. Louis U., 1949; Virginia Tech, 1975

OPPONENTS' FIRST DOWNS

MOST IN A GAME: 30, Virginia Tech, 1972
FEWEST IN A GAME: 3, S.W. Texas, 1947
MOST IN A GAME BY RUSHING: 20, Auburn, 1956
FEWEST IN A GAME BY RUSHING: 0, Wichita, 1949 and 1958; Mississippi State, 1966
MOST IN A GAME BY PASSING: 18, Florida St., 1968
MOST IN A GAME BY PENALTY: 5, Texas A&M, 1955; Florida State, 1966

OPPONENTS' SCORING

MOST POINTS IN A GAME: 61, Texas Tech, 1954
MOST TD'S IN A GAME: 9, Texas Tech, 1954
MOST FG'S IN A SEASON: 11, 1970; 1975

MILESTONE WINS

25th Win - 1951 — UH 20, North Texas 14
50th Win - 1956 — UH 18, Mississippi St. 7
75th Win - 1960 — UH 7, Florida St. 6
100th Win - 1966 — UH 48, Tampa 9
125th Win - 1969 — UH 36, Auburn 7
150th Win - 1973 — UH 27, South Carolina 19
175th Win - 1976 — UH 27, Texas Tech 19

UH ALL-AMERICANS

(Note: Houston first entered intercollegiate athletics in 1946)

Kimmel

H. Wharton

FOOTBALL
1952—J. D. Kimmel, t
1958—Hogan Wharton, t
1966—Warren McVea, hb
1967—Ken Hebert, e
1967—Rich Stotter, g
1967—Warren McVea, hb
1967—Paul Gipson, fb
1967—Greg Brezina, lb
1968—Paul Gipson, fb
1968—John Peacock, db
1968—Royce Berry, de
1969—Elmo Wright, se
1969—Jim Strong, rb
1969—Bill Bridges, ot
1969—Jerry Drones, de
1970—Elmo Wright, se
1970—Charlie Hall, lb
1971—Riley Odoms, te
1971—Robert Newhouse, rb
1973—Deryl McGallion, lb
1973—Robert Giblin, cb
1974—Robert Giblin, cb
1974—Mack Mitchell, de
1976—Wilson Whitley, dt

Odoms

Newhouse

McVea

Brezina

Strong

McGallion

Hebert

Peacock

Bridges

Giblin

Stotter

Berry

Drones

Strong

Gipson

Wright

C. Hall

Whitley

355

SEASON-BY-SEASON LEADERS

TOTAL OFFENSE

YEAR	PLAYER	RUSH-PASS	TOTAL
1976	Danny Davis, QB	420-1348	1768
1975	Bubba McGallion, QB	392- 697	1089
1974	John Housman, FB	988- 0	988
1973	D.C. Nobles, QB	591-1148	1739
1972	D.C. Nobles, QB	289-1351	1640
1971	Gary Mullins, QB	148-1616	1764
1970	Gary Mullins, QB	57-1046	1103
1969	Gary Mullins, QB	398-1433	1839
1968	Paul Gipson, FB	1550- 74	1624
1967	Dick Woodall, QB	39-1224	1263
1966	Bo Burris. QB	180-1666	1846*
1965	Bo Burris, QB	81-1256	1337
1964	Dick Post, LH	528- 2	530
1963	Jack Skog, QB	34-1145	1179
1962	Billy Roland, QB	-14- 952	938
1961	Billy Roland, QB	288- 420	708
1960	Don Sessions, QB	95- 724	819
1959	Lonnie Holland, B	95- 423	518
1958	Lonnie Holland, QB	83- 542	625
1957	Don Brown, RH	378- 25	403
1956	Don Flynn, QB	412- 464	876
1955	Jimmy Dickey, QB	176- 464	630
1954	Jimmy Dickey, QB	181- 474	655
1953	Donn Hargrove, RH	407- 0	407
1952	Bobby Clatterbuck, QB	-34- 736	702
1951	Gene Shannon. RH	1211- 0	1211
1950	Max Clark, LH	860- 35	895
1949	Alan Neveux, QB	36- 939	975
1948	Alan Neveux, QB	209- 549	758
1947	Boyd Tingle, QB-HB	299- 116	415

John Housman

Jim Strong

RUSHING

YEAR	PLAYER	CARRIES	YARDS
1976	Alois Blackwell, RB	151	934
1975	John Housman, FB	107	466
1974	John Housman, FB	192	988
1973	Leonard Parker, FB	224	1123
1972	Puddin' Jones, FB	222	1216
1971	Robert Newhouse, FB	277*	1757*
1970	Tommy Mozisek, RB	153	935
1969	Jim Strong, RB	190	1293
1968	Paul Gipson, FB	242	1550
1967	Paul Gipson, FB	187	1100
1966	Dick Post, FB	185	1061
1965	Dick Post, LH	156	630
1964	Dick Post, LH	116	528
1963	Joe Lopasky, LH	96	353
1962	Bobby Brezina, LH	113	567
1961	Ken Bolin, LH	60	356
1960	Ken Bolin, LH	75	542
1959	Charlie Rieves, FB	87	347
1958	Claude King, RH	76	439
1957	Don Brown, RH	86	378
1956	Don Flynn, QB	90	412
1955	Charley Johnson, FB	82	469
1954	Jack Patterson, FB	77	361
1953	Donn Hargrove, RH	69	407
1952	S. M. Meeks, LH	78	366
1951	Gene Shannon, RH	171	1211
1950	Max Clark, LH	129	860
1949	Gene Shannon, RH	88	498
1948	Jack Gwin, RH-FB	78	357
1947	Boyd Tingle, QB-HB	—	299

Puddin' Jones

Bubba McGallion

PASSING

YEAR	PLAYER	ATT-COMP.		YARDS
1976	Danny Davis, QB	161	77	1348
1975	Bubba McGallion, QB	103	47	697
1974	David Husmann, QB	90	38	524
1973	D.C. Nobles, QB	156	70	1148
1972	D.C. Nobles, QB	209*	101*	1351
1971	Gary Mullins, QB	184	94	1616
1970	Gary Mullins, QB	159	68	1046
1969	Gary Mullins, QB	166	83	1433
1968	Ken Bailey, QB	152	71	1279
1967	Dick Woodall, QB	132	65	1224
1966	Bo Burris, QB	204	98	1666*
1965	Bo Burris, QB	175	81	1256
1964	Jack Skog, QB	55	30	436
1963	Jack Skog, QB	182	100	1145
1962	Billy Roland, QB	140	71	952
1961	Don Sessions, QB	111	48	549
1960	Don Sessions, QB	133	65	724
1959	Lonnie Holland, QB	76	45	423
1958	Lonnie Holland, QB	84	48	542

*—School Record

Joe Lopasky

356

PASSING (Continued)

Year	Player			
1957	Sammy Blount, QB	50	22	306
1956	Don Flynn, QB	53	22	464
1955	Jimmy Dickey, QB	81	32	454
1954	Jimmy Dickey, QB	77	32	474
1953	Bobby Clatterbuck, QB	61	30	276
1952	Bobby Clatterbuck, QB	128	47	276
1951	Bobby Clatterbuck, QB	117	62	1113
1950	Bobby Rogers, QB	61	28	287
1949	Alan Neveux, QB	144	63	939
1948	Alan Neveux, QB	116	46	549
1947	Boyd Tingle, QB	—	—	116

Riley Odoms

PASS RECEIVING

YEAR	PLAYER	NO.	YARDS
1976	Eddie Foster, TE	26	524
1975	Don Bass, TE	38	646
1974	Frank Scalise, FLK	11	251
1973	Bryan Willingham, SE	16	328
1972	Robert Ford, FLK-SE	35	538
1971	Riley Odoms, TE	45	730
1970	Elmo Wright, SE	47	874
1969	Elmo Wright, SE	63*	1275*
1968	Elmo Wright, SE	43	1198
1967	Ken Hebert, SE	28	626
1966	Ken Hebert, SE	38	800
1965	Ken Hebert, SE	24	359
1964	Dick Post, LH	12	100
1963	Clem Beard, RE	19	240
1962	Bill Van Osdel, LE	15	226
1961	Bill McMillan, RH	15	244
1960	Erroll Linden, RE	12	146
1959	Larry Lindsey, LE	11	375
1958	Bob Borah, LE	29	375
1957	Charles Mallia, RE	9	116
1956	Harold Lewis, RH	5	90
1955	Ronnie Emberg, RE	12	173
1954	Ronnie Emberg, RE	12	152
1953	Ben Wilson, RE	12	128
1952	Vic Hampel, RE	19	396
1951	Vic Hampel, RE	25	545
1950	Max Clark, LH	11	203
1949	Maurice Elliott, RE	13	177
1948	Ed Stagg, RE	17	234

Jack Patterson

PUNT RETURNS

YEAR	PLAYER	NO.	YARDS
1976	Elrick Brown, FLK	15	84
1975	Elrick Brown, FLK	16	29
1974	Robert Giblin, CB	7	113
1973	Joe Rust, S	30	98
1972	Robert Ford, FLK-SE	23	236
1971	Pat Orchin, SE	26	189
1970	Robert Ford, FLK	27	214
1969	Calvin Achey, FLK	18	80
1968	Mike Simpson, HB	19	231
1967	Don Bean, FLK	45*	522*
1966	Don Bean, FLK	19	384
1965	Tom Paciorek, HB	14	132
1964	Joe Lopasky, LH	7	76
1963	Mike Spratt, RH	12	123
1962	Gene Ritch, RH	11	63
1961	Bill McMillan, RH	15	77
1960	Larry Lindsey, QB	11	175
1959	Pat Studstill, LE-HB	6	42
1958	Harold Lewis, RH	7	114
1957	Harold Lewis, FB	9	89
1956	Harold Lewis, RH	7	122
1955	Kennie Stegall, LH	7	172
1954	Jimmy Dickey, QB	11	110
1953	Kennie Stegall, LH	5	87
1952	Billy Polson, LH	22	260
1951	Ken Pridgeon, LH	10	105
1950	Carl Mittag, HB	12	143
1949	Jolly Hartsell, QB	16	273
1948	Max Clark, LH	18	176
1947	Jack Gwin, FB-RH	10	129

Robert Giblin

KICKOFF RETURNS

YEAR	PLAYER	NO.	YARDS
1976	Emmett King, RB	14	236
1975	Delrick Brown, QB	13	256
1974	Eddie Foster, SE	15	275
1973	Joe Rust, S	14	267
1972	Robert Ford, FLK-SE	14	331
1971	Willie Roberts, SE	25	579
1970	Willie Roberts, SE	18	375

Eddie Foster

Robert Ford

357

KICKOFF RETURNS (Continued)

Year	Player		
1969	Willie Roberts, RB	20	502*
1968	Jake Green, RB	13	268
1967	Paul Gipson, FB	8	137
1966	Don Bean, FLK	9	214
1965	Warren McVea, WB	17	428
1964	Dick Post, LH	9	168
1963	Joe Lopasky, LH	16	430
1962	Boyd Timmons, LH	6	168
1961	Ken Bolin, LH	18	429
1960	Ken Bolin, LH	9	251
1959	Jim Kuehne, RH	8	183
1958	Claude King, LH	10	291
1957	Harold Lewis, FB	9	185
1956	Harold Lewis, RH	4	105
1955	Donn Hargrove, RH	4	124
1954	Kennie Stegall, LH	6	157
1953	Kennie Stegall, LH	15	270
1952	Billy Polson, LH	9	178
1951	Gene Shannon, RH	16	323
1950	Gene Shannon, RH	12	221
1949	Max Clark, LH	8	173
1948	Max Clark, LH	6	154

Lennard Coplin

SCORING

YEAR	PLAYER	TDs	POINTS
1976	Lennard Coplin, K	0	61
1975	Bubba McGallion, QB	5	34
1974	John Housman, FB	8	48
1973	Leonard Parker, FB	12	74
1972	Puddin' Jones, FB	12	74
1971	Robert Newhouse, FB	12	74
1970	Tommy Mozisek, RB	11	66
1969	Elmo Wright, SE	14	90
1968	Paul Gipson, FB	14	84
1967	Ken Hebert, SE	7	86
1966	Ken Hebert, SE	11	113*
1965	Ken Hebert, SE	4	47
1964	Dick Post, LH	5	30
1963	Mike Spratt, RH	5	30
1962	Joe Lopasky, LH	9	54
1961	Billy Roland, QB; Larry Broussard, FB	4	24
1960	Charlie Rieves, FB	6	38
1959	Charlie Rieves, FB; Larry Lindsey, LE	3	18
1958	Don McDonald, QB	4	35
1957	Don Brown, RH; Claude King, LH	4	24
1956	Don Flynn, QB	4	39
1955	Kennie Stegall, LH	7	53
1954	Jim Baughman, RH; Jack Patterson, FB	3	18
1953	Donn Hargrove, RH	7	42
1952	Ken Pridgeon, LH; S. M. Meeks, LH	5	30
1951	Gene Shannon, RH	13	78
1950	Max Clark, LH	11	90
1949	Alan Neveux, QB	4	53
1948	Alan Neveux, QB	4	39
1947	Boyd Tingle, QB	5	30
1946	Charles Manichia, QB	8	48

* Record

Leonard Parker

PUNTING

YEAR	PLAYER	NO.	YARDS
1976	Jay Wyatt, P	58	2259
1975	Jay Wyatt, P	28	1059
1974	Ken Pridgeon, P	50	1858
1973	Hal Roberts, K	42	1610
1972	Hal Roberts, K	57	2231
1971	Hal Roberts, K	38	1532
1970	Mike Parrott, TE	64	2657
1969	Mike Parrott, TE	46	1874
1968	Mike Parrott, SE	26	941
1967	Ken Hebert, SE	42	1830
1966	Ken Hebert, SE	40	1653
1965	Ken Hebert, SE	75	3147°
1964	Preasley Cooper, QB	44	1666
1963	Morris Wilson, HB	42	1437
1962	Bobby Brezina, LH	64	2226
1961	Larry Lindsey, RH	61	2392
1960	Larry Lindsey, QB	37	1439
1959	Gerald Ripkowski, QB	28	1059
1958	Pat Studstill, QB-HB	28	931
1957	Mike Michon, FB	18	697
1956	Owen Mulholland, FB	16	646
1955	Donnie Caraway, FB	13	538
1954	Jack Patterson, FB	28	1011
1953	Jack Patterson, FB	23	889
1952	Ken Pridgeon, LH	58	2133
1951	Ken Pridgeon, LH	29	1064
1950	Jolly Hartsell, QB	40	1354
1949	Alan Neveux, QB	61	2372
1948	Alan Neveux, QB	66	2399
1947	Roy Wallace, HB	78*	2638

Mike Spratt

Mike Parrott

D.C. Nobles

UH STARS OF THE PAST

Buddy Gillioz

Chuck Odom

Burr Davis

Bob Chuoke

Butch Brezina

ALL-AMERICA

1952—J. D. Kimmel, T	1969—Jim Strong, RB
1958—Hogan Wharton, T	1969—Bill Bridges, OLG
1966—Warren McVea, HB	1969—Elmo Wright, SE
1967—Warren McVea, HB	1970—Elmo Wright, SE
1967—Greg Brezina, LB	1970—Charlie Hall, LB
1967—Paul Gipson, FB	1971—Robert Newhouse, FB
1967—Rich Stotter, OG	1971—Riley Odoms, TE
1967—Ken Hebert, SE	1973—Robert Giblin, CB
1968—Paul Gipson, FB	1973—Deryl McGallion, LB
1968—Johnny Peacock, DB	1974—Robert Giblin, CB
1968—Royce Berry, DE	1974—Mack Mitchell, DE
1969—Jerry Drones, DRE	1976—Wilson Whitley, DT

LOMBARDI AWARD
1976—Wilson Whitley, DT

DANA X. BIBLE AWARD
(Presented by Texas Football Magazine)
1971—Robert Newhouse, FB

ACADEMIC ALL-AMERICA

1964—Horst Paul, E	1969—Elmo Wright, SE
1967—Rich Stotter, OG	1976—Mark Mohr, CB
1968—Chuck Odom, OT	1976—Kevin Rollwage, OT

TEXAS PLAYER OF THE YEAR
(Selected By The Houston Chronicle)

1966—Dick Post, FB	1969—Bill Bridges, OLG
	1971—Robert Newhouse, FB

CHICAGO ALL-STAR GAME

1952—Gene Shannon, B	1967—Bo Burris, QB
1953—J. D. Kimmel, T	1969—Paul Gipson, FB
1954—Buddy Gilloz, T	1971—Elmo Wright, SE
1959—Don Brown, HB	1972—Riley Odoms, TE
1962—Dan Birdwell, C	1872—Robert Newhouse, FB
1967—Tom Beer, E	1975—Mack Mitchell, DE

SHRINE EAST-WEST GAME

1952—J. D. Kimmel, T	1970—Elmo Wright, SE
1958—Burr Davis, G	1972—Puddin' Jones, FB
1967—Warren McVea, HB	1972—David Bourquin, OT
1968—Bill Cloud, OT	

COACHES ALL-AMERICA GAME

1962—Dan Birdwell, C	1970—Bill Bridges, OLG
1966—Tom Beer, E	1971—Charles Ford, LCB
1966—Bo Burris, QB	1972—Tommy Mozisek, RB
1968—Rich Stotter, OG	1973—Steve George, DT
1969—Paul Gipson, FB	

SHRINE NORTH-SOUTH GAME

1958—Harold Lewis, HB	1966—Carl Cunningham, E
Don Brown, HB	1966—Barry Sides, C
1960—Jim Windham, T	1967—Rich Stotter, OG
1966—Bo Burris, QB	1967—Ken Hebert, SE
1966—Tom Beer, E	1970—Earl Thomas, TE

SENIOR BOWL GAME

1950—Max Clark, HB	1968—Paul Gipson, FB
1952—Ken Pridgeon, HB	1968—Johnny Peacock, DB
1958—Don Brown, HB	1971—Riley Odoms, TE
1959—Jim Colvin, T	1975—Mack Mitchell, DE
1962—Byron Beaver, HB	

JAPAN BOWL

1976—Everett Little, OG	1977—Val Belcher, OT
1977—Wilson Whitley, DT	

HULA BOWL

1958—Hogan Wharton, T	1974—Ken Baugh, OT
1966—Tom Beer, E	1974—Deryl McGallion, LB
1967—Warren McVea, HB	1975—Robert Giblin, CB*
1967—Ken Hebert, SE	1975—Larry Keller, DE
1969—Paul Gipson, FB	1975—Mack Mitchell, DE
1969—Johnny Peacock, DB	1976—Everett Little, OG
1970—David Schneider, ORG	1977—Wilson Whitley, DT
1971—Elmo Wright, SE	1977—Val Belcher, OT
1972—Robert Newhouse, FB	

ALL-AMERICA BOWL

1962—Bobby Brezina, HB	1972—Butch Brezina, LE
1971—Richard Harrington, RS	1972—Kent Branstetter, RT

*Injured, did not participate

1958—Bob Borah, E

BLUE-GRAY GAME

1952—John Carroll, T
    Frank James, G
    Vic Hampel, E
    Jack Chambers, C
1953—Buddy Gillioz, T
    Bob Chuoke, T
1954—Jack Patterson, HB
1967—Greg Brezina, LB

1967—Bill Pickens, OG
1968—Chuck Odom, OT
1968—Cliff Larson, DT
1968—Paul Gipson, FB
1968—Johnny Peacock, DB
1970—Charles Ford, LCB
1970—L. D. Rowden, LS

CRUSADE BOWL

1962—Bobby Brezina, HB
    Pete Nikirk, T
    Ken Chancelor, C

Wilson Whitley

ALL-CONFERENCE PLAYERS

1946—All-Lone Star Conference: Quarterback Charles Manichia
1948—All-Lone Star Conference: Tackle Cecil Towns
1949—All-Gulf Coast Conference:
    (Offense) T Cecil Towns, G Mill Myers, QB Alan Neveux,
    FB Aubrey Baker
1950—All Gulf Coast Conference:
    (Offense) HB Gene Shannon, HB Max Clark, G Buck Miller
    (Defense) HB John O'Hara, LB Leo Van Haverbeke

ALL-MISSOURI VALLEY CONFERENCE

(Houston dropped membership in the MVC after the 1959 season.)
1951—(Offense) HB Gene Shannon, G Buck Miller
    (Defense) LB Paul Carr, C Ivis Rister, G Chester Sugarek
1952—(Offense) E Vic Hampel, G Bob Chuoke, HB S. M. Meeks
    (Defense) T J. D. Kimmel, T Buddy Gillioz, LB Paul Carr,
    HB Sam Hopson, HB Jackie Howton
1953—T Buddy Gillioz, T Bob Chouke
1955—QB Jimmy Dickey, FB Curley Johnson, T Lavell Isbell
1956—QB Don Flynn, FB Donnie Caraway, T Dalva Allen,
    G Rudy Spitzenberger
1957—T Hogan Wharton, G Burr Davis, FB Harold Lewis
1958—T Hogan Wharton, G Burr Davis, E Bob Borah

Horst Paul

MVC LINEMAN-OF-THE-YEAR

1957—Tackle Hogan Wharton   1958—Tackle Hogan Wharton

MVC BACK-OF-THE-YEAR

1955—Fullback Curley Johnson

ALL-SOUTHWEST CONFERENCE

1976—DT Wilson Whitley, OT Val Belcher, DB Anthony Francis,
    RB Alois Blackwell, TE Eddie Foster, LB Paul Humphreys,
    DB Mark Mohr

Lavell Isbell

COUGAR CLUB AWARD

*Sideline Coaches Award and L. A. Ehlers Award were replaced
by the Cougar Club Award in 1962.

MOST VALUABLE VARSITY PLAYER:

    1962—Bobby Brezina, Halfback, Louise, Tex.
    1963—Demaree Jones, Guard, Houston (Sam Houston)
    1964—Horst Paul, End, Copperas Cove, Tex.
    1965—Cotton Guerrant, Tackle, Galveston, Tex.
    1966—Bo Burris, Quarterback, Freeport, Tex.
    1967—Ken Hebert, Split End, Pampa, Tex.
    1968—Paul Gipson, Fullback, Conroe, Tex.
    1969—Jim Strong, Running Back, San Antonio, Tex.
    1970—Elmo Wright, Split End, Brazoria, Tex.
    1971—Robert Newhouse, Fullback, Hallsville, Tex.
    1972—Puddin Jones, Fullback, Brady, Tex.
    1973—D.C. Nobles, Quarterback, Lufkin, Tex.
    1974—Bubba Broussard, Linebacker, Brookshire, Tex.
    1975—Wilson Whitley, Defensive Tackle, Brenham, Tex.
    1976—Wilson Whitley, DT, Brenham, Tex.

Demaree Jones

*L. A. EHLERS AWARD
BEST ALL-ROUND BACK (PLAYERS' VOTE):

    1948—Jack Gwin, Halfback, Houston (Lamar)
    1949—Gene Shannon, Halfback, Freeport, Tex.
    1950—Gene Shannon, Halfback, Freeport, Tex.

David Bourquin

L. A. Ehlers Award (Continued)

1951—Gene Shannon, Halfback, Freeport, Tex.
1952—Paul (Rock) Carr, Fullback, Azusa, Calif.
1953—Jack Patterson, Fullback, Brazoria. Tex.
1954—Jim Baughman, Halfback, Vicksburg, Miss.
1954—Jack Patterson, Fullback, Brazoria, Tex.
1955—Curley Johnson, Fullback, Dallas, Tex.
1955—Jimmy Dickey, Quarterback, Galena Park, Tex.
1956—Don Flynn, Quarterback, Tyler, Tex.
1957—Don (First Down) Brown, Halfback, Dayton, Tex.
1958—Billy Ray Dickey, Halfback, Galena Park, Tex.
1959—Charlie Rieves, Fullback, Anguilla, Miss.
1960—Ken Bolin, Halfback, Houston (Sam Houston)
1961—Ken Bolin, Halfback, Houston (Sam Houston)

*L. A. EHLERS AWARD
BEST ALL-ROUND LINEMAN (PLAYERS' VOTE):

1948—Buck Miller, Guard, Wortham, Tex.
1949—Bill Moeller, Tackle, Bay City, Tex.
1950—Buck Miller, Guard, Wortham, Tex.
1951—Buck Miller, Guard, Wortham, Tex.
1952—J. D. Kimmel, Tackle, Texarkana, Tex.
1953—Bob Chuoke, Tackle, Galveston, Tex.
1954—George Hynes, End, Sulphur, La.
1954—Billy McIlroy, Center, Katy, Tex.
1955—Lavell Isbell, Tackle, Corsicana, Tex.
1956—Dalva Allen, Tackle, Gonzales, Tex.
1957—Hogan Wharton, Tackle, Orange, Tex.
1957—John Peters, Tackle, Houston (St. Thomas)
1958—Hogan Wharton, Tackle, Orange, Tex.
1959—Howard Evans, Center, Dallas, Tex.
1960—Jim Windham, Tackle, Colorado City, Tex.
1961—Joe Bob Isbell, Tackle, Little Cypress, Tex.

UNIVERSITY OF HOUSTON TOP 25
SINGLE RUSHING PERFORMANCES

NAME	YARDS	OPPONENT	YEAR
Paul Gipson	282	Tulsa	1968
Robert Newhouse	245	Mississippi St.	1969
Robert Newhouse	237	Cincinnati	1971
Paul Gipson	230	Georgia	1968
Jim Strong	230	Arizona	1969
Paul Gipson	229	Georgia	1967
Paul Gipson	210	Ole Miss	1968
Ted Heiskell	207	Idaho	1968
Robert Newhouse	204	Utah	1971
Robert Newhouse	201	Virginia Tech	1971
Alois Blackwell	200	West Texas St.	1976
Leonard Parker	200	Colorado St.	1973
Donn Hargrove	199	Detroit	1953
Max Clark	198	Wm & Mary	1950
Tommy Mozisek	195	Virginia Tech	1971
Warren McVea	193	Idaho	1967
Robert Newhouse	192	Florida State	1971
Dick Post	187	Kentucky	1966
Puddin Jones	184	New Mexico	1972
Gene Shannon	183	Detroit	1951
Robert Newhouse	182	Alabama	1971
Donnie McGraw	178	Rice	1974
Paul Gipson	173	Texas	1968
Dick Post	172	Utah	1966
Reggie Cherry	170	Florida State	1974
Alois Blackwell	170	Miami	1976

Most Yards In a Game By Three Backs — 436 vs. Virginia Tech, 1971; Robert Newhouse, 201; Tommy Mozisek, 195; Leonard Parker, 40.

Most Backs In a Game Over 100 Yards — 3 vs. San Diego State, 1973; Leonard Parker, 152; Marshall Johnson, 126; Reggie Cherry, 103.

UH-ALL-TIME FOOTBALL SCORES

H—indicates home game

1946: Won 4, Lost 6

UH		OPP
7	S. L. I.—H.	13
14	West Texas	12
32	Camp Hood	7
34	Texas A&I—H	0
14	East Texas	20
7	Texas Western	27
16	S. F. Austin—H	7
3	North Texas—H	7
7	Southwest Texas	21
6	Sam Houston St.—H	28

1947: Won 3, Lost 8

UH		OPP
19	Centenary—H	7
14	McMurry—H	13
35	Daniel Baker—H	12
0	Texas A&I	13
7	East Texas—H	33
0	Trinity—H	20
7	Hardin-Simmons	33
14	S. F. Austin	25
0	North Texas	33
0	Southwest Texas—H	2
0	Sam Houston	23

1948: Won 5, Lost 6

UH		OPP
14	Texas A&I—H	0
7	Texas Western	35
7	S. L. I.	21
40	Louisiana Tech—H	33
18	East Texas	7
7	Trinity	15
13	West Texas	28
13	S. F. Austin—H	21
8	North Texas—H	6
0	Southwest Texas	3
22	Sam Houston—H	13

1949: Won 5, Lost 4, Tied 1

UH		OPP
13	William & Mary—H	14
26	Wichita—H	6
28	S. L. I.	7
14	West Texas—H	13
27	Hardin-Simmons—H	27
21	Midwestern	33
14	St. Bonaventure	20
23	North Texas	28
28	Trinity—H	21
35	St. Louis U.	0

1950: Won 4, Lost 6

UH		OPP
14	St. Bonaventure—H	29
7	Baylor	34
16	Trinity	20
27	Louisville—H	7
13	Hardin-Simmons	14
46	Wichita	6
13	North Texas—H	16
36	William & Mary—H	18
30	Midwestern—H	18
21	Tulsa—H	28

1951: Won 6, Lost 5

UH		OPP
0	Baylor—H	19
33	Detroit	7
6	Texas Tech—H	0
27	Tulsa	46
35	Hardin-Simmons—H	27
27	Villanova—H	33
14	Wichita	19
28	Louisville	35
31	Okla. A&M—H	7
20	North Texas	14
26	Dayton (**Salad Bowl**)	21

1952: Won 8, Lost 2

UH		OPP
13	Texas A&M—H	21
17	Arkansas	7
10	Oklahoma A&M	7
33	Tulsa—H	7
6	Arizona State	0
20	Texas Tech	7
0	Mississippi—H	6
28	Baylor—H	6
33	Detroit—H	19
20	Wyoming—H	0

1953: Won 4, Lost 4, Tied 1

UH		OPP
14	Texas A&M	14
7	Texas	28
25	Detroit	19
0	Oklahoma A&M—H	14
24	Arizona St.—H	20
21	Tulsa	23
37	Baylor	7
21	Texas Tech—H	41
33	Tennessee—H	19

1954: Won 5, Lost 5

UH		OPP
13	Baylor	53
10	Texas A&M—H	7
14	Okla. A&M	7
28	Villanova	7
7	Wichita	9
20	Tulsa—H	7
0	Mississippi—H	26
14	Texas Tech	61
0	Arkansas—H	19
19	Detroit—H	7

1955: Won 6, Lost 4

UH		OPP
54	Montana—H	12
3	Texas A&M	21
7	Detroit	0
21	Oklahoma A&M—H	13
7	Texas Tech—H	0
7	Wichita—H	21
14	Tulsa	17
11	Mississippi	27
26	Villanova—H	14
26	Wyoming—H	14

1956: Won 7, Lost 2, Tied 1

UH		OPP
18	Mississippi St.—H	7
0	Mississippi	14
14	Texas A&M—H	14
13	Oklahoma St.	0
0	Auburn	12
41	Wichita	16
14	Tulsa—H	0
26	Villanova—H	13
20	Texas Tech	7
39	Detroit—H	7

1957: Won 5, Lost 4, Tied 1

UH		OPP
7	Miami, Fla.—H	0
7	Baylor	14
7	Cincinnati	0
6	Texas A&M	28
6	Oklahoma St.—H	6
7	Auburn—H	48
7	Mississippi	20
27	Mississippi So.	12
27	Wichita	6
13	Tulsa	7

1958: Won 5, Lost 4

UH		OPP
39	Texas A&M—H	7
34	Cincinnati	13
44	Wichita—H	0
0	Oklahoma St.—H	7
20	Tulsa—H	25
7	Mississippi	56
6	North Texas	10
37	Miami, Fla.	26
22	Texas Tech—H	17

1959: Won 3, Lost 7

UH		OPP
0	Mississippi—H	16
0	Alabama—H	3
13	Cincinnati—H	12
6	Texas A&M	28
12	Oklahoma St.	19
6	North Texas—H	7
22	Tulsa	13
28	Wichita	13
0	Texas Tech	27
18	Washington St.—H	32

1960: Won 6, Lost 4

UH		OPP
0	Mississippi—H	42
14	Mississippi State	10
20	Oregon State	29
17	Texas A&M—H	0
12	Oklahoma St.—H	7
0	Alabama	14
41	North Texas	16
14	Cincinnati—H	0
7	Florida State	6
16	Tulsa—H	26

1961: Won 5, Lost 4, Tied 1

UH		OPP
7	Texas A&M	7
7	Mississippi State—H	10
21	Boston College—H	0
7	Mississippi	47
13	Cincinnati	7
0	Alabama—H	17
14	Tulsa	2
24	Oklahoma State	28
28	Florida State—H	8
23	Oregon State—H	12

1962: Won 7, Lost 4, Tied 0

UH		OPP
19	Baylor—H	0
6	Texas A&M—H	3
7	Mississippi	40
3	Alabama	14
3	Mississippi State—H	9
0	Boston College	14
7	Florida State	0
35	Tulsa—H	31
27	Louisville	25
42	Cincinnati—H	14
	(**Tangerine Bowl**)	
49	Miami, Ohio	21

1963: Won 2, Lost 8, Tied 0

UH		OPP
14	Auburn—H	21
0	Baylor	27
6	Mississippi—H	20
13	Texas A&M	23
0	Mississippi State	20
13	Alabama	21
0	Detroit—H	18
21	Tulsa	22
6	Memphis State	29
21	Louisville—H	7

1964: Won 2, Lost 6, Tied 1

UH		OPP
34	Trinity—H	7
0	Auburn	30
10	Texas A&M—H	0
9	Mississippi	31
23	Tulsa—H	31
13	Mississippi State	18
13	Florida State—H	13
7	Penn State—H	24
6	Cincinnati—H	20

1965: Won 4, Lost 5, Tied 1

UH		OPP
0	Tulsa—H*	14
0	Mississippi State—H	36
21	Cincinnati—H	6
7	Texas A&M	10
12	Miami, Fla.	44
8	Tennessee	17
40	Chattanooga—H	7
17	Mississippi—H	3
38	Kentucky—H	21
16	Florida State	16

First game in Astrodome.

1966: Won 8, Lost 2, Tied 0

UH		OPP
21	Florida State	13
21	Washington State—H	7
35	Oklahoma State—H	9
28	Mississippi State—H	0
6	Mississippi	27
48	Tampa—H	9
73	Tulsa—H	14
56	Kentucky	18
13	Memphis State—H	14
34	Utah—H	14

1967: Won 7, Lost 3, Tied 0		1970: Won 8, Lost 3, Tied 0		1973: Won 11, Lost 1	
UH	OPP	UH	OPP	UH	OPP
33 Florida State—H	13	42 Syracuse—H	15	24 Rice—H	6
37 Michigan State	7	17 Okla. State	26	27 South Carolina—H	19
50 Wake Forest—H	6	31 Miss. State	14	35 Memphis State	21
6 North Carolina St.—H	16	19 Oregon State—H	16	14 San Diego State	9
43 Mississippi State	6	21 Alabama—H	30	54 Virginia Tech—H	27
13 Mississippi	14	21 Tulsa—H	9	30 Miami, Fla.	7
15 Georgia—H	14	13 Mississippi	24	0 Auburn	7
35 Memphis State—H	18	28 Wyoming—H	0	34 Florida State—H	3
77 Idaho—H	6	26 Wake Forest—H	2	28 Colorado State	20
13 Tulsa	22	53 Florida State	21	35 Wyoming—H	0
		36 Miami	3	35 Tulsa—H	16
				(Astro-Bluebonnet Bowl)	
				47 Tulane	7

1968: Won 6, Lost 2, Tied 2		1971: Won 9, Lost 3, Tied 0		1974: Won 8, Lost 3, Tied 1	
UH	OPP	UH	OPP	UH	OPP
54 Tulane—H	7	23 Rice	21	9 Arizona St.	30
20 Texas	20	17 Arizona State	18	21 Rice	0
71 Cincinnati—H	33	12 Cincinnati	3	3 Miami, Fla.	21
17 Oklahoma State—H	21	34 San Jose St.—H	20	49 Virginia Tech	12
29 Mississippi	7	42 Villanova—H	9	24 South Carolina	14
10 Georgia	10	20 Alabama	34	35 Villanova—H	0
27 Memphis State	7	14 Florida St.—H	7	27 Cincinnati—H	6
77 Idaho—H	3	35 Memphis St.	7	31 Georgia	24
100 Tulsa—H	6	56 Virginia Tech—H	29	13 Memphis St.—H	10
20 Florida State	40	27 Miami—H	6	23 Florida St.	8
		42 Utah—H	16	14 Tulsa	30
		(Astro-Bluebonnet Bowl)		(Astro-Bluebonnet Bowl)	
		17 Colorado	29	31 North Carolina St.	31

1969: Won 9, Lost 2, Tied 0		1972: Won 6, Lost 4, Tied 1		1975: Won 2, Lost 8, Tied 0	
UH	OPP	UH	OPP	UH	OPP
34 Florida	59	13 Rice	14	20 Lamar—H	3
18 Oklahoma State	24	28 Arizona State—H	33	7 Rice—H	24
74 Mississippi St.—H	0	21 Tulsa	0	16 SMU—H	26
34 Arizona	17	27 Virginia Tech	27	0 No. Tex. St.	28
25 Mississippi—H	11	49 San Diego St.—H	14	20 Miami, Fla.	24
38 Miami, Fla.—H	36	14 Miami	33	23 Cincinnati	28
47 Tulsa	14	13 Miss. St.	27	28 Virginia Tech—H	34
34 N. Carolina St.	13	31 Florida State	27	7 Memphis St.	14
41 Wyoming—H	14	48 Colorado State—H	13	22 Florida St.—H	33
41 Florida St.—H	13	33 New Mexico—H	14	42 Tulsa—H	30
(Astro-Bluebonnet Bowl)		49 Cincinnati—H	0		
36 Auburn	7				

(Note: UH was on NCAA probation from 1966 through 1968 and was not permitted to accept bowl invitations.)

1976 results on page 1.

HOMECOMING GAME RESULTS
(16-12-3)

1946 - UH 3, North Texas 7	1962 - UH 35, Tulsa 31
1947 - UH 0, Southwest Texas 2	1963 - UH 6, Mississippi 20
1948 - UH 13, S. F. Austin 21	1964 - UH 13, Florida State 13
1949 - UH 27, Hardin-Simmons 27	1965 - UH 17, Mississippi 3
1950 - UH 36, Wm. and Mary 18	1966 - UH 73, Tulsa 14
1951 - UH 0, Baylor 19	1967 - UH 15, Georgia 14
1952 - UH 33, Tulsa 7	1968 - UH 100, Tulsa 6
1953 - UH 33, Tennessee 19	1969 - UH 25, Mississippi 11
1954 - UH 0, Arkansas 19	1970 - UH 21, Alabama 30
1955 - UH 26, Villanova 14	1971 - UH 14, Florida State 7
1956 - UH 14, Texas A&M 14	1972 - UH 48, Colorado State 13
1957 - UH 7, Auburn 48	1973 - UH 34, Florida State 3
1958 - UH 20, Tulsa 25	1974 - UH 13, Memphis St. 10
1959 - UH 6, North Texas 7	1975 - UH 16, SMU 26
1960 - UH 14, Cincinnati 0	1976 - UH 49, TCU 21
1961 - UH 0, Alabama 17	

UH'S BOWL RECORD

DATE	GAME	OPPONENT	SCORE
Jan. 1, 1952	Salad Bowl	Dayton	26-21
Dec. 22, 1962	Tangerine	Miami, Ohio	49-21
Dec. 31, 1969	Astro-Bluebonnet	Auburn	36-7
Dec. 31, 1971	Astro-Bluebonnet	Colorado	17-29
Dec. 29, 1973	Astro-Bluebonnet	Tulane	47-7
Dec. 23, 1974	Astro-Bluebonnet	North Carolina St.	31-31
Jan. 1, 1977	Cotton Bowl	Maryland	30-21

ALL-TIME COLLEGIATE RECORD

OPPONENTS	W	L	T	Pct.	UH Pts.	Opp. Pts.
Alabama	0	7	0	.000	57	133
Arizona	1	0	0	1.000	34	17
Arizona State	2	3	0	.400	84	101
*Arkansas	1	2	0	.333	24	40
Auburn	1	5	0	.167	57	125
*Baylor	4	5	0	.444	133	165
Boston College	1	1	0	.500	21	14
Centenary	1	0	0	1.000	19	7
Chattanooga	1	0	0	1.000	40	7
Cincinnati	11	2	0	.846	332	211
Colorado	0	1	0	.000	17	29
Colorado St.	2	0	0	1.000	76	33
Daniel Baker	1	0	0	1.000	35	12
Dayton (Ohio)	1	0	0	1.000	26	21
Detroit	7	0	0	1.000	211	77
East Texas	1	2	0	.333	39	60
Florida	0	2	0	.000	48	108
Florida St.	11	2	2	.800	363	221
Ft. Hood	1	0	0	1.000	32	7
Georgia	2	0	1	.833	56	48
Hardin-Simmons	1	2	1	.375	82	101
Idaho	2	0	0	1.000	154	9
Kentucky	2	0	0	1.000	94	39
Lamar	1	0	0	1.000	20	3
Louisiana Tech	1	0	0	1.000	40	33
Louisville	3	1	0	.750	93	74
Maryland	1	0	0	1.000	30	21
McMurry	1	0	0	1.000	14	13
Memphis State	5	3	0	.625	171	120
Miami, Fla.	7	4	0	.636	241	215
Miami, Ohio	1	0	0	1.000	49	21
Michigan St.	1	0	0	1.000	37	7
Midwestern (Tex.)	1	1	0	.500	61	51
Mississippi	3	15	0	.167	157	431
Mississippi So.	1	0	0	1.000	27	12
Mississippi St.	6	6	0	.500	249	152
Montana U.	1	0	0	1.000	54	12
New Mexico	1	0	0	1.000	33	13
North Carolina St.	1	1	1	.500	71	60
North Texas St.	3	7	0	.300	120	165
Oklahoma State	7	7	1	.500	237	195
Oregon State	2	1	0	.667	62	57
*Penn State	0	1	0	.000	7	24
*Rice	4	2	0	.667	130	85
St. Bonaventure	0	2	0	.000	28	49
St. Louis U.	1	0	0	1.000	35	0
Sam Houston St.	1	2	0	.333	28	64
San Diego St.	2	0	0	1.000	63	23
San Jose State	1	0	0	1.000	34	20
South Carolina	2	0	0	1.000	51	33
*Southern Methodist U.	1	1	0	.500	45	32
Southwest La. Inst.	1	2	0	.333	42	41
Southwest Texas	0	3	0	.000	7	26
S. F. Austin (Tex.)	1	2	0	.333	43	53
Tampa	1	0	0	1.000	48	9
Tennessee	1	1	0	.500	41	36
*TCU	1	0	0	1.000	49	21
*Texas	1	1	1	.500	57	48
Texas A&I	2	1	0	.667	48	13
*Texas A&M	6	6	3	.500	186	193
*Texas Tech	6	3	0	.667	137	179
Texas Western	0	2	0	.000	14	62
Trinity (Tex.)	2	3	0	.400	85	83
Tulsa	14	11	0	.560	680	350
Tulane	2	0	0	1.000	101	14
*UCLA	0	0	0	.000	0	0
*Utah	2	0	0	1.000	76	30
Villanova	5	1	0	.833	184	76
Virginia Tech	3	1	1	.700	214	129
Wake Forest	2	0	0	1.000	76	8
Washington St.	1	1	0	.500	39	39
West Texas St.	3	1	0	.750	91	60
Wichita	6	3	0	.667	240	96
William & Mary	1	1	0	.500	49	32
Wyoming	5	0	0	1.000	150	28
UH All-Time Totals	180	131	11	.576	6921	5288

* on 1977 Schedule

ALL-TIME HOME ATTENDANCE

1946— 26,000 (5 games)

1947— 32,000 (6 games)

1948— 29,500 (5 games)

1949— 56,500 (5 games)

1950— 73,842 (5 games)

1951—125,500 (5 games)

1952—183,700 (6 games)

1953— 93,000 (4 games)

1954—122,000 (5 games)

1955—120,000 (6 games)

1956—168,000 (5 games)

1957—101,000 (3 games)

1958—141,300 (5 games)

1959—100,200 (5 games)

1960—128,000 (5 games)

1961— 97,106 (6 games)

1962—104,687 (6 games)

1963— 70,562 (4 games)

1964—109,000 (6 games)

1965—210,106 (6 games)

1966—287,828 (7 games)

1967—274,458 (6 games)

1968—174,695 (5 games)

1969—181,551 (5 games)

1970—214,784 (6 games)

1971—176,060 (6 games)

1972—116,463 (5 games)

1973—157,167 (6 games)

1974— 86,378 (4 games)

1975—131,094 (6 games)

1976—212,015 (6 games)

ALL-TIME ATTENDANCE RECORDS

Home—287,828 (1966)

Away—240,169 (1974)

Total—420,091 (1967)

UH COACHING RECORDS

COACH AND YEARS	W	L	T	Pct.	Pts.	Opp.Pts.
JEWELL WALLACE (1946-47)	7	14	0	.333	236	356
CLYDE LEE (1948-54)	37	32	2	.535	1345	1237
BILL MEEK (1955-56)	13	6	1	.675	361	229
HAROLD LAHAR (1957-61)	24	23	2	.510	712	760
BILL YEOMAN (1962-)	99	56	6	.634	4267	2706
TOTALS	180	132	11	.576	6921	5288

Jewell Wallace

YEAR BY YEAR RECORD

YEAR	W	L	T	UH PTS	OPP PTS	COACH
1946	4	6	0	140	142	Jewell Wallace
1947	3	8	0	96	214	Jewell Wallace
1948	5	6	0	149	182	Clyde Lee
1949	5	4	1	229	169	Clyde Lee
1950	4	6	0	223	190	Clyde Lee
1951	6	5	0	247	228	Clyde Lee
1952	8	2	0	180	80	Clyde Lee
1953	4	4	1	189	185	Clyde Lee
1954	5	5	0	125	203	Clyde Lee
1955	6	4	0	176	139	Bill Meek
1956	7	2	1	185	90	Bill Meek
1957	5	4	1	113	141	Harold Lahar
1958	5	4	0	209	161	Harold Lahar
1959	3	7	0	105	170	Harold Lahar
1960	6	4	0	141	150	Harold Lahar
1961	5	4	1	144	138	Harold Lahar
1962	7	4	0	198	171	Bill Yeoman
1963	2	8	0	149	208	Bill Yeoman
1964	2	6	1	115	174	Bill Yeoman
1965	4	5	1	159	174	Bill Yeoman
1966	8	2	0	335	125	Bill Yeoman
1967	7	3	0	322	122	Bill Yeoman
1968	6	2	2	425	154	Bill Yeoman
1969	9	2	0	422	208	Bill Yeoman
1970	8	3	0	307	160	Bill Yeoman
1971	9	3	0	339	199	Bill Yeoman
1972	6	4	1	325	202	Bill Yeoman
1973	11	1	0	363	142	Bill Yeoman
1974	8	3	1	280	185	Bill Yeoman
1975	2	8	0	185	244	Bill Yeoman
1976	10	2	0	313	217	Bill Yeoman

Clyde Lee

Bill Meek

TEAM CAPTAINS

1946—Center Bill Cook and Tackle Tony Ditta
1947—QB Boyd Tingle and End Evan Weaver
1948—Tackle Cecil Towns and HB Jack Gwinn
1949—FB Aubrey Baker and Tackle Cecil Towns
1950—Tackle Bill Moeller and HB Max Clark
1951—HB Gene Shannon, John O'Hara, G Buck Miller
1952—End Howard Clapp and Tackle John Carroll
    Tackle J. D. Kimmel appointed captain of defense
1953—Tackle Buddy Gillioz and FB Paul Carr
1954—FB Jack Patterson and End George Hynes
1955—Guard Jim Blackstone and Tackle Lavell Isbell
1956—QB Don Flynn and End Ken Wind
1957—FB Mike Michon and End Bob Blevins
1958—T Hogan Wharton, HB Harold Lewis, HB Don Brown
1959—HB Claude King and Center Howard Evans
1960—T Wiley Feagin, FB Jim Kuehne, G Jim Windham
1961—HB Ken Bolin, T Bill Brown, G Joe Bob Isbell
1962—QB Billy Roland and FB Bobby Brezina
1963—E Clem Beard, G Demaree Jones, FB Frank Brewer
1964—E Horst Paul
1965—T Cotton Guerrant
1966—HB Dick Post
1967—E Royce Berry (unable to play because of an injury)
1967—E Ken Hebert and LB Greg Brezina
1968—T Jerry Gardner, T Bill Cloud, FB Paul Gipson
1969—HB Jim Strong and DRE Jerry Drones
1970—OT Craig Robinson, LLB Charlie Hall
    and RS Richard Harrington
1971—FB Robert Newhouse, QB Gary Mullins
    and MLB Frank Ditta
1972—FB Puddin Jones, LCB Randy Peacock
    and ORG David Bourquin
1973—T Ken Baugh, QB D.C. Nobles and LB Deryl McGallion
1974—LB Bubba Broussard, CB Robert Giblin and
    DE Mack Mitchell
1975—LB Paul Humphreys and DT Wilson Whitley
1976—LB Paul Humphreys, DT Wilson Whitley, OT Val Belcher
1977—QB Danny Davis, OG Ramon Rosales, OT Kevin Rollwage,
    DE Vincent Greenwood

Harold Lahar

Bill Yeoman

A

Calvin Achey, 67-68-69
Dalva Allen, 54-56
Will Allen, 63
Jim Arthur, 67-69

B

Tommy Bailes, 52-54
Ken Bailey, 67-68-69
Aubrey Baker, 47-50
Joey Baker, 69
Harlan Baldridge, 51-52
Jack Barbee, 50-51
Mike Barbour, 65-66
Jack Barnes, 53-54
Bob Barnett, 60-61
Dean Bass, 60
Don Bass, 75
Miller Bassler, 73-74
Ken Baugh, 72-73
Jim Baughman, 54
Don Bean, 66-67
Clem Beard, 61-63
Tom Beasley, 58
Byron Beaver, 61-62
Tom Beer, 65-66
Val Belcher, 73-76
Carlos Bell, 67-68
Jim Berger, 65-67
Ken Bergquist, 63
Royce Berry, 65-68
Bill Bidwell, 48-51
Danny Birdwell, 59-61
Webb Bishop, 55-56
Jim Blackstone, 53-55
Alois Blackwell, 75-76
Ed Bleier, 60
Bob Blevins, 56-57
Don Bloom, 54
Sammy Blount, 55-57
Buddy Boek, 55-56
Ken Bolin, 59-61
Mike Bolin, 69-71
Bob Borah, 56-58
Jeff Bouche, 71-72-73
Don Boudreaux, 56-57
David Bourquin, 70-72
Mutt Bowers, 59
Tom Boyd, 56
Elvis Bradley, 76
Joe Bill Bradley, 54
David Bradshaw, 60
John Branson, 59-61
Kent Branstetter, 70-71
James Brasher, 63
Frank Brewer, 62-63
Monroe Brewer, 61
Bobby Brezina, 60-62
Greg Brezina, 65-67
Mark "Butch" Brezina, 70-71
Gus Brezina, 62-64
Bill Bridges, 68-69
Charles Brightwell, 47
Art Briles, 76
David Brooks, 73-74
Bubba Broussard, 72-73-74
James Broussard, 63
Larry Broussard, 60-62
Bill Brown, 58-60-61
Charlie Brown, 48
Charlie E. Brown, 56-58
Chuck Brown, 76
Don Brown, 48
Gene Brown, 53
George Brown, 47
Guy Brown, 74-76
Bob Brumley, 68-70
L. Z. Bryan, 47-49
Mark Bugaj, 68
Bo Burris, 64-66
Les Burton, 53
Bill Butler, 47-49

C

Don Caballero, 64-65
*Deceased

Charlie Caffrey, 57-59
Billy Campbell, 58
Robby Campbell, 48-49
Lee Canalito, 73-74
Don Caraway, 55-56
George Caraway, 66
Mike Carew, 60
Rod Carpenter, 53-55
Paul Carr, 51-53
Sanford Carr, 48-49-51-52
John Carroll, 50-52
Jack Chambers, 49-52
Ken Chancelor, 61-62
Reggie Cherry, 72-73-74
David Childers, 64-65
Bob Chuoke, 52-53
*Howard Clapp, 49-52
Jim Clark, 49-51
Max Clark, 48-50
Rusty Clark, 68-69
Bobby Clatterbuck, 51-53
Bill Cloud, 66-68
Steve Cloud, 69-71
Wendy Collier, 52
Dennis Collins, 64
Jim Colvin, 57-59
Bill Cook, 46-48
Preasley Cooper, 63-64
Lennard Coplin, 74-76
Henry Cowen, 49-51
Danny Cranford, 58-59
Jim Cravens, 54-55
Verle Cray, 52-54
David Cruthirds, 72
Carl Cunningham, 64-66

D

Paul Daulong, 67-68
Burr Davis, 56-58
Danny Davis, 76
Aubra Dean, 46
John Dearen, 54-55
Gerald Deen, 60-62
Joel DeSpain, 70
Billy Ray Dickey, 57-58
Dale Dickey, 70
Jimmy Dickey, 54-55
Donnie Dietrich, 51-53
Tom Dimmick, 54-55
Frank Ditta, 59-61
Tony Ditta, 46-47
Harold Dixson, 46-47
Ricky Domingue, 75
Richard Donley, 46
Randall Dorsett, 58-60
Bobby Dorsey, 53
Gary Drake, 74-76
Jerry Drones, 67-68-69
Jim Dyar, 65-66
Ray Dudley, 63-65
Marvin Durrenberger, 52-53

E

John Eaker, 65
Grady Ebensberger, 76
Howard Ebow, 71-72-73
Ross Echols, 65
Maurice Elliott, 48-49
Richard Elliott, 60-62
Ronald Emberg, 54-56
Calvin Enderli, 63-64
Charles English, 49
Harold Evans, 72-73-74
Howard Evans, 57-59

F

Chuck Fairbanks, 74
Wiley Feagin, 58-60
Calvin Feazle, 47
Leroy Fisher, 71
Don Flynn, 54-56
Don Folks, 52-53

Charlie Ford, 69-70
Robert Ford, 70-72
Buck Foss, 46-47
Eddie Foster, 74-76
Charles Fowler, 64-66
Anthony Francis, 75-76
William Franklin, 74
Basil Freeman, 62-63
Benny Fry, 70
Burl Fuller, 71-72

G

Coy Gammage, 55-56
Jerry Gardner, 66-68
Lee Garl, 52
Wayne Geddes, 53-55
Dick George, 65
Steve George, 71-72
Robert Giblin, 72-73-74
Alonzo Giles, 75
Norman Giles, 56
Ted Giles, 50-51
Buddy Gillioz, 51-53
Steve Gillioz, 75
Paul Gipson, 67-68
Jack Golden, 49-51
Henry Gomez, 46-47
Glenn Graef, 67-68-69
Teddy Gray, 53
Valton Green, 46-47
Vincent Greenwood, 75-76
David Gregg, 48-50
Zane Gregory, 49-52
Charles Guerrant, 64-65
Albert Gustamente, 60
Jack Gwin, 46-48

H

Phill Hahn, 72
Charles Hall, 68-70
Robert Hall, 67
Tommy Hall, 55
George Hamilton, 65
Victor Hampel, 51-52
Bill Hamrick, 71-72
Floyd Hand, 46
Reid Hansen, 75-76
Max Harding, 49
Donn Hargrove, 53-55
Richard Harrington, 68-70
Jolly Hartsell, 48-50
Wyatt Hastings, 47
Ken Hatfield, 76
Ken Hawkins, 46-47
Ken Hebert, 65-67
John Henderson, 58
Ted Heiskell, 69-70
Ronnie Herman, 68-69
Rocky Hernandez, 62
Gerald Hill, 72-73-74
David Hodge, 75-76
Buddy Hodges, 60-61
Lynn Hoffman, 61
Lonnie Holland, 58-59
Bill Hollis, 46-48
Gus Hollomon, 65-67
Bill Hollon, 65-67
Lloyd Holloway, 49-51
Nick Holm, 70-71
Joe Holt, 49-50
Murdoch Hooper, 59-61
Sammy Hopson, 51-53
John Housman, 74-76
Larry Houston, 74
Benny Howe, 60-62
Bill Howell, 61-63
Jack Howton, 51-53
James Humble, 48-49
Paul Humphreys, 74-76
Joe Hurst, 48
Frank Hurtte, 48-49
David Husmann, 74-75
George Hynes, 52-54

(continued on next page)

I

Mike Ilaoa, 74
Joe Bob Isbell, 59-61
Lavell Isbell, 53-55

J

Prentice Jackson, 46
Frank James, 49-52
Bob Jinks, 49-50
Curley Johnson, 54-56
Marshall Johnson, 72-73-74
Roland Johnson, 52-53
*Ronnie Johnson, 61-62
Mike Johnston, 67-68-69
Bill Jones, 73
Demaree Jones, 61-63
Johnny Jones, 64-65
Melvin Jones, 76
Nat "Puddin" Jones, 71-72
Phillip Jones, 68-69
James Joplin, 56

K

Earl Kaiser, 56-57
Tommy Kaiser, 72-73
Larry Keller, 72-73-74
John Kelley, 62-63
J. D. Kimmel, 52
Claude King, 57-59
Emmett King, 76
Dick Kirtley, 59-61
Philip Koonce, 49-50
Louis Kramr, 52
Eugene Krus, 47
Jerry Kruse, 61
Jim Kuehne, 58-60
Bob Kyle, 69-71

L

Marvin Lackey, 49-52
James Landers, 50
Mike Landry, 63
Larry Lantzy, 65
Cliff Larson, 66-68
Robert Lavergne, 74-76
Bill Leech, 60
Bill Lewis, 71
Harold Lewis, 69
Glen Lewis, 69-70
Errol Linden, 59-60
Larry Lindsey, 50-61
Charles Linklater, 52
Charles Little, 73-75
Ronnie Logan, 55
Bob Long, 67-68
Joe Lopasky, 62-64
Carlos Lopez, 69-70
Randy Love, 76
Elliott Loy, 46-47
Wally Ludtke, 62-64
Ted Lutringer, 53
Charles Lynch, 75-76

M

James McConaughey, 51-52
Joe McDaniel, 70
Don McDonald, 57-59
Joe McDonald, 57-58
Bubba McGallion, 74-76
Deryl McGallion, 71-72-73
Donnie McGraw, 73-75
Bill McIlroy, 54-56
Don McIntosh, 72-73-74
Charles McKinney, 74
Dick McKinney, 55-57
Willie McKusker, 50
Bill McMillan, 61-63
James McNeil, 50
Warren McVea, 65-67
Sammy McWhirter, 51-52
John Magee, 61-62

Rickey Maddox, 76
Charles Mallia, 57
Charlie Manichia, 46
Conrad Martin, 60
Jim Martin, 55
Elray Matzke, 53
Richard Mauldin, 58
Roger Mayes, 72-73-74
S. M. Meeks, 52
Gene Meyer, 54
Mike Michon, 56-57
Buck Miller, 48-51
Eddie Mitchamore, 59-61
Mack Mitchell, 72-73-74
Carl Mittag, 49-50
Bill Moeller, 47-50
Mark Mohr, 74-76
Charles Moore, 69-71
James Moore, 50
W. B. Morrow, 47
Tom Mozisek, 70-71
Irwin Muegge, 50
Owen Mulholland, 55-56
Don Mullins, 58-60
Gary Mullins, 69-71
Ray Mullins, 70
Oliver Murray, 57
Phil Muscarello, 56
Bill Myers, 46-49

N

Larry Negriff, 63
Alan Neveux, 48-49
Robert Newhouse, 69-71
Pete Nikirk, 61-62
D.C. Nobles, 72-73
George Nohavitza, 46-47
George Nordgren, 65-67
Jim Norris, 59-61

O

John O'Hara, 48-51
Chuck Odom, 68
Riley Odoms, 69-71
Robert Oglesby, 75-76
Pat Orchin, 70-71
Bobby Orr, 75-76
Paul Otis, 64-66
Randy Owens, 49-51

P

Tom Paciorek, 65-67
Leonard Parker, 71-73
Mike Parrott, 69-70
Charlie Patterson, 58
Jack Patterson, 52-54
Wilbert Patterson, 62-64
Frank Paul, 54-56
Horst Paul, 62-64
Mike Payte, 63-65
Johnny Peacock, 66-68
Randy Peacock, 70-72
Ronny Peacock, 69-71
Terry Peel, 72
Larry Perez, 66-67
Milton Perkins, 60-62
Kenneth Perry, 75-76
John Peters, 55-57
Hubert Peterson, 47-48
Don Petty, 63-64
Tom Petty, 49-51
Wade Phillips, 66-68
Edgar Pichot, 49
Bill Pickens, 66-67
Tom Pierce, 58-59
Billy Joe Polson, 52-54
Dick Post, 64-66
Hilmer Potcinske, 58-59
Ron Powledge, 63
Lester Price, 65
Ken Pridgeon, 51-52
Ken Pridgeon, Jr., 74-75
Sonny Privett, 75
Pat Pryor, 67-68
Bernard Purdum, 47-49

R

Joe Rafter, 63-65
Raymond Ragone, 49
Joe Raitano, 55-56
Loyd Ralson, 49-51
Warren Ramsey, 50-51
Joe Redmon, 75
Gerald Reed, 54
Ken Reese, 51-53
Paul Reinhardt, 62
Bobby Reynolds, 62-63
Donald Rhodes, 50
Billy Richardson, 60
Charles Rieves, 59-60
Gerald Ripkowski, 59
Glenn Riske, 71-72-73
Ivis Rister, 48-51
Gene Ritch, 60-62
Hal Roberts, 71-72-73
Willie Roberts, 69
Craig Robinson, 69-70
Frank Roddy, 48-51
Bobby Rogers, 50-51
Billy Roland, 61-62
Kevin Rollwage, 75-76
Ramon Rosales, 75-76
L. D. Rowden, 69-70
Joe Rust, 73-75

S

Mike Sanders, 63
Robert Sanders, 59
Larry Satcher, 66
Frank Scalise, 73-75
David Schneider, 68-69
Bert Schupp, 72-73-74
Don Sebastian, 76
Carroll Selby, 48-49
John Semian, 58-60
Don Sessions, 59-61
Warren Settegast, 46-47
Gene Shannon, 49-51
Clarence Shelmon, 73-74
Paul Shires, 67-68
Wayne Shoemaker, 52-55
Newton Shows, 52-53
Barry Sides, 64-66
Mike Simpson, 66-68
Jack Skog, 62-64
Billy Smith, 62-64
Joe Bob Smith, 54-56
Manor Smith, 47
Steve Smith, 70
Fred Snell, 76
Bob Snelson, 51
Ray Snokhouse, 51
Rudy Spitzenberger, 55-56
Mike Spradlin, 75-76
Dick Spratt, 64-66
Mike Spratt, 63-65
Skippy Spruill, 66
Ed Staggs, 48-49
Del Stanley, 71-72
*Ken Stegall, 53-55
Otis Stewart, 68-69
Bill Stohler, 71-72-73
Rich Stotter, 65-67
Jim Strong, 68-69
Pat Studstill, 58-59
Luke Stungis, 71-72
Chester Sugarek, 49-51
Allen Sumerford, 68-69
Paul Sweeten, 57

T

Robert Taylor, 62
Rick Terrell, 71-72-73
Buddy Terry, 55-56
Dyral Thomas, 75-76
Earl Thomas, 68-70
Lidney Thompson, 57-58
Mickey D. Thompson, 63-65
Jon Thornburg, 68-69
Boyd Tingle, 47-49
William Tingle, 46-48

(continued on next page)

ALL-TIME LETTERMEN (continued)

°Cecil Towns, 46-49
Robert Turnbull, 54
Joe Tusa, 53

V

James Van Haverbeke, 49-52
Leo Van Haverbeke, 49-50
Bill Van Osdel, 61-62
Max Vater, 73-74

W

Dewey Wade, 57-58
*Bobby Don Walker, 52-53
Leon Wallace, 46

Roy Wallace, 46-47
Gene Ward, 56-57
Milton Ward, 72
Thomas Ward, 70-71
Kenneth Watson, 56
Marty Watts, 72-73-74
Evan Weaver, 46-47
John Welch, 53
Mike Welch, 73
Jim Wells, 75
Hogan Wharton, 57-58
Jim Wheat, 63
Wilson Whitley, 73-76
Don Willhelm, 47-49
Robbie Williams, 67
Theodis Williams, 75
Willis Williams, 76
Todd Williamson, 73-74

Bryan Willingham, 72-73-74
Ken Wind, 54-56
Jim Windham, 58-60
Ben Wilson, 53-54
Morris Wilson, 63
Floyd Winfield, 65-67
Dick Woodall, 65-67
Phil Woodring, 66-68
Elmo Wright, 68-70
Red Wright, 59-61
Tim Wright, 63-65
Jay Wyatt, 76

Y

Ron Yokubaitis, 62-63

STUDENT MANAGERS

Bobby Brown, 46-48
Claude Collins, 49-50
Vernon Eschenfelder, 51-53
Ken Faour, 53-55
Robert Worthington, 54
Charlie Berry, 58
Allen Hawkins, 59
Richard Berry, 62
Ronnie Bowser, 63
Jack Littlefield, 64
Teddy Fisher, 66
Ralph Bearden, 67
Ted Samples, 68
Gary Faour, 68
Kevin McGrath, 69
Bitsy Garcia, 70
Gary Walton, 70
Gary Boyd, 71
Larry Hogan, 72
Trip Bomar, 72
Mike Payne, 73
Mike Brem, 74
Doug McGee, 75
Steve Evans, 75

STUDENT TRAINERS

Jim Ausley, 46-47
Kelsey Goodman, 52
Charlie Miller, 55-56
Bill Bishop, 55-56
Danny Cornwall, 66
Bobby Smith, 67
Jim Lyle, 68
Dick Terry, 68
Greg Bautsch, 68
Hank Birdwell, 71
George Skelton, 71
Robby Powers, 71
Billy Garner, 71
Marshall Priest, 72
Bobby Arriaga, 72
Tee White, 72
Darrell Willis, 74
Randy Worrell, 74